THE CATHOLIC CHURCH
THE FIRST 2,000 YEARS

MARTHA RASMUSSEN

THE
CATHOLIC CHURCH
THE FIRST
2,000 YEARS

A POPULAR SURVEY
AND STUDY GUIDE TO
CHURCH HISTORY

IGNATIUS PRESS   SAN FRANCISCO

Nihil Obstat: Reverend Michael F. McDermott, J.C.L.
              Censor Librorum
              June 9, 2005

Imprimatur: †Most Reverend William J. Dendinger, D.D.
              Bishop of Grand Island
              June 9, 2005

Cover art: Guillaume Pierre de Marcillat (1475–1537)
Pentecost
Cathedral, Arezzo, Italy.
Copyright: Scala/Art Resources, New York

Cover design by Roxanne Mei Lum

ISBN 978-0-89870-969-8
ISBN 0-89870-969-5
Library of Congress Control Number 2003105165
Printed in the United States of America ♾

A. M. D. G.

CONTENTS

PREFACE

History is fascinating when it tells the stories of people who influenced their cultures and when readers understand the connection between what they are learning and their own lives. This book includes many interesting stories and frequent links between historical events and our times. Since the book was written for the convenience of nonscholarly readers, I have used uncomplicated grammar and vocabulary wherever possible. I have usually included explanations of historical or theological terms when they were first introduced, even if most Catholics probably know them. For readers who are unfamiliar with history, I have written brief descriptions of the historical periods in which the events described took place. The book generally follows the chronological divisions found in standard Western civilization textbooks.

Church history is the story of how God works with individuals, societies, and his Church. It is about the way God revealed himself to us in the past and intervened in people's lives. Since this is a Catholic book on the history of the Catholic Church, it includes traditional Catholic interpretations of history. For example, a secular history book might suggest some obvious reasons the Catholic Church survived and flourished for two thousand years, but this book claims God's protection as the primary reason. In addition to giving Catholic interpretations, the book describes the difficult times when scandals or persecution threatened to destroy the Church. Miraculous stories, where they are mentioned, are usually given as they are stated in the original sources and usually include references to the sources in the text. Readers are free to disregard the Catholic interpretations and to refuse to believe the miracles, but it would not be historically accurate to leave them out of a Catholic history book.

The text does not include many direct references to controversial questions of today, such as the possibility or impossibility of ordaining women as priests. Teachers using the book can always start a discussion of these questions, but they should have the option of choosing their own time and method of introducing the subject. The book briefly discusses most historical controversies. For example, there are explanations of the need for Church reform before the Council of Trent, the Inquisition, the Crusades, the treatment of Jews in medieval society, and the historical role of women in society, though the book is too short to devote much space to any of these issues. The discussion questions found at the end of each section are intended to highlight important points found in the chapter and to initiate discussions.

I would like to thank the people who helped me write this book. The most important were my former professors at the University of Colorado, particularly Professor Boyd H. Hill in medieval history and Professor Carl Christensen in Renaissance/Reformation history. In addition to teaching me about history, the evaluation of historical evidence, and how to write about history, they read and commented on parts of the text. However, they are not responsible for its defects or its religious content. Many thanks also to the priests, nuns, teachers, friends, and relatives who taught me, read and commented on the book, or answered my questions about their own lives and experiences.

I

The Church in the New Testament

Featured Saint: Paul

CHAPTER 1

The Church in the New Testament

1. What Is the Church?

Many Catholics think of the Church as an institution or an organization, and this is correct but not complete. The Church was founded by Christ to carry on his work in the world. Each parish church, usually including all of the Catholics in a geographical area and led by a priest, is part of a diocese, which is led by a bishop or an archbishop. Each bishop oversees the parishes in his diocese and is responsible for other Church organizations such as Catholic hospitals, charitable organizations, and schools located in it. He provides leadership in teaching the truths Christ taught us and in explaining the way they should be applied to modern situations.

Often an area with a large population or with geographical or political importance—perhaps associated with an important city—will be made an archdiocese. The bishop of an archdiocese is called an archbishop. He is the leader of the other bishops in the area, but each bishop is responsible for teaching the faith in his own diocese. The leader of the whole Church is the Pope, the Bishop of Rome. All bishops are appointed by him or with his consent and receive their authority from him and from God. The Pope is elected by a group of Church leaders chosen to be cardinals, but he receives his authority from God and is guided by God with special gifts of grace. Each bishop, priest, and deacon is chosen by God through his Church and receives grace from him to carry out his mission. These gifts of grace are imparted by the sacrament of Holy Orders, the action of Christ working through his Church.

The Church is much more than an institution. The Church is a union of Christ and of all of the members of the Church, including people who have died and are in heaven with God and those who have died in God's grace but are not yet united with him in heaven. As baptized members of his Church, believers are united with Christ and with each other in a spiritual sense. Everything they do affects others, regardless of whether anyone besides God knows about their actions, and everything others do affects them. All Christians are part of the Body of Christ, and they are never alone. This teaching is part of the reason Christians believe in the dignity and importance of each individual.

Christ established his Church for several purposes. The Church preaches his message so that everyone may be baptized and find salvation. His sacraments give people his life and grace. He taught believers to turn away from evil and live in peace and justice so that they can be happy in this life and find eternal life in heaven.

The Church has many organizations to carry out the will of Christ and explain his message. For example, Jesus told his followers to care for the sick and feed the hungry, so the Church provides hospitals, nursing homes, and food and shelter for the poor. Jesus told believers to love one another, so Christians try to bring peace to the world by reconciling individuals and nations whenever this is possible. Christ promised that his Church would last to the end of time, so the Church provides for her own survival by ordaining new priests and bishops and baptizing and training new generations of

Christians. Christians believe that Christ taught them the best way of life, so Christians try to create societies in which gospel values are reflected in laws, government structure, and culture.

Since the Church was founded by Jesus Christ and is sustained by God, when believers study Church history they learn about God and the way he has worked with people in the past. History is the story of many individuals and cultures, and readers will find a wide variety of characters, lifestyles, and solutions to apparently impossible problems. Readers who are not Catholics or Christians will find that the study of Church history gives them added insight into secular and religious history and explains many modern controversies.

Discussion Questions

Identify: parish, diocese, bishop, Pope

1. Describe the external structure of the Church.
2. Describe the charitable and missionary activities carried out by the Church.

2. The People of God in the Old Testament

The Catholic Church was founded by Christ about two thousand years ago, but God has been active in history since the beginning. The pre-Christian era was a preparation for Christ, and also for the Church.

The book of Genesis in the Bible tells how God created the universe, the world, and human beings. Though the first people, Adam and Eve, were created good, in God's image, they chose to turn away from God by disobeying his commandment. This sin broke their union with God and deprived them of God's life and grace, and it brought evil and death into the world. God responded by promising to send a Savior.

Much later, about four thousand years ago, God called a man named Abraham to leave his home and go to another land, located in what is now Israel. God promised that if Abraham believed in him, worshiped him, and obeyed him, God would give Abraham the land and many descendants. This promise and Abraham's agreement were a covenant, a binding contract between God and man.

Abraham's faith in God was severely tested. He was already old when God called him, and his wife, Sarah, had not had any children. Many years later, after he had fulfilled God's commands faithfully, he still had no child. Finally his son Isaac was born. After this Abraham's faith was tested again. God asked Abraham to offer up his son in sacrifice. While Abraham must have wondered at this strange command, he did not hesitate, but went to the mountain of sacrifice and prepared to do as God said. At the last moment God stopped him. God said that Abraham had proved that he would obey God's will in everything and that he should not sacrifice his son. Instead, he should sacrifice a ram.

The idea of sacrificing animals or other possessions may seem strange to modern readers. In Old Testament times, offering sacrifices was one way God asked his people to show their love for him. When Christ came to earth, he gave up his life in obedience to God as a sacrifice to bring us salvation and the grace of God. The sacrifices in the Old Testament helped prepare the people of God to understand the sacrifice of Christ. Since the Crucifixion and Resurrection of Jesus, Christians do not offer animal sacrifices to God.

Instead, Catholics worship God through Mass, which re-enacts Christ's sacrifice and brings us his grace. Christians also offer God gifts or sacrifices of money, which are used to support the Church, assist the poor, or help with other good causes. Catholics may sacrifice or give up their possessions or time, as people did in the Old Testament, and they should live their lives in obedience to God's will.

As God had promised, Abraham's descendants became very numerous. They were called the children of Israel after Abraham's grandson, Israel. Later they were called the Hebrews or Jews. They moved to Egypt during a famine and stayed there for four hundred years. At first the Egyptians treated them well, because Joseph, one of Israel's sons, had been sold by his brothers as a slave to Egypt and had become an important official there. After many years the Israelites became even more numerous, and the Egyptians enslaved them.

The book of Exodus tells us that God called Moses to lead the Israelites out of slavery in Egypt, back to the land he had promised to Abraham and his descendants. Moses at first was reluctant to obey God in this, but he finally agreed. With the help of his brother, Aaron, and with many signs and miracles from God, Moses led the Israelites to safety. While they were in the desert on their way to the promised land, God renewed his covenant with them. God told Moses to go to Mt. Sinai, where God gave Moses the Ten Commandments, the basic laws that the Israelites were to follow. When Moses returned, he found that the people had grown tired of waiting for him and had persuaded Aaron to make an idol, a calf of gold, so that they could worship it instead of God. Moses was furious, but he begged God to forgive the people for this sin and to take pity on them. The Israelites all promised to turn back to God and to obey his Commandments. In return, God promised to care for them, to give them a homeland to live in, and to protect them from their enemies, as long as they obeyed his laws and worshiped him alone.

The covenant God made with Abraham, and renewed with Moses, was the basis of God's relations with his chosen people during the years before Christ. God's law became more detailed as he gradually taught his people the way he wanted them to live. At the time of Abraham, God showed his people that he was one God, but they did not have the Ten Commandments. After Moses led them out of Egypt, they were given the Ten Commandments and many other laws, but they did not have the writings about the judges or of the prophets.

The twelve tribes of the Israelites were united under Moses and his successor, Joshua, but as the people increased in numbers and spread through the land, they lost their unity. The tribes had no central government after Joshua died, and each tribe and family did whatever its members wished. The books of Joshua, Judges, and Samuel tell us that God allowed the Israelites to turn away from worshiping him and to pray to the gods of the surrounding pagans. The tribes attacked each other and did many other evil deeds.

Since the Israelites had broken their covenant with God, he let their enemies in nations around them defeat them in battle. He also sent prophets called *judges* to remind the Israelites of their covenant with him. The judges settled disputes among the Israelites, told people God's will for their lives, persuaded them to obey God, and led them in battle against the enemies who were oppressing them. The judges' leadership did not pass on to their descendants. Each time a judge died, the tribes returned to their former state of anarchy.

The last judge was Samuel, a great prophet. When he grew old, the Israelites asked him to appoint a king to rule over them, since they wanted to be like other lands. After praying to God, Samuel anointed King Saul, and, when Saul turned away from God, Samuel anointed King David. Under David's leadership Israel grew to be a strong, wealthy nation. David was devoted to God, and God promised through the prophet Nathan that David's heirs would always rule Israel. Kings who were descended from David ruled Israel for about five hundred years, but the prophecy was completely fulfilled in Jesus, a descendant of David. Jesus Christ established the kingdom of God on earth in his Church and rules over Christians forever.

Many kings after David turned away from God and worshiped idols or oppressed the poor with heavy taxes and unjust laws. Some persecuted the prophets God sent to remind people of his covenant. The tribe of Levi provided priests to offer sacrifice to God, but even these hereditary priests sometimes worshiped false gods. Finally God allowed enemies to conquer the Israelites in wars. The survivors were taken to Babylon as captives.

After several generations the remaining Jews were allowed to return to their home land. At first they were under the authority of Jewish leaders who worshiped the God of their ancestors, though they held their offices from the Persian government. These leaders called an assembly after the Israelites returned and read the whole law of Moses, called the Mosaic law, to the people. Everyone agreed to follow it. This was a further renewal of God's covenant with his people. The law included the Ten Commandments and hundreds of complicated rules for eating, working, keeping the Sabbath, praying, offering sacrifices, marriage, and many other activities. It was easy to become preoccupied with these rules, but many devout Jews understood the spirit of the law and followed God with their whole hearts.

Several hundred years later the Jews were conquered by the Greeks, who persecuted them to force them to follow Greek customs. However, many Jews loved God so much that they were willing to die rather than disobey his laws. After a few Jews had been martyred by the Greeks, they revolted under the leadership of Judas Maccabeus and won their freedom. Later they were conquered and governed by Romans, who allowed them to keep their religion, customs, and some independence, but oppressed them with heavy taxes.

The people of God in the Old Testament were similar in many ways to the Church. The Israelites worshiped the same God, though they did not know that the one God, named *Yahweh*, was a Trinity with Father, Son, and Holy Spirit. They obeyed the Ten Commandments, though Jesus gave a fuller explanation of their meaning to his followers. They had prayer, the Old Testament of the Bible, and worship services. The Jews' beliefs about the creation of the world, angels, devils, the nature and final destiny of human beings, life after death, and the need to avoid sin to please God were the same as or similar to those of Christians. The Jews were waiting for a Messiah who would save them. They were surrounded by nations with different customs and religions, and they knew that God wanted them to obey and worship him rather than to adopt mistaken customs and to worship false gods. The Jews, God's chosen people, had been prepared for the next step in God's plan for the world.

Discussion Questions

Identify: covenant, Abraham, Moses, Ten Commandments, King David, Mosaic law, Judas Maccabeus

1. Describe God's relationship with Abraham.
2. Describe God's covenants with the children of Israel before the time of Christ. What did the people promise to do? What did God promise to do? What happened when they broke their covenant with God?
3. Describe the people of God shortly before the time of Christ.

3. The Church Jesus Founded

The Old Testament had many prophecies about Jesus. Some prophecies spoke of a king who would rule Israel, overcome her enemies, purify her worship, end injustice, and establish a reign of peace and prosperity. At the time of Christ, many Jews thought these prophecies meant that the Messiah would be a military leader like Judas Maccabeus who would free them from the Romans. However, there were other prophecies many Jews ignored. The Psalms and the book of the prophet Isaiah tell of a suffering servant of God, a king who would be rejected, have his hands and feet pierced, be overcome by his enemies, and die a terrible death to ransom his people from their sins. When Jesus came to earth, he fulfilled the second group of prophecies by his Crucifixion and death. Many of the first prophecies were fulfilled after his Resurrection and are still being fulfilled in his Church, and others have not yet been fulfilled. Christians believe that they will be fulfilled at the Second Coming of Christ. Since the Jews did not find in Jesus the military leader they were seeking, and since he spoke against many of their ideas and customs, the majority of the Jews did not believe that Jesus was the Messiah. After Jesus was crucified and rose from the dead, more of them became believers. All of the first Christians were Jews.

The Gospels tell us that Jesus was born by the power of the Holy Spirit from the Virgin Mary. Joseph the carpenter, Mary's husband, was Jesus' foster father. When Jesus was about thirty he began his public ministry, traveling around Israel and preaching to the people.

Jesus gathered a group of disciples and chose a special group of twelve men, the Apostles. Jesus chose St. Peter to be the leader of the Apostles, saying, "And on this rock I will build my church, and the powers of death shall not prevail against it. I will give you the keys of the kingdom of heaven, and whatever you bind on earth shall be bound in heaven, and whatever you loose on earth shall be loosed in heaven" (Mt 16:18, 19). Though Jesus explained his teaching more clearly to the Apostles than to the other disciples, none of them understood it fully until after he rose from the dead.

Though the Jews were God's chosen people, Jesus' teaching was revolutionary for them in many ways. In the Sermon on the Mount he gave them the Beatitudes, which showed that people should follow God more radically than the Mosaic law required. However, the disciples of Jesus were to follow the laws with a new spirit. For example, the Ten Commandments forbid killing people, but Jesus said that people should not even hate their enemies but rather should love them. The Ten Commandments say people should not commit adultery, but Jesus said they should not lust after others. They should control their thoughts as well as their actions. The Jews believed that God rewarded good people by giving them wealth and happiness, but Jesus said that it was harder for a rich man to get into heaven than for a camel to go through the eye of a needle. Living a good Christian life usually makes people happy, but the final reward is in heaven, not in this life. On one occasion, the Apostles asked Jesus how anyone could be saved, since this way of life seemed very difficult. Jesus told them that though this is impossible with men, nothing is impossible with God. Later, with the help of God, the Apostles were able to follow Jesus' teaching, and they gave their lives to bring his word to others.

Jesus was frequently asked where he got the authority to teach. Most religious teachers were Pharisees, who came from famous schools. They based their authority on the prestige of earlier teachers. They thought that since Jesus had not attended such a school, he had no authority to teach. Jesus responded to the question of his teaching authority in several ways. The first was to refer to his miraculous powers. Jesus healed people who had been paralyzed, insane, or sick for years, and he brought dead people back to life. He worked miracles that showed that he had power over nature, such as calming storms, walking on water, turning water into wine, and feeding huge crowds with a few loaves of bread. His miracles helped prove his authority by showing that he had power from God, but they were not the basis of his authority. He gradually revealed to his disciples that he was the Messiah, the Son of God, and that he and God the Father were one. Jesus was God as well as man. This was puzzling to the Jews, who did not have our knowledge that God is a Trinity of Father, Son, and Holy Spirit. Since Jesus was God, he had authority to explain God's laws, to forgive sins, and to make changes in the rules governing God's people. Since he was man, he was able to teach people how to live by his example, and he was able to die for their sins.

Jesus taught his followers many new customs and beliefs. He told them that they must be born again through water and the Holy Spirit, indicating that people must be baptized and live a new life in Christ. The Jews believed that sins could be forgiven only by God; Jesus forgave sins because he was God. After the Resurrection, he gave his Apostles the power to forgive sins in his name through the sacraments of baptism and penance. At the Last Supper, Jesus consecrated the bread and wine so that it became his Body and Blood and gave the Apostles power to do the same thing. This instituted the Eucharist and ordained the Apostles as priests and bishops.

Jesus explained to the Apostles that he must suffer and die, but that he would rise from the dead three days later. He took Peter and two other disciples to a mountain, where he was transfigured and appeared to them in glory with Moses and Elijah, who symbolized the law and the prophets of the Old Testament. Moses and Elijah vanished, leaving only Jesus. This showed that the New Covenant established by Jesus would be permanent and helped the Apostles to believe in the Second Coming of Christ after Jesus had ascended into heaven.

Jesus had many followers, but a few groups actively opposed his teaching. The Pharisees, who were devoted to following the Mosaic laws, with all of the details developed since the time of Moses, often opposed Jesus' teaching, which stressed interior conversion rather than detailed and complicated regulations. The Sadducees disagreed with Jesus because they did not believe in the resurrection of the dead. The Jewish political leaders, especially the high priest, feared that a popular religious leader might undermine their authority and provoke the Romans into destroying their nation. The Roman occupying government was sensitive to any popular movement that might threaten its dominance. Jesus was betrayed by Judas, one of his Apostles, and handed over to the high priest and the Romans, who crucified him. Jesus' death fulfilled the prophecies and gained our salvation. He rose from the dead the third day after his Crucifixion.

When Jesus chose his Apostles and sacrificed his life for us, he changed the worship of the Old Testament. Instead of a hereditary priesthood offering sacrifices, Christians had bishops and priests who had been called to that office and who reenacted the sacrifice of Jesus whenever they celebrated the Eucharist. St. Peter and the other Apostles were the leaders of the Church after Jesus ascended into heaven. As St. Peter was the leader of the Apostles, the successors of St. Peter were the leaders of the bishops—the successors of the Apostles—and of the rest of the Church. Jesus told St. Peter and the Apostles to teach the things he had commanded, which meant that the bishops, led by the Pope, had the authority and the obligation to judge how to apply the teaching of Christ and to preach it throughout the world.

Jesus' own life, death, and Resurrection gave Christians new ideals. He sacrificed his own life to pay the penalty for sins so that believers could have their sins forgiven and become united with God. Christians needed to love Jesus and each other as much as Jesus loved them, enough to give their lives for him or for each other. When Jesus rose from the dead, he showed that God triumphs over obstacles that seem insurmountable and defeats that seem final. Believers did not need to fear death, since it was not the end. If they loved and followed God, death was their birth into life with God in heaven. The good actions of Christians, particularly their love for the poor and for their enemies, were the ways they showed their love for God and followed his commands. Jesus' new ideals were challenging, but Christians throughout the ages accepted the challenge and devoted their lives to serving God and other people.

The Old Testament showed that God loved human beings. He saved his people from slavery, gave them rules to live by so that they could be at peace with each other and

with him, protected them from their enemies, and taught
them to love him and worship him. When they forgot him
or turned away from his laws, he sent judges or prophets to
remind them of their covenant with him. In the New Testament God showed his love by becoming man and living
with his people. He taught them how to live, established the
Church to continue teaching his message, gave us his life in
the sacraments, and died a horrible death to save his people.
He always guides and helps his Church so that Christians
can hear his message and know his will for their lives and
find eternal happiness in heaven.

Discussion Questions

Identify: disciples, Apostles, Beatitudes, St. Peter

1. Who was Jesus?
2. What changes did Jesus make in the way his disciples followed the Mosaic law?
3. How did Jesus show his love for us?
4. What ideals of love do Christians have that were not found in the Jewish religion?

4. The Church in the Acts of the Apostles

After Jesus' Crucifixion and Resurrection, he appeared to
his disciples and the Apostles at various times for forty days.
In his final appearance, described in the book of Acts, he
told them to go to Jerusalem and wait for the Holy Spirit.
The Apostles saw him caught up out of their sight, but two
angels appeared and promised that he would return again.
During the time of prayer and waiting in Jerusalem, Peter,

the leader of the Apostles, said that they should choose a successor to Judas, who had betrayed Jesus and died shortly afterward. They chose Matthias, who was added to the eleven Apostles. This was the first example of apostolic succession, in which the Apostles chose men to succeed them in their office of teaching and governing God's Church. These men were consecrated or ordained as bishops by prayer and the laying on of hands, which is the way bishops are consecrated today in the sacrament of Holy Orders. Bishops in the Catholic and Orthodox Churches are descended through this sacrament from the original twelve Apostles, who were chosen and consecrated by Jesus before he was crucified.

On the Jewish feast of Pentecost, ten days after Jesus ascended into heaven, the Apostles were gathered in prayer with Mary, the Mother of Jesus, and some other disciples. Suddenly they heard a sound like a strong wind, and the Holy Spirit came on them like tongues of fire. They began speaking in different languages and went out into the street, which was filled with people who were gathered in Jerusalem for the feast. Peter preached a sermon to the crowd explaining that speaking in tongues and the death and Resurrection of Jesus fulfilled the Old Testament prophecies about the Messiah. After his sermon, about three thousand people were baptized as Christians.

The Christian community grew quickly because of the Apostles' preaching and working miracles. For example, St. Peter cured a man who had been unable to walk from the time he was born and then preached a sermon explaining that the man was cured through the power of Jesus. About five thousand people became believers because of this miracle. Many believers sold their property, distributed the money to the poor, and lived together in a community. They spent their time in prayer, worship, good works, and preparing for the Second Coming of Christ. Catholic religious orders, which usually ask members to renounce their property and hold all of their possessions in common, look to these early Christians as an example.

As Christians grew more numerous, disputes arose. Some Christians were Greek converts to Judaism, and they complained that Greek widows were being neglected in the distribution of food to the poor. The Apostles chose seven men to be deacons, in charge of distributing food, so that the Apostles could spend their time on preaching and prayer. The deacons were ordained by the laying on of hands. Some of them became noted for preaching, debating, and working miracles.

Jewish officials were very disturbed because the Apostles were preaching that Jesus had risen from the dead. These officials arrested, imprisoned, and whipped Peter and some other Apostles in an attempt to silence them, but the Apostles continued preaching about Jesus. Some Jewish leaders, particularly an influential Pharisee named Gamaliel, recommended leniency toward Christians, but most of the Jewish leaders became more hostile.

The first martyr was the deacon Stephen. The word *martyr* originally meant "witness", and martyrs witnessed to their belief in Christ by dying for him rather than denying him. After St. Stephen's death, a widespread persecution arose against Christians. It became dangerous for them to stay in Jerusalem, so believers scattered to other towns. They spread the gospel to new communities so more people had the opportunity to believe in Christ.

Before the persecution Christians had concentrated on preaching to Jews or Samaritans, who were closely related to Jews. Shortly after this, Peter had a vision in which God showed him that there was no distinction between Jews and the people of other nations. After this vision he preached the gospel to the household of a Roman official who had sent for him. The man became a Christian and received the Holy Spirit with all his family, as converts from Judaism did. The Apostles began preaching to everyone, and many people who were not Jews became Christians.

The greatest dispute in the early Christian community was caused by a group of converts called *Judaizers*. They said that all Christians had to follow the whole Mosaic law. Christians following the leadership of St. Peter and St. Paul believed the entire Mosaic law should not be imposed on converts to Christianity. The Christians in Antioch were confused by this conflict. They sent Paul and other messengers to Jerusalem, where the Apostles held a council to debate the matter. Under Peter's leadership, the council agreed that the Mosaic law was not binding on Christians. The new converts needed only to live a moral life and to follow a few dietary restrictions, such as avoiding meat that had been sacrificed to idols. The Apostles sent a letter to Antioch that said, "It has seemed good to the Holy Spirit and to us to lay upon you no greater burden than these necessary things" (Acts 15:28a). Even with this reminder that the Holy Spirit was guiding the Apostles, some Judaizers did not accept the decision. They continued preaching their own version of the gospel until Jerusalem was destroyed by the Romans in A.D. 70. After that, Christians became more clearly separated from Jews, and the Judaizing faction died out.

St. Peter, St. Paul, and other Apostles wrote letters to their scattered converts explaining how to live the Christian life. Paul specified that Christians must avoid sins such as fornication, homosexual acts, adultery, murder, theft, lying, idol worship, sorcery, forming factions, and receiving the Body of the Lord in an unworthy manner. They needed faith in Jesus Christ, baptism, prayer, good works such as helping the poor, trust in God, and love. The community should be at peace within itself and united with the rest of the Church.

One sign of unity was worship. Christians gathered together each Sunday to pray and sing hymns, read the Old Testament and Christian books such as the Gospels or the Letters of the Apostles, listen to a sermon by the priest or bishop, and join in the celebration of the Eucharist. Early liturgies were rather informal, with interruptions due to charismatic gifts such as prophecy and speaking in tongues. Communities were unified by their help for each other. They collected money, which was used to help pay the traveling expenses of the Apostles, feed the poor, and support the Church in Jerusalem. The Judaizing controversy and the Council of Jerusalem showed that most Christians realized that they needed to find the truth about Jesus from the Apostles and to accept it once they found what it was. This meant that they were unified in their beliefs.

The Council of Jerusalem is not usually counted as an ecumenical council, a meeting of all the bishops of the Church. However, it provided a model for future Church councils. Even though Peter had been chosen by Jesus to be the leader of the Apostles, they all needed to discuss the Judaizing controversy to see the best way to deal with it. Bishops and other Church members were not independent. As a community, one sign of faithfulness to God was unity. After Peter and the council had made a decision, the Christians who refused to follow it were working against the message of Christ and the Holy Spirit.

In the first generation after the Crucifixion and Resurrection of Christ, Christianity spread very quickly. Soon there were communities of Christians in every major city in the Roman Empire. According to tradition, St. Thomas the Apostle founded churches in India, and a convert of the deacon Philip took the gospel to Ethiopia. The last Apostle, St. John the Evangelist, probably died after A.D. 90. By then there were Christian communities throughout the known world. Many factors favored this rapid expansion.

Early Christians had very strong faith. The Apostles had been trained personally by Jesus and had witnessed his death, Resurrection, and Ascension into heaven. They had no doubts about the truth of their message. The first missionaries were often given special gifts, such as the gift of working miracles, that were less common among later Christians. Christians counted it an honor to suffer for Christ and chose to obey God rather than men. When they were persecuted, they moved to new towns and founded new groups of Christians. These dedicated Christians had no difficulty inspiring others to believe in Christ.

The political situation at the time helped Christianity spread quickly. Rome had conquered the countries surrounding the Mediterranean, and the Roman Empire was at peace. Nearly everyone spoke Greek or Latin, so communication was relatively easy. Jews in Alexandria, a Greek city in Egypt, had translated the Old Testament into Greek before the time of Christ, and Jewish theologians had explained their beliefs in Greek philosophical language. When Christians began preaching to Greeks and Romans, they used the Greek translation of the Old Testament and explained some Christian beliefs in Greek terminology. As they traveled, missionaries were always able to find Jewish communities in large Roman cities. The Jews usually heard their message first and helped them preach to the rest of the population, though some Jews opposed Christianity later.

Christians believed that the conditions favoring the quick spread of Christianity were no coincidence. Christ was born on earth at the time chosen by God, and the Holy Spirit guided the Apostles in spreading his message. Christians throughout the ages have been confident that the same Holy Spirit would help them if they were willing to trust him and ask for his assistance.

Discussion Questions

Identify: apostolic succession, martyr, St. Stephen, Judaizers, Council of Jerusalem, St. Paul

1. What happened at Pentecost?
2. Who became leaders of the Church after the death of the Apostles? Who are the successors of the Apostles today?
3. Describe the conflict between the Judaizers and the other Christians. How did the Council of Jerusalem settle the problem? What was the role of St. Peter?

Featured Saint: Paul

St. Paul, originally named Saul, was a Jew born in the city of Tarsus. This meant that he had Roman citizenship, an advantage in his later missionary work. He was educated in Greek culture and language, but he was also trained as a Pharisee, a devout Jew who followed every detail of the Mosaic law. He had been a student of Gamaliel, a famous Pharisee, but he did not imitate Gamaliel's tolerance. Paul joined in the persecution against Christians in Jerusalem. He participated in executing the deacon Stephen, then set out for Damascus to persecute Christians there. However, God changed his plans. Paul told the story in this way:

"As I made my journey and drew near to Damascus, about noon a great light from heaven suddenly shone about me. And I fell to the ground and heard a voice saying to me, 'Saul, Saul, why do you persecute me?' And I answered, 'Who are you, Lord?' And he said to me, 'I am Jesus of Nazareth whom you are persecuting.' Now those who were with me saw the light but did not hear the voice of the one who was speaking to me. And I said, 'What shall I do, Lord?' And the Lord said to me, 'Rise, and go into Damascus, and there you will be told all that is appointed for you to do.' And when I could not see because of the brightness of that light, I was led by the hand by those who were with me, and came into Damascus" (Acts 22:6–11).

A Christian in Damascus named Ananias had a vision in which the Lord told him to go to the house where Saul was staying and heal him. Ananias objected that Saul had come to Damascus to persecute Christians. The Lord told him, "Go, for he is a chosen instrument of mine to carry my name before the Gentiles and kings and the sons of Israel; for I will show him how much he must suffer for the sake of my name" (Acts 9:15–16). Ananias went to him and laying hands on him said, "Brother Saul, the Lord Jesus who appeared to you on the road by which you came, has sent me that you may regain your sight and be filled with the Holy Spirit" (Acts 9:17). Immediately Saul regained his sight and was baptized. After this, Paul was welcomed by Christians, and he seems to have spent several years in the desert, praying and preparing for his mission. Later he conferred with Peter and some of the Apostles in Jerusalem, who confirmed his teaching.

Paul began traveling with some companions to different cities, preaching the gospel. He made many converts, but he usually encountered serious opposition. For example, the silversmiths in one city started a riot and denounced him to the Romans because they were afraid that if people became Christians, no one would buy silver statues of their local god. He caused a riot in another city because he healed a crippled man, and the local pagans, who thought he must be a god, tried to sacrifice a team of oxen to him. One Jewish synagogue leader supported Paul so enthusiastically that his congregation arranged for both of them to be arrested by the Romans. Sometimes Paul converted Roman officials when he was arrested. He was imprisoned many times, whipped, and nearly killed. Other problems were caused by shipwrecks on his travels, hunger, hard work, and the strain of worrying about his Christian friends. In spite of these trials, he rejoiced in God constantly.

Paul's teaching did not always cause conflicts. The book of Acts records a speech he made in Athens, the center of Greek philosophy. Since he used Greek philosophical terms, his audience was supportive at first, but they did not believe in the resurrection of the dead. He made only a few converts there. In another city he preached to the women washing clothes by the river and converted a businesswoman and her household. He encouraged his converts and other Christians by visiting them or writing letters, which were read in Sunday liturgies and later incorporated into the New Testament.

Paul was very humble since he never forgot that he had once persecuted Christians, but he was fearless in preaching the gospel because he knew that Jesus had chosen him. He reproved his converts sharply for their mistakes, but his love for them caused him great joy. Paul's life has inspired Christian converts and missionaries, and his explanations of Christianity are essential in understanding the gospel.

St. Paul ended his life in Rome. He was arrested and beheaded in 67 A.D. during Emperor Nero's persecution, which also caused the death of St. Peter, the Bishop of Rome, and hundreds of other martyrs. The many historical sites and churches in Rome dedicated to St. Peter and St. Paul have been the goals of pilgrimages for most of Christian history and still attract millions of pilgrims and tourists today.

2

The Persecuted Church

1. The Apostolic Fathers
2. Roman Government, Religion, and
   Culture Related to Christianity
3. The Expansion and Persecution of the
   Church in the Roman Empire
4. Early Apologetics: Explaining Christianity
   Correctly

Featured Saints: Perpetua and Felicity

CHAPTER 2

The Persecuted Church

1. The Apostolic Fathers

God is truth and the source of all truth. Christians from the time of Jesus have believed that it is not enough to have a vague general faith. The truth about God and his relationship with human beings is known because he revealed himself through the Old Testament Jews; through his Son, Jesus; and through his Holy Spirit guiding the teaching of the Church. The authors of the New Testament were inspired by the Holy Spirit and were nearly all martyred for preaching about Jesus. It is safe to assume that they were truthful and accurate in relating the events of Christ's life and the earliest days of the Church.

Letters and books written by St. Clement of Rome, St. Ignatius of Antioch, St. Polycarp, and St. Irenaeus of Lyons provide information about the next period in Church history. These bishops and martyrs knew the Apostles or their immediate successors. Their writings tell about the beliefs, customs, and problems of the early Church and indicate how much early Christians loved God. There is also an important anonymous document, the Didache.

St. Clement was the fourth Bishop of Rome, from about 92 to A.D. 101. He knew St. Peter and St. Paul, who were martyred in Rome in around A.D. 67. Clement had heard about disputes in the Church of Corinth and wrote a long letter to the Corinthians. The letter still exists because it was copied and read in worship services at Corinth and other cities, as were the letters in the New Testament. The Church at Corinth had been a model of harmony and good works for many years, but now it was being torn apart by factions. Clement was writing to resolve the quarrel and restore the Church to its earlier state of peace.

Clement's letter is one of the earliest non-biblical Christian documents for which the author and the approximate date is known. The letter reflects conditions in the Church before A.D. 100, less than seventy years after the death and Resurrection of Jesus. Since Clement knew St. Peter, he was only one generation away from the direct words of Christ. His letter may have been written before the book of Revelation, which was probably the last book in the Bible to be written. Clement's letter to the Corinthians is not Sacred Scripture, but it is a valuable witness to the faith and practices of the early Church.

The letter indicates that Clement, the Bishop of Rome, was writing to settle a dispute in the Church of Corinth. Why would Clement do that? Many bishops were closer to Corinth. His action is evidence of the Catholic belief that St. Peter, the first Bishop of Rome, passed on his position of leadership among the Apostles to succeeding Bishops of Rome. Clement's letter is an early example of the Pope guiding the Church, although the theory of the Pope's supremacy is stated more clearly later.

Most Christians in Corinth had rejected the authority of their bishop and priests. To resolve this problem, St. Clement explained the doctrine of apostolic succession. He said that bishops did not get their authority from their community. Christ chose the Apostles, and the office of guiding the

Church was handed down by the Apostles to the present bishops. Since their bishop had been chosen lawfully and ordained by the Apostles and their successors, his authority came from God, and the Corinthians had no right to reject him. Clement asked the Corinthians to put aside their factions and disputes and to live in peace under the leadership of their bishop and his assistants.

Clement's letter mentioned or explained many other Christian beliefs. He praised Christian virtues such as peace, harmony, penance, humility, charity to strangers, forgiveness, discipline, love, and zeal for doing good. These were the virtues the Corinthians needed to resolve their dispute. He asked the Corinthians to avoid the vices of jealousy, envy, disobedience to Church leaders, and the forming of factions. He also mentioned Christian beliefs such as the resurrection of the dead, the goodness and power of God, and the roles of the Father, Son, and Holy Spirit. The advice in the letter is as relevant to problems in the Church today as it was to the problems of the Corinthians.

St. Ignatius, the bishop of Antioch, was arrested by the Romans and taken to Rome to be executed in A.D. 110. As he traveled, he wrote letters to seven churches. One of his letters was addressed to St. Polycarp, Bishop of Smyrna, who had been a disciple of St. John the Evangelist.

Before Polycarp was martyred in 156, he had been a teacher of St. Irenaeus of Lyons, located in modern-day France, who had originally lived in Smyrna. Irenaeus, who was active in A.D. 180, was the most influential theologian in the second century and is an important source of information about the early Church.

One important anonymous document was published in 1883, after it was discovered in an ancient Greek monastery. It is usually called the *Didache*, although its complete title is

"The Lord's Instruction to the Gentiles Through the Twelve Apostles". It was probably written between A.D. 60 and 150. It is important because of its description of the structure of the early Christian community, its explanation of liturgical celebrations such as baptism and the Eucharist, and its teaching about the Trinity and other Christian doctrines. The Didache shows that early Christians were expected to follow the same moral code Christians are expected to follow today, with the help of God's grace and the sacraments. The Didache emphasizes the love and obedience Christians should have for Christ and his Church.

The early Church had the same basic structure, beliefs, liturgy, and moral code as the present Church, though some aspects of these that were not well developed then are more clearly defined now. The Church has been called *Catholic*, which means universal, from the time of Ignatius of Antioch (about A.D. 110). Catholics have always believed that they are the Church founded by Christ, and the earliest historical literature supports this tradition. Other churches broke away from the Catholic Church at later times.

Clement's letter to the Corinthians and the writings of Ignatius of Antioch, Polycarp, and Irenaeus of Lyons may still be read for instruction and inspiration in living the Christian life. This is a characteristic of the writings of the Apostolic Fathers, well-known Christian writers who lived a few generations after Christ and handed on his teaching faithfully. Not all Christians writing at that time are called Apostolic Fathers, because some of them adopted beliefs that were not consistent with Christ's teaching. Writers who taught errors were called *heretical*, from the word for error. A heresy is an erroneous belief about the truths Jesus taught or about Christ himself. True beliefs about Christ taught by God and the Church are called orthodox beliefs, so beliefs that are

contrary to the truths taught by Christ could be called unorthodox (or heterodox) as well as heretical. Some unorthodox writers deliberately rejected part of the Christian message,
but others made mistakes because they did not know how to
apply the gospel teaching to questions that Christ had not
answered. The Apostolic Fathers often discussed issues regarding truths that were not clearly defined until hundreds
of years later. Some have never been defined. Christ gave
the Apostles the guidance of the Holy Spirit to judge matters of faith and morals, not to answer every question that
could ever be asked.

By the time of Irenaeus, the Christian writings that were
eventually accepted as Sacred Scripture were the most important sources for knowledge of the faith. The writings of
the Apostolic Fathers were also regarded as authentic explanations of the Christian faith. Books written by some other
authors had a variety of problems. Many of them were so
full of errors that they were not preserved. Christians know
about them only because they were quoted by theologians
who were explaining Christian beliefs in order to refute these
authors' errors. However, some books contained so many
helpful things in addition to their errors that they were copied by monks in the Middle Ages, whereas many manu-
scripts from the ancient world that were not copied were
lost forever.

Church leaders did not make the final selection of books
for the New Testament for hundreds of years after the death
and Resurrection of Jesus. In their Sunday liturgies, early
Christians used the Greek translation of the Old Testament
(called the Septuagint), the four Gospels, the book of Acts,
the letters in our New Testament, the book of Revelation,
and letters by writers such as St. Clement. About A.D. 400,
a Church council formally ratified the tradition that Christians

would use the Greek translation of the Old Testament. The books in the New Testament were chosen because they were written by one of the Apostles or Evangelists and because they were accepted by most Christians. The writings of the Apostolic Fathers were used outside of the eucharistic liturgy to clarify the meaning of the Scriptures and to explain some questions that the Sacred Scriptures did not resolve.

Discussion Questions

Identify: St. Clement of Rome, St. Ignatius of Antioch, St. Polycarp, St. Irenaeus of Lyons, Apostolic Fathers, heretical belief, orthodox belief

1. What can Christians learn from the letter of Clement of Rome about the authority of the Bishop of Rome? About the virtues needed to live in a Christian community?
2. Why is it important to know which ancient Christian writers are Apostolic Fathers and which are not?

2. Roman Government, Religion, and Culture Related to Christianity

The Roman government persecuted Christians from the early days of Christianity. This persecution was not characteristic of Roman culture, which was intolerant only of foreign religions that were considered threatening to the stability of the empire. Romans who converted to foreign religions were sometimes considered eccentric or unpatriotic, but Christianity seemed dangerous for several reasons. Christians condemned some Roman cultural practices and refused to join in the patriotic worship of the Roman emperor. Because of mistaken ideas about Christian beliefs and liturgies, many

Romans believed that Christians were extremely immoral. In addition, Christians began converting Romans to their religion. Christianity taught many good moral qualities admired by Romans, so some of the persecution was inspired by misunderstanding or deliberate falsification regarding Christian beliefs and practices. It is ironic that Christians preserved many Roman achievements after the Roman Empire had ceased to exist in the West.

The Roman reaction to Christianity was influenced by Roman culture and history. The city of Rome was founded about B.C. 750. At first it was governed by kings, then by a type of democracy called a *republic*. Rome gained control over Italy, then began finding excuses to invade other countries. This was not difficult. Most countries were ruled by kings or groups of wealthy nobles and had no orderly means of succession for their governments. Dissatisfied individuals who thought they ought to rule their nation could ask Rome for military assistance. Romans invaded the countries and put these individuals in charge of the government in exchange for favorable trade and taxation agreements. Roman armies were usually able to defeat the armies of other nations because of the Romans' superior military tactics, soldiers, weapons, and discipline. Since the new rulers needed continued support from Roman armies, Roman officials were able to demand increasing control and taxes. Eventually they ruled a huge empire of conquered countries.

Many Roman generals became wealthy from plundering subject nations. They began fighting each other to gain control of Rome, and the republic was torn apart by civil war. A few years before Christ, a ruler named Caesar Augustus gained supreme power. He preserved many features of republican government, such as the Senate, but he was the emperor and had complete authority over the government of the Roman Empire.

Most of the empire outside of Italy was ruled by Roman officials appointed by the emperor. Their main functions were to support local rulers favorable to Rome, to preserve peace, and to collect the taxes and send them to Rome. Since the native rulers who cooperated with the Romans were allowed to keep some of the taxes, they became powerful and loyal to Rome, so the Roman system was usually effective and permanent. Some officials attempted to squeeze as much money as possible out of conquered nations, but others were more moderate and allowed local manufacturing and farming to flourish. The peace imposed by Rome allowed widespread travel and trade, in turn promoting a unified culture, common languages, and economic prosperity. These benefits were so obvious that most countries eventually supported Roman rule.

Since wars meant spending money instead of collecting taxes, Roman officials were more concerned with keeping the peace than with justice. For example, even though he knew Jesus had done nothing that deserved death, Pontius Pilate, the Roman governor in Jerusalem, had Jesus crucified. He thought this judgment would keep the peace by pleasing local religious and political leaders, even though he knew Jesus had done nothing that deserved death. However, Roman officials who were too lawless or who extorted too much money from native people could be recalled to Rome by the emperor and might be prosecuted for crimes they had committed. The character of local governments was influenced by the character of the ruling Roman emperor. An honest, efficient emperor such as Augustus tried to appoint honest officials who would rule subject nations fairly. In contrast, under an emperor such as Nero, who was dishonest and incompetent, Roman governors were unlikely to face any consequences for their actions.

Many ideals of Roman culture were similar to the ideals of Christian culture. The Romans believed in honesty, family life, personal responsibility, and loyalty to the government. They thought that parents should be just and kind to their children and slaves. Children should be obedient to their parents, and slaves obedient to their masters. Idealistic Romans admired bravery in war, hard work, a simple lifestyle, and public service for the good of Rome. They believed that these virtues were good in themselves, pleasing to the gods, and necessary for a strong country.

While most Romans admired ideals similar to those of Christianity, Roman laws and customs were often contrary to them. Roman fathers had absolute authority over their wives and children, and parents could sell their children into slavery or kill them. Men were not expected to be faithful to their wives, though it was considered admirable if they were. Women were expected to be faithful to their husbands, but many of them did not attempt to live up to this standard. Roman women could have abortions or use drugs or sorcery to try to avoid having children. Monogamy, marriage between one man and one woman, was the general rule, but divorce and remarriage were frequent. Wealthy Romans owned many slaves. The slaves had practically no legal rights and could be abused or killed by their owners, though they were protected to some extent by public opinion and the cost of replacing them.

The traditional religion of Rome was polytheistic, with many gods. These included Jupiter (or Jove), the king of gods; Juno, his wife; Mercury, his messenger; Minerva, a virgin huntress; Mars, the god of war; and dozens of minor gods and goddesses. Romans believed that their gods did not always require moral behavior among human beings, but that they did like prayers and sacrifices. By the time of Christ, few Romans had much faith in their gods, though official sacrifices and prayers continued in pagan temples in Rome until about A.D. 400.

Though traditional Romans considered the worship of foreign gods to be somewhat impious, many Romans followed innovative philosophies. Many educated Romans became disciples of the Greek philosopher Plato or other Greek or Roman teachers. Their philosophical systems often required strict morality and fidelity to duty. These systems offered peace of mind and the satisfaction of being virtuous. Some of them had a vague belief in reincarnation or an impersonal supreme being, but at the time of Christ their main focus was on behavior in this world. Romans sometimes joined imported mystery religions such as the cult of Mithra from Persia, the cult of Osiris and Isis from Egypt, or the Eleusinian mysteries from Greece. These religions offered secret rites and ceremonies and promised their followers a better life after death. Political traditions included the belief that the emperor was a god, or at least had godlike qualities. Statues of the emperor were set up in temples and offered sacrifices of incense, like statues of the gods. These philosophies and religions were not exclusive. A Roman could sacrifice to the gods of Rome and the emperor, belong to several mystery cults, base his behavior on Platonic philosophy, and imitate the virtues of his ancestors.

As time passed, religious beliefs in the Roman Empire changed. Believers of the old pagan religions began to teach that all of the gods were subordinate to one supreme god. These believers became more concerned with moral behavior and life after death. Teachers of Greek or Roman philosophy tried to experience unity with the supreme being, and this supreme truth began to take on the characteristics of a supreme God surrounded by celestial forces and powers. After a majority of

Romans became Christians, pagan religions and philosophies began to resemble or imitate Christianity.

Since there were communities of Jews in most Roman cities, many Romans knew about the Jewish religion. Some admired it, and a few became Jews, though the Mosaic law posed such a severe challenge that most Romans were unwilling to follow it. The government disapproved of the Jewish religion because it was exclusive. Jews believed that their God was the only God and that all other gods were either nothing at all, or demons. Jews would not allow non-Jews into their temple and would not even pretend to worship other gods. Since Roman civic life included sacrifices to the gods of Rome and the emperor, Romans regarded Jews as unpatriotic because they would not participate. At first Christians were disliked as a new Jewish sect, and later Christians were persecuted when it became evident that they followed a separate religion, which the Romans regarded as more dangerous than Judaism.

At the time of Christ, the city of Rome was filled with masses of poor Romans who were unable to find work because they had lost their farms to land speculators and were unable to compete with slaves for other jobs. Some of these people joined the army, but the Roman government supported thousands with free grain from Egypt and free entertainment. Many Roman officials were elected by the people of Rome, who usually voted for the candidate who promised them the best horse races, plays, and gladiator fights. Much of this entertainment was immoral. Many of the plays would have been X rated today, and the gladiator shows sometimes required slaves who were trained warriors to fight to the death with each other or to attack wild animals. Sometimes condemned criminals were forced to fight with gladiators or were burned or torn apart.

In spite of these negative aspects, Roman culture had many good qualities. Under Roman rule, Europe was peaceful and united. Roman government, particularly the modified democracy of the republic, influenced the U.S. Constitution and most other modern constitutions. Roman ideals of bravery, honesty, and public service remain necessary for any society. Roman engineers built the best roads and aqueducts and the most comfortable buildings in Europe before modern times. Roman law, art, and literature have been very influential. Christians preserved the good characteristics of Roman culture and condemned the worst parts of it.

Discussion Questions

Identify: republic, mystery religion

1. How did Rome grow from a city to an empire?
2. Which aspects of Roman culture were similar to Christianity?
3. What foreign religions and philosophies were popular in pagan Rome?
4. In early Rome, would you have gone to see gladiator fights? Why or why not?

3. The Expansion and Persecution of the Church in the Roman Empire

Soon after the death of Jesus, Roman officials began to realize that Christians were different from Jews, who did not accept Christ. Jews lived quietly and kept to themselves, but Christians preached the message of Christ to everyone. This sometimes caused riots or other disturbances in Roman towns. The Apostles and later missionaries traveled throughout the known world preaching the gospel. Christian lay people also traveled, gathered in communities, and attempted to evangelize their friends and neighbors. They kept in touch with Jerusalem, and soon with the Church in Rome. Most Christian communities were relatively small in comparison with the total population of their cities, and early converts were often slaves or poor people. Roman officials characterized Christians as poor foreigners who formed small exclusive groups, held secret worship services, made many converts, caused riots, and subverted public order. They believed that Christians must be doing something shameful since they kept their worship secret. Some believed they were a new mystery cult. Other pagans thought that Christians were atheists since they did not worship the Roman gods. Later the pagans accused Christians of cannibalism and incest, perhaps because of inaccurate rumors about the Eucharist and Christian ideals of loving everyone. When Christians became more numerous and gained converts among the upper classes, government officials thought the sect was becoming dangerous and ought to be outlawed.

The first major persecution by the Romans, in A.D. 64, was caused by a bizarre set of circumstances. The Roman emperor was Nero, who was probably the worst ruler in Roman history. Famous for a number of irrational acts, he was eventually assassinated. According to a Roman historian, Nero set fire to some districts of Rome. To avoid being blamed for this crime, he accused the Christians. Many Christians in Rome were arrested on the charge of setting the fire or of being enemies of the human race. Some of these victims, both men and women, were forced to dress as mythological beings or in animal skins and then were torn to pieces by dogs. Others were crucified or covered with pitch and burned in Nero's gardens. People in Rome felt sorry for the Christians even though they thought that the Christians were guilty of criminal behavior. After this, it was made illegal to be a Christian, and the persecution spread to other parts of the Roman Empire. St. Peter, the Bishop of Rome, and St. Paul were put to death in Rome about A.D. 67. St. Paul was beheaded, and St. Peter was crucified. At his request, he was crucified upside down, because he said he was not worthy to die like Christ.

Roman government officials under Nero became increasingly arbitrary, greedy, and provocative. The Jews living in Judea rebelled against Roman domination, and Rome crushed the revolt ruthlessly. Jerusalem and the Temple were completely destroyed around A.D. 70. Jesus had prophesied that Jerusalem would suffer destruction (Mt 24:2), and most Christians left before it was surrounded by Roman armies. Josephus, a Greek-educated Jewish historian, related the horrible details of the siege in his book *The Jewish War*. Josephus commanded a detachment of Jewish troops who were defeated and decided to commit suicide rather than surrender to the Romans. Josephus tried to talk them into surrendering, but when they refused, he arranged to be the last one to die. After the others had killed themselves, he surrendered to the Roman general Vespasian. The general intended to send Josephus in chains to Rome, where he might have been enslaved, fed to the lions, or killed by gladiators. Josephus avoided this by telling the general that he had surrendered because he dreamed that he saw Vespasian as emperor of Rome. Pleased with this favorable prophecy, the general put Josephus on his staff, where he was able to help negotiate with the Jewish rebels. Vespasian became Roman emperor in A.D. 69, after the death of Nero. His later leniency toward Christians and Jews may have been caused by his respect for Jews such as Josephus.

Because of the nature of Roman government, persecution of Christians was never universal or consistent. Even if an emperor started a general persecution, one governor might not prosecute known Christians, while another might pay informers to find them. After Nero's reign, Christians were usually left alone until the reign of Domitian, from A.D. 81 to 96. After that, they were persecuted with varying degrees of severity. Though most Christians did not have to worry too much about being arrested, their peace was always precarious. Much of the earliest Christian literature is concerned with preparing for being arrested, persecuted, or martyred.

The letters of St. Ignatius of Antioch, written as he was being taken to Rome to be executed, show the Christian attitude toward martyrdom. For him, death was the gate to life with Christ, and his sufferings were united with the sufferings of Christ. He did not fear fire, the cross, lions, or cruel tortures, as long as he made his way to Jesus Christ. If Christ gave him strength, he would endure all things. Evidently Christ strengthened his martyrs, since they died bravely. Many were filled with joy from God and joked with the men putting them to death or converted their jailers. One might expect bishops such as Ignatius to be heroic, but ordinary Christians, even young people and children, showed the same faith and courage. Many saints, such as Tarsicius, Perpetua, and Felicity, were young martyrs who freely gave their lives rather than deny their faith and love for Christ or break his commandments.

Why were these people willing to give their lives for Jesus? Denying Christ is a major sin that cuts people off from God's grace and love. The martyrs were aware of their personal relationship of love with Jesus, who lived within them and to whom they were committed. They were willing to suffer with him, since it brought them closer to him, rather than lose the relationship by denying that it existed or committing some other sin. They knew that they would be united with Christ in heaven after their death. St. Polycarp told his judge that he had served Christ for eighty-six years, and Christ had done him no wrong, so he could not blaspheme his name. St. Perpetua said that she could not deny that she was a Christian when that was what she was. St. Tarsicius, a young man carrying Holy Communion to the sick, was beaten to death because he refused to tell some pagan soldiers what he was carrying, to prevent them from mocking Jesus.

There were frequent minor persecutions, and occasional severe ones that affected the whole Roman Empire with varying degrees of intensity. Between A.D. 249 and 258, the emperors Decius and Valerian made a concentrated effort to exterminate Christianity. By then Christians had become numerous, and many held influential positions in the government. However, Christians were still a minority. Commissions were set up in every town, and everyone was required to sacrifice to the emperor. Bishops were expected to give up the Sacred Scriptures and the vessels used in celebrating the Eucharist. Many Christians refused to comply and were martyred, but some local officials provided Christians with false certificates saying they had sacrificed. Many Christians denied their faith and made the sacrifice, but later regretted it and wanted to return to the Church. Normally they were excluded from the Eucharist for years before they were allowed to receive Holy Communion again. However, some Christians at this time believed that major sins committed after baptism could never be forgiven. Consequently, they believed that Christians who had committed the sin of sacrificing to the emperor were permanently cut off from God's grace. The Church eventually defined the doctrine that all sins committed after baptism can be forgiven if the person is sorry for them, confesses them, and is reconciled with the Church.

In spite of persecutions and errors, Christians were becoming numerous and well established in society. Catholic beliefs and practices were gradually being more fully defined and explained. While many Roman officials were hostile, others were sympathetic to Christianity or were Christians themselves. One Roman emperor included a statue of Christ in his private chapel among the statues of various gods, and it was rumored that another emperor was a secret Christian. Some theologians wrote defenses of Christianity and addressed them to sympathetic emperors. At times it seemed that Christians would gradually be accepted as part of Roman culture.

However, sympathetic emperors were succeeded by others who persecuted Christians. Roman rulers had several reasons to persecute Christians besides disliking or fearing them. According to Roman law, the property of condemned people could be confiscated by the government and sold, so a persecution could be used to solve a financial crisis. Another motive was provided by the frequent economic problems, famines, and barbarian invasions. Most Romans believed that general prosperity was a sign the gods favored the emperor and were pleased with Rome. During an economic crisis, emperors sometimes persecuted Christians as a propaganda device. Emperors hoped that people would think that the gods were causing misfortune to punish the behavior of the Christians instead of thinking that the misfortune was caused by the emperors' mistakes.

The last and most serious persecution occurred in the reign of Diocletian, 284 through 305. By this time there were separate rulers in the eastern and western sections of the empire.

Diocletian reigned in the east, where the persecution was most severe. Many Christians were executed, enslaved and forced to work in the mines, or fined. One of these was St. Nicholas, an eastern bishop who became so famous for giving gifts to the poor that he was popularized many years later as Santa Claus. A few years later, however, the emperor Constantine became a Christian, and Christians were no longer persecuted by non-Christian emperors.

Discussion Questions

Identify: Nero, Josephus

1. Describe the persecution of Christians under Nero, Decius and Valerian, and Diocletian.
2. Why were the persecutions against Christians not continuous? Why did they often take place when Romans were suffering from famines or economic problems?
3. For what was St. Nicholas noted?
4. Why were Christians faithful to Christ during persecutions? Are these motives still a part of Christianity?

4. Early Apologetics: Explaining Christianity Correctly

Christian apologetics involves explaining Christianity to people who do not understand it, of justifying it to people who are hostile to it, or of removing misconceptions about it. Apologetics is also used to point out inconsistencies in other religions and philosophies. Christian apologists show that Christians lead happier, better, and holier lives than non-Christians and that Christianity is beneficial for the government and society in general. These explanations and demonstrations are needed so that Christians will understand what they believe and non-Christians will give the message of Christ a fair hearing. Jesus and the Apostles used these approaches in their preaching.

Though early Christians knew Christ and had the guidance of the Holy Spirit, they needed a new vocabulary and generations of experience living the Christian life before some doctrines could be explained fully. Some Christian beliefs can never be fully understood because our minds are limited and God is infinite. However, some explanations are better than others, and some are completely wrong.

After the Judaizing controversy, the next major challenge to Christian doctrines came from Gnosticism. The Greek word *gnosis* means wisdom or knowledge. Gnostics believed they had secret knowledge about angels, devils, and other celestial beings, and a secret way to God. Some Gnostics thought that these spirits were more important than Christ, and the most radical ones reinterpreted the Christian story as a struggle between angels and devils in which Christ was unimportant. They rejected much of the New Testament because it did not agree with their beliefs. In the Letter to the Hebrews, St. Paul or one of his disciples explained that Christ is above the angels and the angels are subject to him, as they are to God (Heb 1:4–14). St. Irenaeus of Lyons and other early theologians wrote extensively against Gnosticism. Besides repeating the arguments Paul used, they said that the Church has always taught that the angels were subordinate to Christ. Some Gnostic leaders insisted that they were in possession of secret teachings about angels from Christ and knew more than the bishops. The Apostolic Fathers argued that if Christ had imparted secret teachings to anyone, it would have been to his twelve Apostles, who would have passed the knowledge down to the present bishops.

Excessive preoccupation with angels, devils, and other supernatural spirits is not uncommon in the modern world. Many New Age leaders and others seek, and claim to find, various types of spirits who will speak through them and lead them. Christians today need to be as knowledgeable about the correct relationship between Christ and the angels as their ancestors in the early Church.

Another heretical group was founded by a man named Montanus. He believed that Christ was coming again very soon and that everyone should give up marriage, hold their possessions in common, and live lives of strict self-denial. He thought that major sins committed after baptism could never be forgiven. Montanism was such a strict sect that it did not gain many converts, but it did convince Tertullian, a famous theologian. Tertullian had always insisted on the strictest possible interpretation of Christian doctrines, and he recommended that Christians study nothing but the Bible. By this time, most Christian theologians were well educated in Greek and Roman pagan literature and philosophy as well as in knowledge of the Bible and the Apostolic Fathers. Tertullian finally left the Catholic Church and became a Montanist. His Catholic writings were still read, since they contained many helpful explanations of Christian teachings.

From the time of Christ, the Church has taught that when people deliberately rejected the teaching of Christ or the authority of the bishops, they were departing from the Catholic Church. Groups such as the Montanists were Christians, though mistaken ones, and they were clearly distinguished from non-Christians, such as Jews and pagans. People who had been baptized and had promised to follow Christ could never undo their action and return to their original state. Even if they turned against Christ or his Church, they could never be in the same position as unbelievers who never knew him. Catholics made every effort to persuade other Christians to come back to the Church.

Errors such as Gnosticism and Montanism forced Catholics to explain what they believed. Persecutions established the principle more firmly that Christians should give their lives rather than deny Christ or his teaching. Stories about the martyrs and other literature show that early believers were deeply aware of their personal and loving relationship with Jesus. The early Christians laid a firm foundation for all succeeding generations of Christians to build on.

Discussion Questions

Identify: Christian apologetics, Gnostics, Montanists, Tertullian, Perpetua and Felicity (see below)

1. What did the Gnostics believe? What did St. Paul say about angels and celestial beings?
2. What did Montanus teach?
3. Why was the Montanist sect attractive to Tertullian?

Featured Saints: Perpetua and Felicity

The second and third centuries are often called the *age of martyrs*. More Christians were killed then than at any other time in Church history until the twentieth century. Many bishops and priests were executed, but most of the martyrs were ordinary Christian men, women, and children. Two of the most famous martyrs were young women named Perpetua and Felicity, from Carthage in Africa.

In A.D. 203, Emperor Severus instituted a new type of persecution to discourage people from becoming Christians. Most of the victims were new converts. Perpetua, Felicity, and three other Christians were arrested in Carthage. Perpetua was twenty-two years old, married to a wealthy man and the mother of a young son. Felicity was a young slave who was about to become a mother. Saturus, a layman who was instructing them in the faith, voluntarily joined them in prison. Perpetua's father, who was not a Christian, begged her to save herself by giving up her faith, but she refused. Shortly after this the five new converts were baptized in prison. After Perpetua obtained permission for her baby to remain in prison with her, she was so happy that she said she would rather be in prison than anywhere else.

After Perpetua was baptized she had several visions or dreams. In the first, she saw a golden ladder reaching to heaven, surrounded by terrifying swords, daggers, and hooks. Saturus climbed the ladder safely, then turned and called to Perpetua. She was afraid to follow because a large dragon appeared at the bottom, but when she said the name of Jesus, the dragon put his head down at the foot of the ladder. She stepped on it and climbed to the top, where she found a man dressed as a shepherd and thousands dressed in white eating a delicious banquet. When she awoke, she could still taste the sweetness of the food. They knew that this dream meant that they would suffer martyrdom.

At their trial, held on a huge platform in public, the prisoners continued to state firmly that they were Christians, and the judge condemned them to be torn apart by wild beasts in the arena on a pagan feast day. He also ordered the men to be scourged and the women to be hit in the face. Shortly after this, the prisoners' warden changed his attitude and became very helpful and friendly. Later he became a Christian, since he realized that these prisoners had some great power within them. Perpetua's father continued begging her to give up her faith, but she refused. She said that he was the only one in the family who would not rejoice when they were with Christ.

Perpetua had another vision, in which she saw that she would be fighting not with wild beasts, but with the devil, and that she would be triumphant. Saturus had a vision in which he was led by angels to a beautiful garden, where they met many martyrs and other Christians. These visions strengthened the Christian prisoners to look forward to their martyrdom with joy, in spite of the gloomy prison and their other trials.

Perpetua wrote about their imprisonment and her visions, and Saturus wrote of his vision. An eyewitness told the rest of the story. Felicity gave birth to a daughter, who was adopted by another Christian, and the next day they were led into the arena. Saturus and the other men were killed quickly by leopards and bears. Perpetua and Felicity were attacked by a wild cow, and both were thrown down unharmed. Getting up, they quickly straightened their clothing and hair to await the next attack. The mob began shouting that this was enough, and the two were led out of the arena. Perpetua spoke to the Christians waiting there and encouraged them to be faithful and love Christ, who had strengthened Perpetua and Felicity to face the wild cow without fear. The crowd's mood changed and they began shouting for their death, and the women were taken back and executed by gladiators.

This story, especially the visions, became so famous that St. Augustine had to remind his congregation that it was not as authoritative as Sacred Scripture. The names of Perpetua and Felicity are recited in the liturgy, along with a few other saints, every time a priest uses the first Eucharistic prayer at Mass. The bravery and grace of God in the trials and death of Perpetua and Felicity have inspired countless Christians to be faithful to God in spite of persecution by the government or opposition to Christianity by their families.

3

Christian Rome

CHAPTER 3

Christian Rome

1. The First Christian Emperor

When the emperor of Rome, Constantine, converted to Christianity in A.D. 312, he began a new era in the Church. Christianity was encouraged, instead of being persecuted or tolerated by the government. New difficulties became evident immediately. Would Christian emperors accept the authority of bishops to direct the Church? What would happen if an emperor disagreed with the bishops? Would people without faith become Christians in order to gain good positions in the government?

Diocletian, the pagan emperor who died in 311, thought that it was impossible for one man to rule the whole Roman Empire effectively. He ruled the Eastern empire, and he appointed a co-ruler, Maximian, to govern the Western empire. They adopted their chief military officials as their heirs to rule after them. Roman emperors had usually designated their successors by adopting them as sons or marrying them to their daughters. However, the system broke down after Diocletian and Maximian abdicated in 305. Galerius and Constantius Chlorus, their successors who ruled jointly with them, were unable to appoint their own successors, because they had sons who intended to rule.

Constantine was the son of Constantius Chlorus. His mother was a Christian named Helena. According to rumor, she was a barmaid before marrying Constantius, but she was evidently a remarkable woman. After Constantine became emperor she spent the rest of her life in the Holy Land searching for relics of Jesus and early saints, founding churches, helping the poor, and praying. When she died she was considered a saint.

Constantine's father was not a Christian, and Constantine was not raised as a Christian. He spent his early life learning to lead soldiers in battle and to run the government. At this time, soldiers usually had greater loyalty to the general who commanded them than to the ruling emperors. Since Constantine was supported by his army, he took control of the government in England without much opposition in 308.

Maxentius, the son of Maximian, seized power in Rome. Constantine and Maxentius were unable to influence the Eastern part of the empire, so Licinius, another general, took control there. However, no one believed that the empire should be divided into three parts. In 312, Constantine decided to attack Rome in order to make his position more secure by becoming the only ruler in the West.

This battle was the occasion of Constantine's conversion to Christianity. When he was preparing to attack Rome, he found that Maxentius had more soldiers and was likely to defeat him. Shortly before the battle, he had a vision or dream in which he saw a Christian symbol, the chi rho, and heard the words "in this sign you will conquer". He told his soldiers to paint the symbol on their shields, and unexpectedly they won the battle. After this Constantine became a Christian catechumen, although he did not take the step of being baptized until he was about to die. Twelve years later he defeated Licinius in the East and became the sole ruler of the Eastern and Western Roman Empire.

Roman emperors had always regulated the worship of the pagan Roman gods. Old Testament stories seemed to set a precedent for Christian rulers to intervene in Church affairs. For example, Israelite kings such as David were expected to support the worship of God and suppress idol worship. Kings who neglected this duty were partly responsible for the misfortunes of the whole nation. Both traditions encouraged Constantine to take some responsibility for supervising Christian worship and belief. The emperor was an unbaptized layman, so he chose bishops as advisors and moved very cautiously at first. He legalized Christianity and included more Christians in his government, but he did not attempt to influence the Church or to outlaw other religions. After he became the sole ruler of Rome, he turned his attention more fully to Church affairs.

Though the Church was rapidly gaining new members and wealth, a serious problem was developing. A new heresy was being preached that had a more destructive impact on Church life than any in the past. Arius, a priest in Alexandria, Egypt, had begun teaching that Christ was not God, but was something between God and man. Many people believed him. The bishop of Alexandria and his young deacon, Athanasius, repeated the constant teaching of the Church that Jesus was fully God. At that time, most bishops were uninfluenced by Arius and believed that they needed to define the traditional teaching more clearly to refute his errors. This situation led to Constantine's first major attempt to guide Christianity. He and the bishops who advised him called for a Church council to meet in Nicea, in 325, to discuss the Arian problem. After this council, which condemned the teaching of Arius, Constantine used imperial forces to ensure that the council decrees would be followed.

Constantine was one of the most capable and successful emperors in Roman history. He was the sole ruler of the Roman Empire for the last twelve years of his life and continued Diocletian's administrative, military, and financial reforms. When he died, the empire was secure and prosperous. He saw that Rome, located in Italy, was in a bad strategic position to be the capital of the Roman Empire, so he founded a new capital, Constantinople, the modern Istanbul. It was located between the Black Sea and the Aegean Sea and was much more easily defended and accessible than Rome. The city was thoroughly Christian, with beautiful churches instead of pagan temples. The new capital flourished from the beginning and remained one of the most prosperous cities on the Mediterranean for more than a thousand years. In spite of these achievements, some of the precedents Constantine set caused serious problems for the Church after his death.

Discussion Questions

Identify: Constantine, St. Helena, Constantinople

1. How did Constantine become the sole ruler of Rome?
2. What might have influenced Constantine to intervene in Church problems?
3. What did Constantine do as a Christian emperor?

2. The Council of Nicea and the Arian Conflict

The Council of Nicea, held in A.D. 325, was the first ecumenical council, a general council of the whole Church. (As mentioned in chapter 1, the Council of Jerusalem is not generally considered an ecumenical council, though it was the first example of a Church council settling a dispute about Christian teaching.) The Council of Nicea was convened in 325 to deal with the Arian problem. Arius taught that Jesus, the Son of God, was subordinate to the Father and had been created by him in time. Since he was created by God, he could not be fully God. Furthermore, the Holy Spirit was sent by the Father, so the Holy Spirit could not be fully God. Arius thought that Jesus was especially close to God and had extraordinary gifts, but he had done God's will by his own choice, in the same way that ordinary Christians try to do God's will. He could not save people by giving them God's life and grace, although he could help them by his example and teaching.

The teaching of Arius denied several fundamental Christian doctrines. The Apostolic Fathers wrote that God became man so that man might become God. In other words, since Jesus was God who became man, he could enable people to be forgiven for their sins, to live Godlike lives, to have God's life and grace within them through the sacraments, and to be united with God forever in heaven. If Jesus were not fully God, he could not do any of these things. Christians who understood their faith saw that if Arius were correct, people could not be forgiven their sins or receive God's grace, so no one could be saved.

Arius began spreading his beliefs by every possible method. Arius was a fascinating conversationalist, a magnetic preacher, and an engaging writer. His religious songs quickly spread throughout the Greek-speaking part of the empire. Many Egyptians adopted his beliefs, and the controversy became very widespread and intense among ordinary Christians.

Alexander, the archbishop of Alexandria, took action quickly. When Arius refused to stop teaching his new doctrines, he was forbidden to act as a priest. Since this did not prevent him from converting people, Alexander called for a council of Egyptian and Libyan bishops to discuss the problem. Over a hundred attended. They supported Archbishop Alexander's actions against Arius, who was forced to go into exile. Arius found a supporter in Eusebius, the bishop of Nicomedia. Eusebius was a member of an earlier movement, called *Subordinationism*, which was centered in Antioch and believed in some modified Arian doctrines. Arius stayed with Eusebius and wrote a book promoting his teaching. Since the Egyptian bishops had not been able to end the controversy and Arius had found several bishops to sponsor him, Constantine and his advisors called a general council.

More than four hundred bishops attended the Council of Nicea. After a long debate, they agreed to a document that explained that the Father and the Son are of the same nature or substance, but distinct in Persons. This meant that Jesus is fully God and has existed with God the Father from all eternity. Jesus is equal to the Father but is a separate Person from him and from God the Holy Spirit. There is one God, but there are three Persons. The council also condemned Arius. Though all except two bishops signed the council documents explaining the nature of God, three more refused to condemn Arius, and a few others thought that there might be some common ground between the two beliefs. Nevertheless the council was a triumph for the unity of the Christian faith and showed that Christian believers and their bishops had survived three centuries of persecution with their faith nearly intact. They did not do nearly as well in the decades that followed the council. Constantine supported their decisions by issuing an imperial decree exiling Arius and the bishops who had not signed the Council documents.

The *Nicene Creed*, which is recited in the Sunday liturgy, is based on the documents of the Council of Nicea and portrays the relationship of Jesus to the Father as "God from God, light from light, true God from true God, begotten not made, one in being with the Father". The Apostles' Creed, which is used in the baptism liturgy and which Catholics usually recite before saying the Rosary, is older and shorter. Later creeds became more specific and longer, in order to explain the faith in the light of new controversies. Creeds are concise summaries of the Christian message. When Christians recite a creed, they recommit themselves to God and reaffirm their faith. The Church recommends that all Christians study their faith, so that they will be able to understand and believe all of the articles in the creeds.

Discussion Questions

Identify: ecumenical council, Council of Nicea, Nicene Creed

1. How did the beliefs of Arius differ from traditional Christian beliefs?
2. Describe the relations of God the Father and God the Son based on the definitions established by the Council of Nicea.

3. Politics and Belief After Nicea: Athanasius to Ambrose

The first ecumenical council was a triumph of unity and faith in the Church, but the decades after Nicea were some of the worst in her history. The most notable characters at that time were two great bishops and saints, Athanasius and Ambrose, and a pagan emperor, Julian. Most emperors and bishops after Constantine were anything but exemplary. The Catholic faith survived because a few heroic bishops and most lay Catholics held on to their traditional faith in spite of Arian emperors and many cowardly or unorthodox bishops.

The Arian conflict was renewed three years after Nicea. Constantine's sister, who admired Arius and believed in his teachings, and a few semi-Arian bishops persuaded Constantine to pardon Arius. He recalled the Arian bishops he had banished and ordered them reinstated in their dioceses. Later, Arians persuaded the emperor to exile some orthodox bishops, and Arius began to prepare for a triumphant return to Alexandria. Athanasius had recently succeeded Alexander as archbishop of Alexandria. He refused to allow Arius to enter the city, in spite of Constantine's decree. After a long succession of unfounded lawsuits against Athanasius, Constantine banished him. Arius was about to enter Alexandria in triumph when he unexpectedly died. Many people believed that his death showed that God had condemned his teachings, but his faction continued to gain strength.

Constantine remained Catholic, but during his reign Arians became more numerous and powerful. Many became bishops. Some modern historians believe that Constantine did not understand the Arian controversy. Though he was decisive regarding other subjects, he changed his religious policy many times, following the views of the various bishops or other people advising him.

The successor of Constantine, Constantius II, became an Arian. He attempted to impose the Arian faith on the whole Church by using a variety of tactics. He forced the election of Arians as bishops and tried to persuade the other bishops to become Arians. He held many local Church councils, packed them with bishops loyal to him, and used them to issue documents repudiating the Council of Nicea. Bishops who refused to cooperate were arrested. After many years of harassment only Pope Liberius and a few bishops had refused to sign Arian professions of faith. They were exiled or imprisoned, sometimes for many years, and their dioceses were given to Arian bishops. As St. Jerome said, "The world groaned and marvelled to find itself Arian." Catholics rioted and refused to recognize the Arian bishops, but this did no good since the bishops were supported by imperial soldiers. Catholics could choose between attending churches controlled by Arians and not worshiping in a church at all. When Constantius II died in 361, he believed that the empire was firmly Arian.

Constantius was mistaken. The events of the next few years justify our faith in Jesus' promise that "the gates of Hell" will not prevail against the Church (see Mt 16:18). The next Roman emperor was Constantius' nephew, Julian, who had been raised as an Arian Christian. After he became emperor, he repudiated Christianity and followed a mixture of pagan worship and neo-Platonic philosophy. His friends and family thought he was eccentric, because of his philosophic idealism, since he lived very simply, dressed in a plain tunic like a philosopher, avoided court ceremonial and banquets, and lived a celibate life after his wife died. Like all successful emperors at this time, he was a brave soldier, a good general, and a powerful orator. His authority was based as much on the loyalty of his armies as on his family connections.

Julian wanted to put an end to Christianity, but he knew that he was not strong enough to attack the Church directly. He decided to weaken the dominant Arians by allowing the return of exiled Catholic bishops and the free election of new bishops. Imperial troops would no longer be used to enforce religious beliefs. He reopened pagan temples, appointed new priests to sacrifice to the gods, supported mystery cults, encouraged the study of pagan philosophy, and promoted pagan government officials.

Julian ruled for a few years, then he was killed in battle. According to an old story, as he was dying of his wounds, he realized that Christianity would triumph and said, "Galilean, you have conquered." Julian's attempt to revive paganism was a failure. The old religion had been declining for many years before Constantine, and Julian could not find enough dedicated pagans to accomplish his reforms. Christianity was so widely respected that pagan temples were forced to adopt many Christian functions, such as caring for the poor, to compete with Christianity. Many of the pagans Julian appointed to his government became Christians after he died.

When Julian allowed the exiled Catholic bishops to return, Catholics began practicing their faith again. Bishops who had been forced to sign Arian professions of faith often repudiated them and returned to the faith defined at Nicea. However, many bishops and lay people remained firm Arians, so the change back to traditional belief was slow in some places and occasionally violent. Some cities had both Arian and Catholic bishops for many years. Julian was followed by a number of Catholic and Arian emperors, each of whom ruled for a short time. Each emperor promoted his own faith, and the rapid changes caused more conflict. Christians began to realize that Church doctrines should not be determined by Christian secular leaders.

The imperial family often stayed in Milan, Italy. Milan reflected the religious struggles throughout the empire. When the city's Arian archbishop died in 374, the Catholics were determined to elect a Catholic bishop. At that time, bishops were chosen by popular elections, which were influenced by the recommendation of the preceding bishop, the public's knowledge of the candidate's life, and the fact that bishops could not take office unless they were consecrated by other bishops. Since communications were very unreliable, local people usually knew more about the life and faith of potential bishops than the Pope in Rome, who might be months or years away in travel time. Government leaders sometimes chose the bishops, though this was considered unethical. Since the Catholics and Arians in Milan both intended to elect a candidate of their own faith, and the Arian imperial family was away at the time, the election seemed likely to cause a riot. The governor of the province, a popular young man named Ambrose, went to the cathedral to keep the crowd calm. When he entered, people began shouting his name, and he found himself elected.

Ambrose was astonished. He was a Christian, but he was an unbaptized catechumen; he knew very little about his religion, and he had never intended to be a bishop. However, he regarded his election as the voice of God. In a few days he was baptized, ordained, and consecrated archbishop. He chose a saintly old bishop as an advisor, sought out orthodox commentaries on the Bible, and took up his new duties with the same courage and tact he had shown as governor. He said later that he learned his faith at the same time he was teaching it to his congregation.

Ambrose had some advantages that many bishops lacked. Since he had been trained to be a governor, he was an outstanding orator. This was essential in any public office since the few books available were expensive, and most people could not read. Ambrose's family connections put him on the same social plane as the imperial family and other rulers. He was an experienced administrator, and he was very popular in Milan. Before his election he had been famous for Christian virtues such as charity to the poor, chastity, and refusing to authorize judicial torture, which was routine in the Roman legal system. His faith was strong, and he prayed to God for help in every difficulty.

Milan was peaceful after Ambrose was consecrated, and he gave all of the churches to Catholics. After a few years the imperial family returned. The emperor was a young boy named Gratian. He was under the authority of his mother, Justina, a firm Arian. Justina asked Ambrose for a church to use for Arian worship. He refused. Justina ordered imperial troops to take over the cathedral, and Ambrose and his congregation barricaded themselves inside. Justina was unwilling to order the soldiers to attack, so she stationed them around the cathedral. After several weeks, since the Catholics showed no indication of wavering, she ordered the troops to withdraw. Justina's decision showed the increasing prestige of Ambrose, and of bishops in general. In the past rulers had used their armies to force bishops to conform to the rulers' decisions. Justina's decision also showed that the Catholics in Milan had most of the local population on their side.

By A.D. 400 the Arian religion was declining rapidly among Roman Christians, but it lasted for several hundred years among barbarian tribes. Today no major denomination is Arian. Some people who call themselves Christians do not believe that Christ was divine, but they are different from the Arians because they usually believe that Christ was no more than an exceptional human being. Catholics and the major Protestant denominations have held firmly to their belief in the Trinity. The final result of the Arian heresy was that most Christians have a better understanding of the relationships of the three Persons of the Trinity.

After Gratian began ruling as emperor, he became a Catholic. He often turned to Ambrose for advice. During his short reign he put an end to many pagan ceremonies, which previous emperors had left alone. The title *pontifex maximus*, high priest of the pagan religion, was finally dropped from the emperor's official name. He removed the pagan altars and statues from the Senate in Rome, in spite of objections from a few pagan senators. The symbolic value of these changes was very important. Constantinople had been founded as a Christian city, and now the ancient city of Rome was also thoroughly Christian.

A crisis involving one of Gratian's successors, the Spanish general who became Theodosius I in 394, allowed Ambrose to establish a more important precedent. Like Gratian, Theodosius was a personal friend and admirer of Ambrose. He was a baptized Catholic, although he did not always follow the teaching of Christ. On one occasion he ordered the massacre of seven thousand civilians. When Ambrose learned about this, he excommunicated Theodosius. This was the first time that a bishop had asserted so much authority over an emperor, but Ambrose explained that he could not do otherwise without abandoning the office given to him by Christ. When Theodosius protested, Ambrose said that if he wanted to receive Holy Communion, he would have to enter the Church as a penitent and be reconciled like any other sinner. Theodosius finally agreed, did his required penance, and was reconciled to the Church. This established the principle that emperors were subordinate to the Church regarding their personal morality and showed that the intentional massacre of innocent civilians was absolutely forbidden in Christian society.

Some people might wonder why Pope Damasus and his successor, Pope Siricius, allowed the archbishop of Milan to take such an influential role. Ambrose was able to accomplish more than the Bishop of Rome because of his connections with the imperial family, his diplomatic experience, and his personal holiness. From the time of the Apostles to the present, the most influential leaders of the Church have often been bishops, priests, or lay people rather than Popes. The authority that comes with the office of the Successor of St. Peter is not the same as holiness, charismatic gifts of leadership, political skills, intelligence, or training in theological debate, though most Popes have had many of these qualities. Popes resolve disputes, judge new movements, exercise authority, and defend the faith. They are the only individuals with the gift of infallibility in teaching faith and morals, but there has always been a great need for leadership from others.

Ambrose was one of the most outstanding and influential bishops in the history of the Church. Since the time of Constantine, secular rulers had been trying to control the Catholic faith. Ambrose enforced the old tradition that bishops have full authority in Church affairs and are entitled to judge the faith and moral lives of all Christians, including government leaders. As the power of secular rulers declined, the Western Church was able to follow the example of Ambrose and maintain her independence from the government.

Discussion Questions

Identify: Constantius II, Julian, Ambrose, Justina, Theodosius I

1. How did Constantius II spread the Arian faith?
2. Since most of the bishops at the death of Constantius II were Arian, how did the Catholics return to their original faith?
3. What could Catholics have done if their bishop was exiled by the Roman government and a new bishop was escorted by soldiers into their cathedral? Did they have any alternatives to supporting the new system?

4. Life in Christian Rome

Pagan Roman families about A.D. 350 had many similarities to families today. Idealistic Romans married with the idea of forming a permanent relationship with their spouses and having children. While fathers had complete authority over their wives and children, they were expected to be fair, and there are many stories of the love between husbands and wives and their children. Wives and unmarried women could own property and had authority over their children and slaves. Divorce and infidelity were common. Roman women sometimes tried to avoid having children by having abortions or using drugs or sorcery. Unwanted children could be left to die or sold into slavery. Prostitution was very common, and ambitious young Roman men often had long-term unmarried relationships with poor women or slaves and abandoned them later to marry into wealthy families. The children born to these relationships were not usually able to inherit property from their fathers, even if their mothers were not slaves, and these children were often cast out with their mothers. Poor people or slaves might never be able to marry. Homosexual and lesbian activity was not uncommon. Some idealistic pagan emperors had tried to discourage divorce and to promote healthy families, but their laws and good examples were not very effective. Other emperors had led the way in immorality.

Dedicated Christian families at that time were characterized by love, fidelity, self-control, permanence, and openness to children. Jesus had explained that divorce was not part of God's original plan for men and women. If spouses separated, they could not marry new spouses without committing adultery. Jesus taught that celibacy—giving up marriage and sexual relations for the purpose of prayer and of serving God better—was good and holy, but marriage was good in itself. Since Christians did not believe in having abortions, they often had many children. Many people who became Christians, or wanted to convert, were living in immoral sexual relationships against their will. For example, a Christian slave woman might be forced into an unmarried relationship with the man who owned her. Since Christianity forbid these relationships, women were given hope of eventually gaining an honorable life and security for themselves and their children through marriage. Christians who were legally married to non-Christians when they converted were expected to stay married and try to convert their spouses. It was considered best for Christians to marry Christians. Most marriages were arranged, but parents usually tried to find spouses who would please their children.

As Christian ideals penetrated society, the absolute authority of fathers and parents became modified. Children gained the right to refuse undesirable marriages, and parents were not allowed to sell daughters into prostitution. Women gained more rights in divorce, more control over their property, and some protection from abusive husbands. These laws reflected Christian ideals, but the laws were not designed to force everyone to adopt Christian marital beliefs. Remarriage after divorce was allowed for centuries after Rome had become predominantly Christian.

Some social conditions helped Roman families. Fathers usually trained their sons to follow in their occupation, since there were few other economic opportunities. Mothers usually trained their daughters. Since most people lived all their lives near the place they were born, many people had extended families with dozens of uncles and aunts, cousins, grandparents, nieces, nephews, and in-laws. Married children could ask their relatives for help if they had any problems.

There are other ways to follow Christ besides marrying and raising a family. From the time of Jesus, some individuals chose not to marry because they wanted to consecrate themselves completely to Christ instead of spending time caring for spouses and children. The Acts of the Apostles contain stories of virgins who were dedicated to prayer and prophecy and associations of widows who did charitable works. St. Paul and many other men imitated Jesus by living celibate lives. Single people and hermits began to form groups of monks and nuns, but many people lived consecrated lives in their families or as part of the general Christian population in society.

Christians who were especially holy and faithful to their vocations were sometimes given charismatic gifts. These included miraculous powers such as healing, prophecy, and the gift of converting sinners or pagans. At times God gave these graces to people who were in consecrated states of life or about to be martyred and also to holy married people. Christians prayed to them after they died, and many miracles proved that God continued to answer the prayers of his saints or of the people who asked the saints to intercede for them. Relics of saints were preserved and credited with miraculous healings and conversions, in the same way as the touch of Jesus' cloak healed the sick woman in the Gospels.

Becoming a Catholic was a slow process. Converts went through a long period of instruction called the *catechumenate*. They were usually received into the Church during the Easter vigil. This ancient practice has been revived in the Rite of Christian Initiation for Adults (RCIA). After converts were baptized they received more instruction about the sacraments, and they were expected to pray, do charitable works, and live moral lives. They attended Mass on Sundays and the feast days of saints, which were often celebrated very elaborately. Sermons had to be long and informative since there were few other opportunities for Christians to learn about their faith. People who wished to postpone baptism could remain catechumens for years. Children might be instructed in the faith by their parents or by religious men and women, deacons, priests, or tutors. However, many children were raised with little religious instruction and were left unbaptized until they were adults.

Christ instituted all of the seven sacraments while he was on earth, but it took the Church many years to explain the powers Christ gave her. There are references in the New Testament to baptism, laying on of hands for confirmation, the Eucharist, ordaining bishops, the anointing of the sick, confessing sins, and matrimony. Infant baptism was practiced from the earliest days of the Church, since there are references to whole households being baptized, but many catechumens in the later Roman Empire postponed baptism until they were close to death. The sacrament of penance was very severe at that time. Yearly or more frequent confession became common in the Middle Ages, and the easy penances given now are relatively modern. The sacrament of confirmation was often given to infants along with baptism instead of being postponed for years, as it is now in the Western Church. The Eucharist was established with readings, a sermon, the offertory, the prayers of the Sacrifice of the Mass, and Communion from the time of the Apostles. By A.D. 400 the liturgy could be very elaborate, and priests often celebrated Mass several times a week. Later they said Mass every day, and many lay people attended Mass daily. The anointing of the sick became commonly reserved for people near death.

Early Christians had a great reverence for sacramentals such as relics, blessed objects, and holy places. They used devotional practices such as celebrating the feast days of saints, asking for their intercession, walking in religious processions, fasting, praying the Psalms, and giving alms to the poor. Modern Catholics sometimes understand the sacraments better than they understand these other aspects of Christian life.

Jesus chose the Apostles, led by St. Peter, and their successors to be bishops, leaders of the Church. The Apostles also chose deacons to help them. The duties of deacons have changed over time. In the early Church some women were called *deaconesses*, but they did not have the share in the sacrament of Holy Orders that deacons did. Deaconesses helped distribute food to the poor, prepared women for baptism, and did other works of charity. Later the word *deaconess* was sometimes used for the leader of a community of nuns. In the Latin language, the same word was often used for a large number of unrelated offices, jobs, or titles.

Shortly after the Apostles chose deacons they began ordaining priests, who shared more fully in the powers of bishops. Priests were able to administer all of the sacraments except for ordaining priests and bishops, though priests did not usually administer confirmation. At first some married men were chosen as priests and bishops, but in the Western Church this practice changed very quickly. Priests were soon required to be celibate in many dioceses, and bishops had to be celibate. Sometimes married men were elected to be bishops, but they were expected to stop living with their wives when they took up their new office. This was hard for the bishops and also for their wives, who often joined religious communities. Soon bishops were chosen only from unmarried men. The Catholic Church and most of the early heretical sects ordained only men as priests and bishops, even though some pagan cults had women priestesses. The Church was following the example of Christ, who chose only men to be his Apostles, though many women were his followers and friends. Ultimately, all priests and bishops are chosen by God acting through his Church. Many successors of the Apostles have not been very heroic or have completely betrayed their office. This is not surprising, since Judas, who was personally chosen by Christ, betrayed him, and the rest of the Apostles abandoned Jesus when he was arrested. The weakness of human leaders shows the power of God, which has preserved the Church for two thousand years.

By A.D. 400 the Church was well established, with large cathedrals, elaborate rituals, a formal hierarchy, and many dedicated Catholic lay people, monks, and nuns. In the Western Roman Empire, most Catholics believed that the secular government should not control Church doctrine or policy. Even though the proper relationship between the two powers was still unclear, the Catholic Church was free to follow the teaching of Christ.

Discussion Questions

Identify: Athanasius, ascetical, St. Jerome (see below)

1. What did Athanasius accomplish besides remaining faithful to Christ?
2. How did the Church benefit from the Arian controversy?
3. Which sacraments were administered differently in some ways in the early Church than today? Which have changed very little, or not at all?

Featured Saint: Athanasius

St. Athanasius was born to Christian parents in Alexandria in Egypt about 297. He is best known for his defense of

Christian faith in the divinity of Christ during the Council of Nicea. However, his life encompassed several other movements: the development of formal monastic life, the increasingly firm belief that bishops and not secular rulers should explain the teaching of Christ, and the continued effort to maintain Christian unity.

As a young man, Athanasius lived in the desert and gained a reputation for fasting, prayer, and ascetical living. (The word *ascetical* came from a Greek word for athletic training and indicated that Christians used self-denial and spiritual exercises to become stronger in the struggle to imitate Christ.) Athanasius was well educated in philosophy and the pagan classics and was famous for his knowledge of the Bible and Christian literature. He attended the Council of Nicea as a deacon. Several years later, when he was less than thirty years old, he became the archbishop of Alexandria in Egypt.

Like Jesus, Athanasius experienced some of his most painful trials because of the treachery of Christians who should have supported him. The disciples of Arius were determined to force Athanasius to deny the traditional faith in Christ and agree with their new views or else to give up his position as archbishop to someone more sympathetic to them. They resorted to some very dishonest tactics. They were unable to shake the popularity of Athanasius in Egypt among the Catholic population, so they began bringing false charges against him. They accused him of a number of crimes, such as destroying the sacred vessels used for their liturgies and murdering one of their bishops to use his hand for magic. Athanasius was able to prove that these accusations were unfounded, particularly since the Arian bishop was alive and in hiding, as the Arians knew. They claimed that Athanasius had immoral relations with a woman, but at the trial she was not able to identify him. Eventually they accused him of trying to prevent the grain ships from sailing to Rome. This was a very serious charge, since the city of Rome faced famine if the grain ships did not arrive on time. Constantine believed this accusation and banished Athanasius. When the political situation changed, Athanasius was able to return to Alexandria, only to be banished again by Constantius II. He was banished from his diocese five times, but he never denied his faith. He died in 373.

Since Athanasius spent so much time at councils and in exile and was so knowledgeable about Egyptian religious life, he helped the monastic movement come to maturity in other parts of the Christian world. Many Western saints were inspired by the tales of heroic Egyptian Christians who gave up everything for Christ and went into the desert to fast and pray. Western Catholics such as St. Jerome, who made an excellent Latin translation of the Bible called the *Vulgate*, were inspired to travel to the East for study and brought back theological books and traditions that had a profound influence on the Western Church. Athanasius and other exiles kept the Eastern Church informed about the West, where bishops were more independent of government control. The travels of bishops attending councils or being exiled brought gains in unity that influenced all future development of the Church.

Athanasius had a reputation for personal holiness from the time he was a young man, and the reputation increased as he remained faithful to Christ in spite of opposition. It was no coincidence that the most fearless defender of the faith lived a good moral life and frequently fasted and prayed. One who has given up everything for Christ, and who knows and loves Christ through continuous prayer, is unlikely to abandon him because of threats or exile.

4

Augustine and the Decline of Rome

Featured Saint: Benedict

CHAPTER 4

Augustine and the Decline of Rome

1. Augustine's Early Life and Conversion

St. Augustine wrote some of the most beautiful and inspiring books about God that have ever been written. He is the best known author from the early Church except for the writers of the New Testament. In his *Confessions* he tells readers about his early life and his conversion to Catholicism. Augustine's book praises God's mercy in saving him after he had done so much that was wrong and made so many mistakes, and it tells of the great joy of seeking and finding God. It has been called the first autobiography, and it is still a fascinating story.

When Augustine was born in about 354 in a small town in Roman Africa, the Roman Empire was flourishing and becoming thoroughly Christian. When he died in 430, nearly all of Western Rome had been overrun by barbarian Germanic tribes, and northern Africa was being devastated by the Vandal tribe. Today that area is a desert of drifting sand and rocks, but in Roman times there were many towns and estates with olive trees, grapevines, grain, and other crops. Many of the people were of mixed Roman and African descent, and the culture was thoroughly Roman.

Augustine's mother was St. Monica, a devout Catholic married to a pagan named Patricius. Monica did not have

Augustine baptized, but she taught him prayers and blessed him with the sign of the Cross and hoped that he would grow up to be a good Christian. However, early in his life Augustine turned away from God. There were several reasons for this. As a boy he and his friends enjoyed adventures such as stealing, and when he was sixteen he formed an immoral relationship with a woman who later bore him a son. He knew that these activities were against the laws of Christianity. In addition, the translation of the Sacred Scriptures then used was very badly written according to the classical standards Augustine was learning in school. He rejected the gospel message because he was interested only in literary style. He stopped going to church and trying to live a Christian life. Patricius was not concerned with his beliefs, and Monica could do nothing but pray for him.

Augustine was very ambitious, and Patricius was able to pay for a good education. After Augustine had completed school in his home town, he went to Carthage, the most important city in Africa, for an advanced degree. When he had finished his education he began teaching in Carthage.

After rejecting Christianity, Augustine joined the Manichees, a non-Christian sect that originated in Persia. This sect believed that the universe was controlled by two equal powers. The evil power, the power of darkness, controlled the visible material world, and the good power controlled the spiritual world. This belief in two equal but opposing powers is called *dualism*. The moral code for their elite, a small group of supposedly perfect Manichees, was extremely strict, but ordinary Manichees were not expected to follow all the moral laws. Since they believed that the material world was evil, they recommended abstaining from marriage, from having children, from eating most foods, and from many other activities. Augustine did not intend to marry the woman he was living with, so he had no problem conforming to the loose moral code by which most Manichees lived. He knew that he did not understand all their doctrines, but he believed that if he could meet the most important leaders they would know the answers to his questions.

After teaching several years in Carthage, Augustine heard that there were many opportunities in Rome for teachers. He collected letters of introduction from his influential friends and set sail. He soon established himself in Rome as a teacher and a successful orator and made some acquaintances among the influential pagan senators and government officials.

Augustine dropped out of the Manichee sect after he moved to Rome. Their doctrines were inconsistent and irrational, and the famous Manichees he met were not able to answer his questions. Their elite were hypocrites, unable to follow the strict rules they professed. He was interested in astrology, but he gave it up when he found that children born at the same time had completely different destinies. In Rome he became interested in another group, the Neo-Platonists. These philosophers believed that there is one supreme good, like a supreme god, and that it is our destiny to seek him and to find him through meditation, prayer, and living a good life. As Augustine studied Neo-Platonism and talked with members of the group, he found himself wanting to seek this supreme good. Later this desire helped lead him to Christianity.

Several pagan senators suggested that Augustine move to Milan and look for a job with the imperial court. He established a household there with his mother and his son. Monica went to church whenever they had Mass or prayers and became quite devoted to St. Ambrose, the famous archbishop of Milan. She was also busy with plans for helping Augustine's career and improving his moral life by finding a suitable wife for him. He agreed to marry a young woman from a wealthy family, but this family insisted that he must first separate from the lower-class woman with whom he had lived for sixteen years. This was considered reasonable in Roman society, and Augustine sent her back to Africa, though he was very unhappy about separating from her. The woman was heartbroken and swore that she would never form a relationship with anyone else. After she was gone, Augustine found it impossible to live a single life while waiting for his marriage. He began a secret relationship with another woman, though he despised himself for his weakness and lies.

So far Augustine had done nothing to indicate that he would ever become a Christian, much less a bishop and a saint. However, many Catholic saints have been converted from similar or worse lives. Once they turned toward God and began trying to obey him, God gave them the grace to give up their sins and become new creatures in Christ.

Augustine soon found a group of friends in Milan who were working for the government and who were interested in neo-Platonic philosophy. Many of them were also interested in Christianity, and they often discussed their religious beliefs. When Augustine began going to church to hear the sermons of Archbishop Ambrose, who was an excellent orator, he learned that Christianity was a logical, supernatural religion. It avoided the irrationality and hypocrisy he had found in the Manichees, fulfilled the desire of the Neo-Platonists by uniting Christians with the supreme goodness of the Holy Trinity, and told the truth about God and the universe. He considered becoming a Christian, but he did not believe that he would be able to live according to Christian standards. As he learned more about Christianity, he became very depressed because of his moral weakness. Neo-Platonism had given him some good ideals but not the strength to live by them.

On one occasion Augustine invited several friends to meet a government official who had come from Africa. This man told them that two of his colleagues there had been so moved by the story of St. Anthony Abbot, a famous Egyptian monk, that they had given away all of their possessions and become monks. Augustine was torn with remorse because these men had given up everything to follow Christ, but he was too weak to give up his sins. He left his friends and threw himself down under a tree in the garden, weeping. Then he heard the voice of a child singing something like a child's chant, "Take and read, take and read", and he picked up a copy of St. Paul's letters, lying on a table in the garden. Opening this book, he read that God asks man to put on Christ and to live in purity. When Augustine read this, a tremendous confidence flooded his soul. He knew that with God's help he would be able give up his sins, and he was filled with joy. He resolved to follow God completely by living a celibate life. Augustine did not have enough strength on his own to give up his immoral relations with women, but through faith he found the grace to remain celibate the rest of his life. He, his son, and a friend were baptized during the Easter Vigil by St. Ambrose.

Monica was delighted with her son's new resolutions. Though she had spent years trying to arrange a good marriage for him, she was happy to give up her plans now that he had resolved to devote his life to God through monastic prayer and contemplation. Monica died shortly after Augustine became a Catholic. She had become a saint by praying constantly, attending Mass and other church services, loving God, and doing God's will by patiently caring for her family. Augustine's father, Patricius, had become a Catholic about a year before he died. Augustine's son, whom he dearly loved, died soon after Monica, during the long trip back to Africa with Augustine and some of his friends and relatives.

After Augustine returned to Africa, he and some of his friends lived on his property and spent their time in prayer, fasting, religious conversation, and contemplation. By living this semi-monastic life he experienced the goodness of God so intensely that he said that God is better than anything people can see or imagine. He is more beautiful than the most beautiful scenery, more satisfying than the most satisfying human relationship, more sweet than the sweetest scent or taste, and as much superior to everything as the Creator is superior to the things he creates.

In spite of the quiet life Augustine adopted, he was well known in Africa because of his earlier career and his conversion to Christianity. Several years after he returned he visited the town of Hippo. When the people recognized him they organized a demonstration to induct him as a priest, so that he would succeed the old bishop when he died. Augustine saw that this was the will of God and accepted. He was unhappy that his concerns as a bishop prevented him from spending much time in prayer and contemplation, but he realized that he would be able to do more for God as a bishop than as a monk.

Discussion Questions

Identify: St. Augustine, *Confessions*, Monica, Manichees, Neo-Platonists

1. Describe Augustine's background, education, and career.
2. What are some of the things Monica did that made her a saint?
3. Describe Augustine's conversion. Include his reasons for leaving the Manichees and Neo-Platonists and for losing interest in astrology.

4.   What did Augustine have in common with Ambrose be-
     fore he was elected bishop? How did they differ?

2. Augustine's Work as a Bishop

A bishop's most important works are preaching and administering the sacraments. Augustine wrote many collections
of sermons, so much is known about his preaching and his
audience. Some of the sermons lasted so long that he suggested that the people take a short break. The audience
sometimes interrupted him with applause, comments, or
weeping. He must have been a magnetic preacher. Since he
traveled to every church in his diocese frequently, he spoke
to a great many people. Like modern priests, he usually
discussed the Bible readings for the day and used them to
explain Christian principles, moral living, or different aspects of the faith.

Augustine's life as a bishop was similar to the lives of modern bishops, who have the same responsibilities for their
churches as he did. Augustine frequently traveled to neighboring dioceses or to Carthage to assist in ordaining bishops
and to attend episcopal conferences, formal groups of bishops from the same geographical area called together to discuss Church policies. He supervised the priests, monks, and
nuns in his diocese and was responsible for overseeing the
correct administration of the sacraments by his priests. He
held debates with the leaders of other religions and wrote
books to answer their criticisms of the Catholic Church and
to demonstrate the mistakes in their beliefs. He was in charge
of administering Church property, which was extensive, and
overseeing the funds for the poor. Finally, he was responsible
for his own prayer life and his relationship with God.

At that time, bishops had many duties that are now performed by secular officials. Bishops judged legal cases between Christians and assisted government and army officials in many ways. Since the government was Catholic, most officials believed that it was their duty to promote Catholic worship. Augustine and the other bishops were often asked to suggest laws to support Catholicism and discourage other religions. The laws were enacted and enforced by government officials. Many local councils of bishops were held to discuss this issue. Augustine argued that the best way to convert non-Christians and members of heretical or schismatic Christian sects, such as Manichees and Donatists, was to hold debates with their leaders and persuade them of the truth of the Catholic faith. However, the other bishops believed they needed assistance from the government in dealing with these sects, and Augustine reluctantly went along with them. It had been illegal to be a Manichee for many years, because the Manichees' teachings about marriage were detrimental to society. Now Donatists, a large group of schismatic Christians in Africa, could be fined or arrested. Several years later Augustine barely escaped being attacked by Donatists and learned that some fanatical Donatists would beat or kill their members who returned to the Catholic Church. Several Catholic bishops were badly beaten by Donatists. After this, Augustine became more reconciled with laws against the sect.

The Donatists were very similar to the Catholics in their doctrines and liturgy. They believed that the archbishop of Carthage, who had jurisdiction over all of northern Africa, had denied Christ during the persecution of A.D. 250. The Donatists thought that because of this sin, Christ could not work through him, and all of the sacraments he administered after that were invalid. They thought that the priests and bishops he ordained had no special powers from God, so their Masses and other sacraments had no effect. Donatus was their first archbishop, and their hierarchy all traced their ordinations back to him. They said Donatus was consecrated correctly as a bishop, so the Donatists had valid sacraments. Their church, however, was schismatic, split apart from the Catholic Church. Except for their beliefs that Christ could not work through a sinful priest or bishop and that serious sins committed after baptism could not be forgiven, they did not disagree with the Catholics on major doctrines.

The Pope and the rest of the Church supported the Catholic archbishop of Carthage against Donatus and his followers. Even if the Catholic archbishop had committed the serious sin of denying the faith, the sacraments he administered would still have been valid, because the sacraments come from Christ and not from the holiness of the priest who administers them. The archbishop was eventually tried and acquitted on the charge of lapsing during the persecution, but the Donatists still refused to be reunited with the Catholics.

By Augustine's time the Donatist sect had been in existence for more than a hundred years. The Donatists were very numerous in Africa, but there were scarcely any in other countries. They were used to being cut off from communion with all the other Christians in the world, and they had no inclination to return to the Church. While some Donatist leaders were sincere, others realized that there was very little reason to continue the schism. They prolonged it because they were afraid that if they became Catholics, they would lose their positions. During Augustine's long rule as a bishop, he persuaded many Donatist leaders and their congregations to return to communion with the Catholic Church. However, the sect did not come to an end until many years later, when the wars and persecution by Arian Vandals made the Donatists realize that their superficial differences with Catholics were unimportant.

Because Augustine had been converted from the Manichees and from Neo-Platonist philosophy, he wrote many books explaining the truths of the Christian religion in terms Manichees and Neo-Platonists would understand. He refuted the errors of these groups, but he was always careful to show which of their teachings were found in Christianity or could be reconciled with Christian doctrines and used to explain Christianity more clearly.

Augustine entered into a debate with another group, the Pelagians. Pelagius was a Catholic priest from England who believed that men could live good lives and be saved by their own efforts. He did not believe that men needed grace from God. He denied the Catholic belief that men are weakened by original sin, the sin committed by Adam and Eve and passed down to everyone. Catholics believe that people have good qualities and are capable of doing good with the help of God's grace, but cannot be saved or do good without him. Augustine obtained copies of the writings of Pelagius and wrote a refutation. After some years, the Pope and a council of bishops also condemned the errors Pelagius was teaching.

Most Pelagians returned to the Church. Augustine's writings helped prevent his errors from being revived for hundreds of years, but some of his views are popular today among social planners, who believe that people are fundamentally good and become bad only because of bad social conditions. Though there is some truth in their belief, since God created human beings to be good, they are now weak and selfish because of their fallen nature. The best environment would not make people saints without the help of God's grace, and in any case, there are no perfect people to create a perfect environment. People need discipline, effort, and God's grace to live good lives.

Augustine wrote many books that answered pagan objections to Christianity and offered a Christian explanation for the decline of Roman civilization and the success of barbarian invaders. This was an important question. Barbarian tribes had been entering the Roman Empire for hundreds of years, but during the lifetime of Augustine they began winning substantial victories in battle with Roman forces. Africa was one of the last Western territories to remain free from invasion, but finally the Germanic barbarian Vandal tribe crossed the straits of Gibraltar and began traveling east toward Carthage. The Vandals plundered every town and estate, massacred or enslaved the people, and tortured the bishops they captured to find where they had hidden the reputed wealth of their churches. Augustine died of a fever in A.D. 430, during the siege of Hippo. Nearly everything he wrote was saved by his friends and disciples who survived the siege.

Discussion Questions

Identify: episcopal conference, Donatists, Pelagians, Vandals

1. What were Augustine's duties as a bishop? How were they different from the duties of modern bishops?
2. Why did the Roman government pass laws against the Manichees and the Donatists?
3. Why did Augustine disagree with the other bishops about the laws against Manichees and Donatists?

3. The Fall of Rome, *The City of God*, and the Vandal Invasion of Africa

The Western Roman Empire lasted over a thousand years. During that time Rome had grown from a small town to a huge empire circling the Mediterranean Sea. Constantine had founded a second capital, Constantinople, in the East. The Eastern empire used the Greek language, and Latin was spoken in the West. The original languages in many of the conquered countries had fallen out of use, which promoted unity in each half of the empire, but the two halves were unable to communicate with each other freely. They had divergent cultures and traditions, separate agricultural and economic bases, and different external enemies.

The Western empire included modern Britain, France, part of Germany, Italy, Africa, and part of the Balkans and Slavic areas of Europe. The Western empire had a very long northern border, running from Scandinavia through Germany and farther east. The rivers that protected it could be crossed by invaders with boats or on the ice in cold winters. Many tribes lived north of the borders. They spoke different Germanic and other languages and had long traditions of fighting wars to gain food, plunder, and glory. Britain was bordered by pagan tribes living in Wales, Scotland, and Ireland. Roman Africa was protected to the south by deserts.

Invaders from the north threatened the Eastern Roman empire, but they were never able to gain permanent control there. The Persian empire, east of Israel, was a more serious threat, but since Persia and Rome were separated by a desert, there were seldom any major battles or invasions. Egypt, which was surrounded by impassable deserts, was nearly safe from attacks as long as Rome controlled the Mediterranean.

Though the Roman upper class had once considered military training essential, by Augustine's time most men had little knowledge of warfare and no intention of fighting. The best Roman generals were usually Germans, or Romans who had spent years with German tribes and had learned their military tactics. Many common soldiers were Germans, and there were few Roman troops. Expelling all German invaders from Western Rome was impossible. The Eastern empire had similar difficulties, but Eastern emperors were more successful in recruiting loyal soldiers and Roman generals, so they were often able to defeat invaders in battle. They had other advantages over the Western emperors. Since the East had a richer economic base and more wealth, emperors were often able to buy off invaders or to hire them to fight other tribes, which was more economical than fighting them with government troops.

Members of German tribes had been entering Rome to trade or enlist as mercenary soldiers for hundreds of years. Inside the empire they found rich farmland and other economic opportunities, protection from warlike neighbors, and many other advantages. Entire tribes, with all of their people, livestock, and possessions, began trying to enter the empire. One of the first was the Franks, a pagan tribe that crossed the borders about A.D. 250. Like most tribes, they were ruled by kings and assemblies of nobles. At first the Franks lived by attacking towns or estates and living from the plunder. They had to fight occasional battles with local Roman armies or larger forces led by generals from Rome, but often they were able to escape with their plunder. After many years they worked out an agreement with the Roman government and settled down permanently in France. They continued speaking their own language at first and following their own laws and customs. Some of them were farmers already, and some acquired slaves or took over entire estates. They were excellent soldiers, and they maintained their military traditions, although they gradually began adopting some Roman customs.

After 350 more tribes began moving west and south. Population increases, pressure by new tribes such as the Huns, and the weakness of Roman armies encouraged them to settle inside the Roman Empire. Some of them had become Arian Christians, converted by Wulfila, a missionary from the Germanic tribe of the Goths. However, their religion did not help them live peacefully with the Romans, who were predominantly Catholics. One Arian tribe entered the empire with the permission of Emperor Valens, an Arian emperor, but in 378 they defeated and killed him in battle because he did not give them the provisions he had promised. Other tribes were hired to fight earlier invaders. Since no Roman leader was strong enough to defeat the invaders in battle and force them to leave, these newcomers settled in any undefended area they chose or traveled from place to place living on plunder. In 410 the ancient city of Rome was defeated and sacked by the Visigoths, distant relatives of the well-established Goths. The Visigoth victory shocked the whole Roman Empire. It was an unmistakable sign that the world had changed forever.

What were Christians to think of these events? The pagan statues had been taken out of the Roman Senate less than twenty years earlier. Were the angry pagan gods responsible? Modern historians blame military or economic forces for the disaster, but these explanations were no more satisfying to the Romans than they are to many people in similar circumstances today. Bishops pointed out that the barbarian tribes were often more virtuous than Christian Romans, who did not practice their faith or live by the Commandments. Bishops also criticized the Roman government, which had many oppressive laws and taxed people so heavily that they were better off when they had been conquered by barbarians. St. Augustine wrote one of his most famous books, *The City of God*, to explain that the heavenly Jerusalem, to which Christians are called, was not the same thing as the Roman Empire. The kingdom of God will never be found in any society or political system on this earth. All human governments and societies are imperfect and will come to an end, but the kingdom of God will last forever.

After Rome was sacked, the barbarians withdrew. Roman government continued in the West, but the most powerful people in Rome were usually Gothic generals. Roman senators and emperors kept some authority, and a few Romans maintained their wealth and power. Some became successful generals, fighting with the same methods as the Germans. The Goths were Arians, but they seldom attempted to interfere with the Catholic religion. As the Roman government became increasingly ineffective, Catholic bishops, who were usually upper-class Romans, took over more responsibilities formerly managed by the secular government.

One of the last provinces to be conquered was Africa, which was invaded by ruthless Vandals. They took control of all the land and established a kingdom that lasted over a hundred years. Europe was occupied by different tribes living among old Roman families who still owned some property. This peaceful arrangement was the result of diplomacy. Most barbarian tribes respected the traditions of Roman power, and they were not so numerous that they needed all of the land. They were often willing to leave the Romans some property in return for recognition from the Eastern emperors as legitimate rulers. Frequently the land was divided, with some going to the invaders and the Romans keeping the rest. As time passed, the different nationalities learned each other's languages and began to intermarry, though the religious differences between Arians and Catholics caused constant friction. Many years later the Frankish king Clovis converted with his tribe to Catholic Christianity and conquered most of the other tribes in France. After this the Roman and German peoples gradually fused into a unified civilization.

Discussion Questions

Identify: Franks, Wulfila, *The City of God*, Goths

1. What military and economic factors led to the barbarian invasions and conquest of Western Rome?
2. Why was the Eastern empire successful in resisting invasions of barbarians?
3. Why was the fall of the city of Rome so shocking to Christians?
4. Describe the distribution of land to Romans and barbarians after the barbarian invasions. How was this a help in the eventual formation of a new culture?

4. Monastic Life: Christianity Preserved and Lived More Fully; Conversion of Ireland

The Gospel of Luke tells the story of a rich young man who asked Jesus what he should do to inherit eternal life. Jesus told him that he should obey the Commandments. He should not commit adultery, kill, steal, or bear false witness, and he should honor his father and mother. The young man said that he had been doing these things all his life. Jesus said, "One thing you still lack. Sell all that you have and distribute to the poor, and you will have treasure in heaven; and come, follow me" (Lk 18:22). The young man in the Gospel went away sad, because he had many possessions. He was not willing to follow Jesus' invitation to live a more perfect life of poverty with him, even with the promise of being rewarded in heaven.

Several hundred years later, a young man named Anthony walked into church when that Gospel was being read. He heard the words as though they were spoken to him personally by Jesus. Unlike the man in the Gospel, he did exactly what Jesus said. He sold his family property, gave away the money, and went to the desert of Egypt to live as a hermit. Anthony followed Jesus by praying, fasting, meditating on the Bible, and helping other hermits. After many years he became famous for his holiness and wisdom. He was chosen to be the leader of a community of monks. Today he is known as St. Anthony Abbot, a founder of religious life.

Religious life began to assume its modern form between A.D. 250 and 400. Earlier in the history of the Church, religious life included people in a wide variety of vocations, such as consecrated virgins or hermits, men and women gathered in small informal communities, traveling pilgrims, and church workers of various types. It was evident by St. Anthony's time that these people, who gave away their possessions and left "the world", needed more religious guidance than the Gospels provided. Many people began such lives with good intentions, but ended them as wandering beggars who did not follow the Ten Commandments or Christ's teachings. Even the ones who remained faithful to Christ made many mistakes. A few dedicated monks and nuns fasted too strictly and died or grew too preoccupied with bizarre ascetical practices and refused to listen to advice. Monks who were sincerely following Christ began to see that they needed formal plans or rules to help avoid these errors.

Monastic rules became important first in Egypt, the center of early monastic life. Hermits living there gathered around leaders such as St. Anthony. The leader, or the religious superior, was called an *abbot*, from the word for father. He established rules and governed the community. Some abbots wrote down their rules, which regulated prayer and work, the procedures for admitting new members, and other practical advice about the spiritual life and community business.

Nuns were led by abbesses, who arranged for priests to administer the sacraments and usually took care of the rest of their business themselves. When leaders died, communities elected successors, who normally followed the same rule as the former superiors.

Rules gradually became more explicit, though superiors always had the authority to adapt them to new conditions. Monks and nuns began taking vows to be celibate, to live a life of poverty with no possessions except for the community property, and to obey the superior in everything except commands that would be sinful. People were required to try the monastic life for some time before taking vows so that they would be able to leave if they were not suited to this life. After they took vows, monks and nuns could be freed, or dispensed, from their vows only by the abbot or the local bishop. The vows laid an obligation on the monks and nuns to stay in the community and obey the rules, but the vows also gave them some rights. They were able to elect new superiors and to remain in the monastery even if they became old and unable to work. Superiors had the obligation to regulate community life according to the rule and to do everything in the best interests of the community. These rules established permanent religious communities devoted to serving God. They could be adapted to a wide variety of cultures, situations, and needs. The rules were so practical that some religious communities have lasted from the end of the Roman Empire until today.

The main purpose of monasteries was to help monks and nuns give their lives to God, by helping them seek and find a closer relationship of love with him. Many communities met in their church seven times a day for community prayers. Once a day they had Mass, and members were expected to spend some time every day reading and meditating on the

Bible or some other spiritual book. Most of the remaining time was spent working. Monasteries in the West had to be self-sufficient after the fall of Rome. There was little trade, and the monks had to make or grow nearly everything they used, so they were trained in a wide variety of jobs. Some monasteries became famous for scholarship and writing. Monastic instructors taught the other monks, future priests or bishops, and lay people. Monks also became artists, farmers, craftsmen, cooks, builders, or experts in other trades. Nuns were expected to have the same intense prayer life as monks. Some nuns were educated well enough to write elegant histories or religious plays, which they produced in their convents. Others taught girls, copied books, or specialized in trades such as weaving, making vestments, and baking.

Monasteries became increasingly important as parishes and dioceses were impoverished by the invasions and settlements of barbarian Arian tribes. Earlier bishops and priests had been educated in Roman schools located in large towns, but the towns became smaller, and it was difficult to find schools. Fewer men were able to read liturgical books, say Mass, or read the Bible. The only education available in most parts of Europe became centered in the households of bishops and in monasteries.

Children attending monastic schools who were talented scholars often remained in the monasteries as monks and nuns all of their lives. In large, prosperous monasteries it was not unusual to find teachers who were fluent in Latin and Greek and who had read all of the classical literature and Christian commentaries in their libraries. Many monks spent their working hours copying books, so that they would not be lost forever when the current volumes wore out. These books preserved Greek and Roman knowledge and provided the foundation of science, mathematics, medicine, engineering, and literature for later civilization. Since monasteries were more stable than any other institution, they were essential in maintaining Christianity and became centers of missionary activity to non-Christian nations.

The conversion of Ireland provides a good example of the influence of monasteries. The great apostle of Ireland was St. Patrick. He was a Roman from Britain who was kidnapped by Irish raiders when he was sixteen, probably about A.D. 400, and was sold as a slave in pagan Ireland. He had been indifferent to Christianity, but his years of slavery taught him to pray constantly and to rely on God for everything. He escaped after seven years and made his way back to Britain. Eventually he became a priest and a bishop and returned as a missionary to Ireland, where another missionary bishop had just been martyred. Patrick was more successful. In his long life, he traveled to every part of Ireland and converted nearly all of the local kings. He made certain that these conversions were permanent by traveling with groups of monks, some of whom settled in each area he converted and trained the local people in Christianity. He found so many men who wanted to become monks and priests, and women who wanted to become nuns, that Ireland soon became one of the most thoroughly Christian nations in Western Europe. Ireland escaped devastation from invaders at this time, and later Irish monks traveled to many countries in Europe to found monasteries, revive local Christianity, and evangelize pagan nations. When Patrick was very old, he said that he gave thanks to God for chastening him by allowing him to be taken captive. God gave him so many benefits and graces through the experience that St. Patrick looked forward to praising the Holy Trinity for these gifts forever.

Discussion Questions

Identify: St. Anthony Abbot, abbot, monastic rule, St. Patrick, St. Benedict, St. Scholastica

1. How could a person join or leave a monastery?
2. Describe the conversion of Ireland.

Featured Saint: Benedict

St. Benedict is often called the father of Western monasticism. His rule for monks was used in most Western monasteries and convents for six hundred years, and it is still followed by thousands of Benedictines all over the world. Much is known about Benedict because Pope St. Gregory the Great, who lived in a Benedictine monastery a generation later, included some stories about him in his *Dialogues*. Benedict was born to wealthy parents in Italy in A.D. 480 and went to study in Rome. The city was then ruled by Arians and pagan barbarians, and the Catholics living there were not usually living lives that reflected their faith. Benedict's classmates tried to persuade him to join in their immoral practices. Benedict was afraid that if he stayed, he might not be able to resist temptation, so he left Rome. He met a monk in a wild area called Subiaco. The monk gave Benedict a religious habit, showed him an isolated cave, and agreed to leave his monastery every day and bring Benedict part of his food. Benedict lived there alone in prayer and fasting for three years.

Eventually Benedict was discovered by some shepherds. They were impressed with his holy life and began spreading stories about him. A community of monks that had recently lost its abbot asked him to come and rule over them. According to Pope Gregory, Benedict told them that they would not like his ways, but they insisted, and he came with them.

However, they grew so exasperated with his strict rules that they put poison in his wine. When he made the sign of the Cross over it before drinking it, the jug broke, and he realized their intention. He suggested that they find an abbot they liked better, and he attempted to return to his solitary life.

Since stories about Benedict's holiness were widespread, he soon found himself surrounded with disciples and established a group of monasteries. Monks in Europe had been following a variety of rules imported from the East or written by bishops. Benedict wrote a rule for monks that was practical, concise, and easy to understand. Much of this rule pertained to the spiritual life and was little more than a string of quotes from the Bible regarding virtues suitable for monks. The rest outlined monastic prayers, meals, government, and other practical matters.

St. Benedict and his twin sister, St. Scholastica, were famous for many miracles. St. Scholastica founded a community of nuns. They followed the same rule as the men, under the authority of their abbess, but the communities had little contact with each other. One day she went to see Benedict. They met outside of his monastery in a small house and talked for hours about God and religious life. Finally Benedict got up to leave, since it was getting late. Scholastica begged him to stay longer, but he refused. She bowed her head and prayed. Suddenly a huge storm broke, with thunder, lightning, and torrents of rain, so that it was impossible to leave. "God forgive you, Sister. What have you done?" Benedict said. "I asked you to stay, but you did not listen; so I asked God, and he did listen", Scholastica replied. They remained talking far into the night. A few days later Scholastica died. Benedict saw in a vision a great light traveling toward the heavens and knew the vision meant that his sister was rejoicing with God.

Benedict accepted monks who were rich or poor, Roman or barbarian, and refused to distinguish between them. All did the same manual labor and received the same food and clothing, depending on their health and strength. Many people sent their sons to his monasteries to be educated, and the monks had many visitors of all nationalities. In addition to being centers of prayer and education, Benedictine monasteries were models of Christian love and brotherhood. Benedict died in 547, but his spiritual influence is still important to Christians.

5

Christianity in the East

CHAPTER 5

Christianity in the East

1. Conflict in the Eastern Church

Communication between the Eastern and Western halves of
the Roman Empire was slow and difficult in A.D. 400. There
was some trade and travel, but not enough to create a unified culture and philosophical outlook. The empire had been
governed by two rulers for nearly a hundred years, and local
government officials normally served in their native countries. Greek was the predominant language in the East, and
Latin in the West. Official documents were issued in both
Greek and Latin, so governors did not need to know both
languages. The empire had nearly separated into two different nations united by one government and religion.

The Church in the empire was united, but she suffered
from the same difficulties in communication between the
East and the West as the government. Most bishops were not
able to read both Greek and Latin. There is no record that
St. Augustine ever read anything written in Greek, in spite
of his thorough education and ambition. He was limited to
reading translations of Eastern councils and theological books,
when these were available. Most bishops lacked his education and his interest in controversies in the other half of the
empire.

Popes attempted to keep in touch with the Eastern part of the Church, but some of them did not speak Greek. All of them were forced to communicate with the East by sending letters or representatives, called *legates*, who had authority to speak for them in councils and negotiations. Travel was too slow and dangerous for Popes to make the long journey to the Eastern empire. In addition, Popes were very reluctant to come within the reach of the Eastern emperors. During the Arian controversy, the Pope had been imprisoned for years and treated very harshly by the Arian emperor, Constantius II, and many other bishops had suffered greatly in prison in Constantinople. Church leaders had learned to avoid taking useless risks whenever possible.

The Church in the Eastern empire was thriving. The Arian heresy had very few followers left there. Most people in the East were Catholics, though there were still some pagans, Jews, and members of other religions. Constantinople and the other cities had many beautiful churches. Convents and monasteries were filled with monks and nuns. Bishops in the East were usually well educated in one of the great philosophical or theological schools. Education and society were becoming thoroughly Christian.

The Bishop of Rome was acknowledged to be the Primate, or leading bishop, of the whole Church. However, archbishops from the important cities of Constantinople, Antioch, Alexandria, and Jerusalem thought that they were nearly as authoritative as the Pope. The primates of these cities were often called *patriarchs*, because they ruled very old, important churches and had jurisdiction over extensive land and many other bishops. Since Constantinople was the Eastern capital, the patriarch of Constantinople was second in honor in the empire.

Eastern emperors watched over the Church as carefully as Constantine. The emperors' interference often caused serious problems, since some of them were not orthodox Catholics, and they had more power over local bishops than Constantine had claimed. A number of heroic bishops resisted unjust or erroneous emperors, but the Eastern part of the Church was never able to become as independent of the secular government as the Western part.

The Eastern Church had other problems. Christian rulers often gave large donations of money or art to churches but completely neglected the poor. Emperors levied high taxes, which were detrimental to family and social life and bankrupted many people. Rulers thought that these taxes were necessary to pay for running the government and to defend the empire against barbarians. However, the taxes also supported public entertainment and maintained an elaborate court, with many officials and expensive ceremonies to increase the prestige of the emperors. There was constant dissatisfaction because of oppressive officials and unjust laws even during the reigns of good emperors. Since the poor and the victims of unjust laws came to the Church for help, Church leaders were usually aware of their suffering. Bishops spoke out against unjust laws, high taxes, and immorality such as adultery, theft, murder, idol worship, and other sins. However, a few emperors followed Christ sincerely by helping the poor, repairing churches, and supporting good bishops against their enemies.

The Arian conflict, which began during the reign of Constantine, affected the whole empire. Later errors were usually confined to the Greek or the Latin half of the Church. The Pelagian and Donatist movements, which were important in the Western Church, were condemned by Eastern councils following the Pope's lead and never became major threats in the Eastern Church. Speculation on the nature of Christ led to two erroneous movements that were influential in the East. They affected the West primarily because the participants in each controversy tried to persuade the Pope to support their views. The Church remained united in doctrine in spite of the different problems, cultures, and languages in each half of the empire.

Catholics believe that Christ is fully God and fully man. He has two natures, a divine nature and a human nature, but he is only one Person—the divine Person of God the Son. However, it is difficult for us to understand how one Person can have two natures. People from the theological school at Antioch in Syria usually stressed Christ's human nature, and people educated in Alexandria in Egypt usually stressed his divine nature in their faith and devotion. What began as a difference in outlook gradually widened into two contradictory beliefs about who Christ is and how he can save us. The first error came into focus when Archbishop Nestorius, the patriarch of Constantinople, supported a priest who told his congregation to stop calling Mary the Mother of God. Nestorius reasoned that Mary was only a creature made by God, and God could not be born from a creature. He said that he could not worship an infant two or three months old as God. He believed that Christ's divine nature was completely separate from Christ's human nature. Jesus was two Persons, and the divine and human natures were united only by love. In Jesus' nature as God, he could not suffer. Mary was not the Mother of God, but only the mother of Jesus. This belief denied the doctrine of the Incarnation, that Jesus is God who became man. It went against tradition, popular devotion, and the writings of the Apostolic Fathers. If the teaching of Nestorius had been true, our salvation would have been impossible, since the infinite sacrifice of Jesus who is God is necessary for our salvation. The divine Person of the Son suffered in his human nature, as the Catholic Church teaches.

St. Cyril of Alexandria pointed out that the new teaching was heretical, since it denied the Incarnation, one of the major doctrines in Christianity. He emphasized that Mary was the Mother of God. He appealed to the Pope, who condemned the doctrines of Nestorius. However, Nestorius did not accept the condemnation. He claimed that Cyril taught that Christ had only one nature. This confused the question, and both patriarchs requested a council to settle the matter. It was held at Ephesus in 431 at the invitation of the emperor, Theodosius II. The council was held without the patriarch of Antioch, who was very late. Cyril, who represented the Pope, led the council, which condemned the views of Nestorius and deposed him as archbishop of Constantinople. The Catholics in Ephesus were delighted, because they believed Jesus was God and Mary was the Mother of God. They held a torchlight procession and a celebration for the bishops when the council was over.

The patriarch of Antioch arrived several days later. He did not believe that Nestorius taught that Christ was two Persons, so he convened a council with the bishops from Syria who had accompanied him and deposed Cyril as archbishop of Alexandria. Since the patriarchs and councils could not agree on a decision, Theodosius II imprisoned both Cyril and Nestorius. After talking to them he gave his judgment in favor of Cyril. Nestorius was deposed and sent to a monastery in Antioch. Cyril wrote several public letters explaining his beliefs about Christ more carefully, so that people could see that he held the same faith in Christ as the rest of the Church. The letters persuaded the patriarch John of Antioch that Cyril was orthodox, and the two signed a decree of union several years later. St. Cyril lived peacefully in Alexandria until his death in A.D. 444. Bishops who were saints were unusual at that time. Cyril was noted for his holy life, his strong defense of the faith, and his attempts to be reasonable and win over his opposition.

The Nestorian heresy lasted about fifty years in the empire, but some Nestorians went to Persia and continued teaching Nestorian beliefs, although they modified them to be more similar to the faith of the Church. Nestorian Christianity still exists today.

The Nestorian controversy and the Council of Ephesus helped to define the doctrine of the Incarnation. However, subsequent events showed the weakness of the Eastern part of the Church, both internally and in relation to the government. The dispute between Cyril, the patriarch of Alexandria, and Nestorius, the patriarch of Constantinople, had been judged by the Pope and the Council of Ephesus, but since the patriarch of Antioch rejected their decisions and held his own council, the final judgment was made by the emperor. He came to the same decision as the Pope and the Council of Ephesus, but the situation reinforced the bad tradition set by earlier emperors, who imposed their views on the Eastern Church.

Discussion Questions

Identify: legates, patriarchs, Nestorius, St. Cyril of Alexandria, Council of Ephesus

1. Why were the Eastern and Western halves of the Church not usually affected by the same errors?
2. What were some strengths and weaknesses in the Church in the Eastern empire before Nestorius?
3. What did Nestorius teach that was different from traditional Catholic faith?

4.   Describe the Council of Ephesus and its outcome. How
was the dispute about the "persons" of Christ finally settled?

2. The Monophysite Controversy

The Monophysite conflict began in Alexandria after the death
of St. Cyril. Dioscorus, the new patriarch of Alexandria, did
not believe that the early supporters of Nestorius had honestly accepted the decisions of the Council of Ephesus. Many
of them had retained their positions in the Church, and he
began attacking them. He gathered a group of followers who
believed that Christ's human nature was so completely ab-
sorbed into the divine nature that Christ had only one nature, which was neither divine nor human. It was both,
blended together. There were several different varieties of
the Monophysite, or one nature, heresy. It was the opposite
of the Nestorian heresy, which claimed that Christ's
divine and human natures were so distinctly separated that
he was two Persons. Catholics believed that Christ was one
Person with two natures, divine and human, but at that time
this belief had not been fully and completely defined and
explained.

The patriarch of Alexandria began attacking former Nestorians through a friend and supporter, the monastic leader
Eutyches. This man was more interested in making important friends and increasing the influence of the patriarch of
Alexandria than in living a monastic life. He had allies at the
emperor's court and monastic friends in other cities, and he
did everything in his power to persuade them to support
Dioscorus and organize attacks on his enemies.

Eutyches caused so much trouble that a regional council
at Constantinople condemned his Monophysite views. He

appealed to the emperor and many other influential people, including the Pope, St. Leo. The emperor called another council. Leo sent a long letter, later called the Tome of St. Leo, to Flavian, the patriarch of Constantinople. The Pope's legates at the council were instructed to read the letter, which repeated the orthodox belief that Jesus is one Person with two separate natures, united but not mixed or blended. However, neither Flavian nor the Pope's legates had a chance to speak. A number of monastic leaders who supported Eutyches brought large delegations of monks, who refused to admit the supporters of Patriarch Flavian and the enemies of Eutyches. Some monks were so violent that the council turned into a riot. Flavian was attacked and badly beaten, and he died three days later. The Pope's legates escaped, but over a hundred bishops were forced to sign decrees acquitting Eutyches. When the Pope heard about the affair he called it a council of robbers. Since the Pope never signed the decrees, the council was not considered an ecumenical council, and it usually has been called the Robber Synod. It was one of the low points in Church history and religious life.

Pope Leo and the emperor called another council, which met at Chalcedon in 451. Emperor Theodosius II, who usually supported the Monophysites, had died. His successor allowed the bishops to convene in a legitimate council with the Pope's legates presiding. Six hundred and thirty bishops attended it. They all accepted the Tome of St. Leo and signed the Chalcedon council decrees, which stated clearly that Christ was one Person with two natures. This was the doctrine that had been taught by the Council of Ephesus (which had condemned Nestorius) and by St. Cyril and Patriarch Flavian.

Unfortunately the Council of Chalcedon did not state clearly that it was supporting the Council of Ephesus and the teachings of St. Cyril, and a large party of Monophysites claimed that the new council had confirmed their beliefs. Many Monophysites refused to accept the theological definitions of the Council of Chalcedon. Later emperors tried to formulate a compromise between the Monophysites and the Catholics, but this only made the dispute more complicated and bitter.

The Monophysite sect was strongest in Egypt. Eventually most Monophysites converted to the Muslim faith after the Arabs conquered Egypt in 642. Some Monophysites returned to the Church many centuries later, and some still exist as separate sects today. The group split into several branches with slightly different beliefs, and the Monophysites who survived were less radical than Eutyches and his friends.

The Nestorian and Monophysite heresies caused the Eastern Church and the empire severe damage, but they also had some good effects. The controversies helped Christians learn more about the nature of Christ and of the Mother of God, and people learned more about the Church. Everyone had to accept the unfortunate truth that patriarchs, bishops, and monks could be as unorthodox and violent as emperors. St. Cyril of Alexandria set a good example as a firm defender of the faith who was willing to express his beliefs more clearly so that everyone could see that he was orthodox.

In the Nestorian conflict, the patriarch of Constantinople had fallen into heresy, and in the Monophysite conflict, the patriarch of Alexandria had done the same. Neither was influenced by coercion from hostile emperors, erroneous translations, or misleading accounts of events. The conflicts damaged the prestige of the patriarchs of both cities. The Bishop of Rome was never judged heretical by the Church or by later Popes. Some Popes were more courageous in defending the faith than others, but none adopted heresy, as had other bishops, even though a few of them lived sinful lives. In 451, when the Council of Chalcedon was held, Attila the Hun was threatening to invade Italy and the Western empire had nearly ceased to exist. Nevertheless the Pope's legates were given the place of honor, and his decisions were accepted as correct by the bishops in the Council of Chalcedon. Eastern Christians gained more respect for the Pope through these controversies.

Discussion Questions

Identify: Dioscorus, Eutyches, Monophysite, Tome of St. Leo, Robber Synod, Council of Chalcedon

1. Describe the views of Eutyches and the Monophysites. How do they differ from traditional Christian beliefs?
2. What happened at the Robber Synod? Why wasn't it accepted as an ecumenical council?
3. What was the outcome of the Council of Chalcedon?
4. The vow of obedience taken by monks and nuns obliges them to obey superiors in everything except commands that would be sinful. What events in the Robber Synod show that this exception in the vow of obedience was necessary?

3. Justinian and Theodora

Eastern emperors were usually the sons or relatives of earlier emperors or generals who married into the imperial family. Nearly all of them faced problems from religious disputes, invasions, and a lack of sufficient funds. Many were young and indecisive or had no experience in running the government. Public policy was often managed by career bureaucrats, men who went into government service hoping to gain wealth and power. These men were frequently dishonest and greedy and were hated by most of the population. Emperors usually distrusted capable generals or diplomats, since these men might lead revolutions and take power themselves. The more successful they were, the more dangerous they seemed to the emperors.

In the Western empire, a young ruler faced by these problems arranged for his most loyal and effective Roman general to be assassinated. The Goths took complete control of the city of Rome a few years later, in 476. In the Eastern empire, the government was very unstable, but it survived. It was shaken by disputes in the imperial family, dishonest or fearful generals and treasury officials, religious disputes, rebellious taxpayers, plagues, famines, and wars. The government gradually changed. After about A.D. 400, the Roman Empire in the east was called the Byzantine Empire. The Eastern emperors maintained imperial authority there, but they could do little to affect the West for many years. They were forced to authorize victorious Goths in Rome and barbarian leaders in other countries to act as rulers under their authority. This policy maintained the concept of a unified empire for more than a hundred years after the reality had ceased to exist.

The dynastic method of succession and the influence of Christianity led to an increase in the influence of women in the government and society. From the time of St. Helena, royal women were active in supporting Christianity, influencing the government, choosing their spouses and thus the successors to the throne of the empire, or running the government in the name of children who were the next in line of succession. Women were normally crowned as empresses when their husbands became emperors. This gave these women a good deal of power over government officials, though the amount of authority depended on the character of the empress and her husband. Sisters and other relatives of the emperors could be very influential if they wished, since they could often persuade the emperors to follow their advice, and it was always possible that their husbands or sons might become emperors. For example, one of the royal women in the Western empire insisted on marrying a Gothic leader. He was soon killed, and after her second husband had died, she ruled the West in the name of her young son. Other women influenced religious policy by persuading emperors to follow Christian moral laws, to call Church councils, or to pardon bishops who were out of favor. In the East, several victorious generals became emperors because they married women in the imperial family. Though they ruled the empire, their wives had their friends appointed to office and their enemies banished or executed, influenced legislation and foreign policy, and managed public works or charities. Since these women had the power to influence appointments and policy, men and women made every effort to please them by giving them gifts or by doing what they asked.

In 517 a new general took power in the East. He was prudent, thrifty, and popular because he restored stability. His son, Justinian, was even more capable. Justinian showed his wisdom by marrying a very unusual wife, the popular actress Theodora. She was intelligent and ambitious, and the crowds in Constantinople loved her. Soon after he took power, Justinian was faced with a revolt in Constantinople and planned to escape from the city. Theodora persuaded him and his advisors to stay and fight the revolt with their available forces. They bribed some of the rebel leaders, and a loyal general named Belisarius took his German troops and defeated the rest. After this victory, Justinian allowed Theodora to have unprecedented power and to control the revenue from large estates he gave her.

The empress gathered a group of loyal friends and supporters, which included Belisarius and his wife and many other officials. Since Justinian did not always follow Theodora's advice, she frequently worked against his policies secretly. Their enemies accused them of manipulating public opinion by this means. For example, Justinian insisted on harsh tax laws, but Theodora appeased public opinion by using some of the money to help the poor or to found homes for reformed prostitutes. Justinian once guaranteed the safety of the queen of the Goths, but it was rumored that Theodora persuaded Justinian's envoys to do nothing to help her, and the Gothic queen's enemies assassinated her. Whether or not this was true, the two remained united until Theodora's death many years later. They were the most effective rulers of the Eastern empire for generations.

Justinian soon felt secure and began looking for ways to expand the empire. His first step was to attack the Vandal kingdom in 533. Vandals had occupied North Africa since 430. They had never been recognized as lawful rulers by the Eastern emperors and they had never returned any of the property they had conquered from the Romans. Justinian's best general, Belisarius, sailed with an army to Africa. The Vandal king was a young man with no military experience. Belisarius defeated him in several quick battles that prevented the Vandals from uniting for a counterattack. The general used some of the Vandal wealth to pay his army and sent the rest to Justinian and Theodora. His representatives returned property to the heirs of the original owners and repaired or established new Catholic churches. North Africa remained predominantly Catholic and under Byzantine control for a hundred years.

A few years later, Belisarius attacked the Goths, who controlled Italy. He quickly established Justinian's authority over Rome and the surrounding areas, though he spent many years enlarging and consolidating his victories. Later he attacked the Visigoths, who had conquered Spain, and established an outpost there. Belisarius was one of the greatest generals in history, and his long, loyal service to Justinian was nearly unequaled in Byzantine diplomacy. The emperor was secure enough to have little fear of a rival, and Theodora supported the general and his wife. After Theodora died, Belisarius lost favor. The Byzantine Empire lost control of some of the lands he had conquered after the death of Justinian.

Justinian's conquests caused major problems for the Pope. The Arian Goths had seldom interfered with the Catholics, and the Pope had been free to send legates to Eastern councils without risking being imprisoned, exiled, or mistreated in other ways by the overbearing Eastern emperors. When Justinian controlled Rome, he sometimes harassed and imprisoned Popes and other Church leaders. Justinian was a Catholic, but he often listened to the advice of Theodora, who supported the Monophysites. Since this sect had been condemned by several councils, she was limited to finding men who were sympathetic to Monophysites, having them elected as bishops, and preventing the laws against the sect from being enforced. She and Justinian manipulated Church councils and forced them to pass decrees lenient toward Monophysites. She maneuvered the election of a sympathetic candidate as Pope, but after his election, he refused to cooperate with her plans, even though she arranged to have him arrested and imprisoned for years. She hoped to reconcile Monophysites and Catholics, but this was impossible because the two beliefs were fundamentally different. Radical

Monophysites would not agree to the most conciliatory state-ments orthodox bishops could sign without abandoning their faith.

Besides prolonging the Monophysite struggle, Justinian and Theodora's interference in religious affairs led to several schisms in Italy, which lasted for at least thirty years. Re-gional churches split away from the authority of the Pope, since they believed that he was influenced by rulers sympa-thetic to Monophysites. The Church was also damaged by long military campaigns. Most cities in Italy were conquered and sacked, which led to famines, disease, and a breakdown of government and social life. The reconquest of Italy by Catholic rulers led to far more problems than Italy's first con-quest by Arian Goths.

By 600 it was evident that the Eastern and Western halves of the Church had worked out different relations with sec-ular rulers. In the West, the Church was independent of gov-ernment control in proclaiming doctrine, although Eastern emperors occasionally tried to influence Popes for the next four hundred years. Most Western Catholics believed that the Church should be free from secular control in choosing bishops, although some local rulers forced the election of their own candidates. The Pope in Rome was clearly the leader of the Church.

The tragedy of the Monophysite conflict gave the Church two more saints, Maximus the Confessor and Pope Martin I. (When "Confessor" is used in the title of a saint, it means that the saint was as heroic in proclaiming or confessing his faith as the martyrs.) In the year 653, the Eastern emperor attacked Rome and captured Pope Martin, hoping to force him to approve a new offshoot of the Monophysite heresy. Since St. Martin refused, he was beaten and starved to death. St. Maximus was an important Eastern abbot who was in

Rome for a council at the time Martin was captured. Maximus was famous for his spiritual writings, his defense of the true faith, and his support of the Pope as the leader of the whole Church. Even though he was seventy-three, he was arrested by the emperor and banished. After Maximus endured years of increasingly harsh exile and imprisonment, the emperor ordered that he and a few companions should have their tongues and right hands cut off to silence them and should be imprisoned for life. St. Maximus died in the year 662. He is honored by Eastern and Western Christians for his profound books on the spiritual life and his heroic defense of the Catholic faith.

In the East, the feuding patriarchs had given the Eastern emperors the opportunity to control the Church, both in determining doctrine and in selecting bishops. Most of the patriarchs continued to respect and follow the Pope. Eastern Church leaders tried to assert their independence from government control, but they were never able to maintain it. The Eastern Orthodox Church and the other churches descended from it, such as the Russian Orthodox Church, were generally more submissive to government control than the Western Church.

Discussion Questions

Identify: Goths, Justinian, Theodora, Belisarius, Maximus the Confessor

1. Describe problems that caused changes in the Byzantine government.
2. Describe the conquests of Belisarius.
3. How did Justinian, Theodora, and Belisarius cause problems for the Church in Italy and the Pope?

4. The Eastern Empire and Muhammad

Muhammad was born in Arabia in 570. The few inhabitants of Arabia were predominantly pagan, with some influence from Judaism and Christianity. Muhammad began by working for a wealthy widow as a camel driver on her caravans. Later he married her. He lived a quiet life and spent his time in prayer and meditation. One day he had a vision in which he thought he saw the Angel Gabriel, who told him that he was chosen as a prophet. Muhammad claimed to have other revelations, which were written down in a book, the Qur'an. Despite some opposition when he destroyed the pagan statues in Mecca, he converted many followers to his new religion.

This religion has a number of attractions. Muslims worship one God named Allah, and Muhammad was his prophet. Allah is quite similar to the Jewish God, and Muslims use much of the Old Testament. For Muslims, Jesus is a lesser prophet than Muhammad, and they believe that Mary was always a virgin. Muslims are expected to pray five times a day, fast one month a year, give to the poor, and make a pilgrimage to Mecca. They believe that God punishes evil and rewards good, particularly when the good are Muslims who encourage the worship of Allah. The rewards provided by Allah are partly tangible; good Muslims expect to gain wealth, prosperity, and material comfort. Men are allowed to have four wives, and women are expected to obey their fathers and husbands. Paradise is described as a material heaven with delicious food, peaceful gardens, and many beautiful women for the men.

After Muhammad died, the religion was controlled by officials called *caliphs*, who were also secular rulers and military leaders. Religious, secular, and military authority were normally united in the same person in the Muslim religion. (In Christianity, Church officials such as bishops were not usually secular rulers or military leaders.) The Muslim caliphs began wars of conquest. Between 632 and 644 they conquered the remaining Arab tribes, Persia, the Holy Land, and Egypt.

The Muslims were aided by several events. The Persians had attacked Constantinople, and the Byzantine emperor had defeated Persia in 628. The Persian government collapsed, leaving the country open to conquest. Most people living in the Eastern empire had no military training or experience in war. In the Holy Land, modern Israel and the surrounding areas, and in Egypt, people were still suffering from religious disputes and high taxes. At first the Muslim Arabs usually did not try to force Christians to abandon their faith. Monophysites, Nestorians, and members of non-Christian religions had no loyalty to the Byzantine rulers, who harassed them with repressive laws. They did little to defend themselves against the invaders. Catholics who were discouraged by high taxes and unpopular bureaucrats were reluctant to fight the Arabs, who seemed to be constantly victorious. The desert nomads moved more quickly than the Byzantine armies. They conquered the Holy Land and Egypt before the emperor could send enough soldiers to defend them. Within ten years, the Byzantine Empire had lost two of its largest provinces.

Emperors were unable to recapture these lands, and the empire soon suffered further losses. The Muslims gradually moved west from Egypt. They conquered all of North Africa by 690 and invaded Spain. Their faith, the promise of gaining wealth and land from their victories, their superior military tactics, and the lack of effective opposition encouraged them to conquer a huge Muslim Arab empire. It was composed of separate kingdoms ruled by caliphs. Christianity survived for hundreds of years in some conquered countries. In a few places it never died out, but eventually most Christians in Muslim lands were taxed, enslaved, forcibly converted, or legislated out of existence.

Discussion Questions

Identify: Muhammad, Qur'an, caliph, St. John Chrysostom

1. Briefly describe the Muslim religion.
2. What weaknesses in the empire made it vulnerable to conquest by the Arabs?
3. Describe the spread of the Muslim religion.
4. What happened to Christians in the lands conquered by Muslims?

Featured Saint: John Chrysostom

St. John Chrysostom was born about 350 in Antioch. His father died when he was very young, and he was raised by his mother, a devout Christian. After receiving a good classical education, he spent some years in a monastery. When he was about thirty he was forced to leave religious life because of bad health. He returned to Antioch and was ordained a priest. The archbishop chose John to be his chief assistant, and John became famous as an eloquent preacher and orator. The name Chrysostom means golden mouth, and he earned it because his speeches were as beautiful as gold. He frequently spoke out on political subjects, as well as moral questions and basic Christian teaching.

In 397, St. John was chosen to be patriarch of Constantinople, where he soon became as famous and controversial as he had been in Antioch. His sermons and charitable deeds reminded people that the care of the poor was one of the main duties of Christians. The saint enforced strict standards among priests, monks, and nuns, and his sermons attacked the chief sins of the people in Constantinople. He often preached against immodest clothes, expensive jewelry, and immoral plays, games, and races, as well as condemning more notorious sins. John was very harsh with sinners who refused to repent, but kind to people who were trying to reform their lives. On one occasion an unpopular politician fled to his church for refuge from a furious mob. St. John preached an eloquent sermon on forgiveness, calmed the crowd, and saved the man's life.

St. John had many devoted friends, especially among communities of nuns and women doing charitable works. However, his sharp criticisms made him many enemies. Even St. Cyril of Alexandria, who spent some time in Constantinople before going to Egypt, sometimes disagreed with him. The two enemies who caused John the most trouble were Theophilus, the patriarch of Alexandria at that time, and Empress Eudoxia. The empress wore fashionable clothes, which meant that she was often very immodest, and she spent a great deal of time and money on jewels, makeup, and hairstylists. She was so egotistical that she had a silver statue of herself put up in front of one of the main churches in Constantinople. Eudoxia took John's sermons as personal attacks, especially when he spoke out against the immoral entertainment at a ceremony in her honor and preached against a "Jezebel", an evil Israelite queen in the Old Testament. The empress persuaded Archbishop Theophilus to accuse John of a number of crimes, such as deposing bishops and priests for frivolous reasons. Theophilus arranged for a small council of bishops to convict him, and the emperor banished him.

St. John was soon recalled. A small earthquake terrified Eudoxia, who thought that God was angry with her because of her attacks on the saint. She persuaded the emperor to revoke the decree banishing the archbishop. However, John preached another sermon that offended her, and she persuaded the emperor to banish him again. The people in Constantinople began rioting in John's favor, and the emperor sent troops to arrest John in his church. The saint appealed to many influential politicians and prelates, including the Pope, but this did no good, because the emperor imprisoned their legates. John died in 407 as he was being transported to his place of exile.

St. John Chrysostom was one of the most courageous bishops in history. Few Church leaders have continued speaking out against those in power when they knew that the rulers would have them exiled. John set a good example by living a modest life as archbishop and helping the poor. Wealthy people in Constantinople often followed his advice and used their money for charitable purposes instead of buying expensive clothes or estates. Later bishops sometimes followed his precedent in speaking out against evil when there was little chance of improving the current situation and every chance of being thrown in prison. Finally, St. John left the memory of his golden speeches, which inspired the people of Constantinople to do good and avoid evil.

6

Clovis to Charlemagne: The Early Middle Ages

1. The Conversion of the Barbarians
2. Pope Gregory the Great
3. Charlemagne: Protector of the Church
4. The Iconoclast and *Filioque* Controversies

Featured Saint: Bede

CHAPTER 6

Clovis to Charlemagne: The Early Middle Ages

1. The Conversion of the Barbarians

During the Middle Ages, the Church in Europe was forced to adapt to a new culture. The Roman Empire had been ruled by emperors, who appointed officials to govern provinces. Medieval society was based on the feudal system. Feudal society was usually ruled by kings, who were chosen because they were sons or relatives of earlier rulers, and the provinces of their kingdoms were administered by knights, who were strong military leaders. They swore oaths of homage and became the king's vassals, or loyal followers. The usual qualifications for being a knight were birth into the noble class and ability to fight for the king in wars. How was the Church to survive in this military society?

The new culture developed gradually. After A.D. 400 Western Rome gradually fell into the hands of barbarian tribes. The Franks, a pagan tribe, first entered the Roman Empire in Gaul, modern France, about A.D. 250. They had always been warriors. During the new invasions, they fought in wars to defend their territory or to assist the Romans, who were attacked by new tribes that were more hostile. The Franks were ruled by kings and assemblies of nobles, like most tribes.

Kings who led their men in successful battles gained wealth, military glory, and security. Unwarlike kings were often attacked by their neighbors or overthrown by enemies in their own tribe. At this time, fighting was normally done on foot, with swords, axes, lances, and some armor. It was not difficult for a man to be both a farmer and a warrior, and all Frankish men were expected to know how to fight.

Justice in barbarian tribes from Germanic backgrounds was provided first by one's relatives. If someone was murdered, his relatives were responsible for avenging the murder. However, they could accept financial compensation from the murderer instead. The compensation was regulated by law or set by the king, and it was usually a large sum of money. The system of compensation was not ideal, but it ensured that justice was done and helped deter people from committing crimes. In spite of Frankish laws, there were many feuds, since some relatives refused to accept compensation and tried to kill the people who had injured them. A person with no relatives could easily be robbed or murdered. Such a person would often put himself under the protection of someone stronger by agreeing to work or fight for him. This would ensure that the person had some protection against violence and some security.

Another drawback to Frankish justice was that the rulers were usually stronger than anyone else, so they could commit crimes with relative safety. Many rulers were assassinated by subjects who had no other means of protection against the rulers.

Romans living among barbarian tribes continued to follow Roman law, which was usually administered by Roman officials or bishops. However, Roman society was changing, affected by the prevailing lawlessness. Bishops were expected to maintain public order, but they had severe limitations. Arian barbarian rulers often stole Church property, taxed Romans heavily, or confiscated their possessions. If the Romans had no military power they were nearly helpless. Roman men were forced to learn how to fight so that they could defend their property, but they were unable to defeat their Germanic rulers.

No early Frankish kings were weak, but an exceptionally strong king came to power in 486. St. Gregory of Tours, a bishop, wrote about this king in *The History of the Franks* in about A.D. 594. Clovis, the new king of the Franks, combined fighting strength with intelligence. He was a capable leader and very unscrupulous in getting his way and eliminating enemies.

Clovis married Clotilde, a beautiful princess from the Burgundian tribe. She was as strongwilled and intelligent as Clovis. Her parents were Arians, but she had become a Catholic. She began trying to convert her husband, who was a pagan like most Franks. The queen insisted on having their first child baptized, and it died immediately in its white robes. Clovis was furious with her, thinking that the pagan gods could have saved it. He frequently murdered people who opposed him, but Clotilde managed to pacify him. She said she was pleased that God had judged her worthy that her child should be with him in heaven. When they had another child, she had him baptized. The child began to get sick, but he was cured by her prayers, according to Gregory. Clotilde was nearly the only woman in the entire *History of the Franks* who openly opposed her husband in anything, and her courage and prayers were soon rewarded.

Clotilde often argued with her husband, saying that his pagan gods were nothing but wood and stone and could not help him, but the Christian God would listen to his prayers. Once when the king was about to lose a battle, he prayed to the Christian God for assistance, then unexpectedly won. However, he did not become a Catholic immediately. After talking to St. Remigius, a holy bishop sent to Clovis by Clotilde, he called together his warriors in an assembly to talk over the advantages of becoming Catholic. He found that they were in favor of converting. Clovis and three thousand of his chief fighters were baptized together on Christmas day, A.D. 496. After this, all the members of the tribe were officially Catholic, but it was many generations before the Franks learned their faith thoroughly.

When Clovis became a Catholic, he adopted some Christian practices, such as forbidding his soldiers to plunder Church property, sending gifts to the churches dedicated to his favorite saints, and giving money to the poor. These practices won him the support of his Roman subjects and gave him an advantage over neighboring Arian tribes, who were opposed by their Roman subjects and bishops. Since Clovis wanted to increase his power, he found excuses to attack the other tribes, and he was usually victorious. He did not give up his unscrupulous tactics with his conversion. For example, he suggested to one king's son that he have his father assassinated, so that he would be king. After the son did so, Clovis arranged to have him murdered. Then the Frankish king came to the town with his army and called an assembly. Clovis said that since the old king and his son were both dead, it would be best for everyone if they proclaimed Clovis king. The people agreed, and he added that town to his possessions. After he had defeated the rulers of Arian tribes, the Arians eventually became Catholics. St. Gregory of Tours was pleased with this result, but it did not justify the king's treachery and murders, and Gregory criticized them very harshly.

When Clovis died, his wife, Clotilde, devoted the rest of her life to living as a nun, with occasional trips to help her family. She spent so much time praying in the church she had built, and did so many good works, that she is regarded as a saint. Her sons each received part of their father's kingdom, and her daughters married rulers of neighboring tribes. The royal family was very numerous, but many of the men died in wars to gain more land, wars of vengeance, or by assassination or disease. A few Frankish rulers controlled most of France by the time Gregory finished his *History*.

Since the religious difference between Franks and Romans was no longer a barrier, the two nations began to intermarry and form a unified society. The Franks gradually began living more civilized and less violent lives under the influence of Christianity. In St. Gregory's time, a few Franks still practiced sorcery and worshiped pagan gods. Many Franks obeyed God's laws because they thought that the saints would arrange for their death if they did too many evil deeds, rather than obeying out of love of God or even because of fear of hell. Often the bishops could do little except try to persuade Franks to attack their enemies instead of their families and friends and to use legal means of justice against criminals instead of assassinating them or torturing them to death.

Franks and Romans believed firmly in the intercessory power of saints. Some of them carried this belief to extremes. St. Gregory was once accused of slandering a Frankish queen, and he had to take oaths that he was innocent and say Mass on the altars of several different saints to prevent her from having him arrested and possibly killed. She thought that Gregory would not commit perjury and risk the vengeance of such powerful heavenly intercessors. Many Catholics believed that the patron saints of churches, monasteries, and church personnel would send misfortune to anyone who harmed them and give good fortune to anyone who protected them. This belief helped the Church survive in the relative lawlessness of the early Middle Ages. It was true that rulers who were good Catholics often enjoyed more good fortune than the others. They were supported enthusiastically by their bishops, subjects, and families. They were relatively safe from assassination by fearful or injured subjects, one of the leading causes of death among Frankish rulers. Living a Christian life had many advantages besides gaining the favor of God and his saints, but few Franks could resist the temptation to enlarge their possessions by murder and unjust conquests.

After the Franks became Catholics, some of them became bishops. These bishops were not always exemplary, and most bishops in Gregory's time were still chosen from the available Roman candidates. Some of them were no better than the Franks. Gregory related stories of Roman and Frankish bishops who used their offices to become alcoholics or gluttons, illegally accumulate land and valuables, seduce women, or plot against priests or neighboring bishops. Other bishops, like Gregory, became saints. Bishops were murdered occasionally, but Gregory said that their murderers quickly died or were killed, since God avenged their deaths.

Dealing with Frankish Catholics was so difficult that conscientious bishops and priests frequently gained reputations for holiness. For example, Gregory related the story of a priest who interceded for two slaves who had married without their owner's permission. Such a marriage was unlawful, though unauthorized marriage was not regarded as a serious crime, and the Frankish owner was furious. The priest persuaded the slaves' owner to agree that they would not be harmed and would never be separated. When the priest left, the Frank had them buried alive together in punishment. As soon as the priest heard this he returned and persuaded the owner to have the slaves dug up, but only the man was still alive.

Gregory's efforts to reconcile quarrels or stop battles among the Franks were not always successful and made him some dangerous enemies, but his *History* shows that he had a sense of humor about the outrageous situations and violent people he encountered. Unlike some Romans, he was able to appreciate the virtues of the Franks while encouraging them to give up their injustice and immorality.

A few Frankish leaders were good Christians. They helped make life in France more peaceful and secure by reconciling enemies, preventing battles, protecting the poor and Church property, and setting examples of good Christian living. Some gave money or land to the Church or joined convents or monasteries. Gregory praised kings and queens who followed Christian laws and respected the Church, even if they were not exemplary rulers. His *History of the Franks* was influential for hundreds of years and encouraged many rulers to live moral Christian lives. Gregory was unhappy that the civilized Roman world had ended, but his goal of persuading Franks and Romans to live together in Christian unity helped form medieval civilization.

Discussion Questions

Identify: Franks, St. Gregory of Tours, *The History of the Franks*, King Clovis, Queen Clotilde

1. Describe Frankish society at the time of the conversion of King Clovis.
2. Why did Clovis become a Catholic?
3. Why were Catholic beliefs about the intercession of the saints so important at this time?
4. How did the conversion of the Franks to Catholicism help Frankish and Roman society? How did it help the Church?

2. Pope Gregory the Great

Pope St. Gregory was born in the city of Rome in 540, about the same time St. Gregory of Tours was born in France. Both were from upper-class Roman families and were related to many government leaders and bishops, and both were fairly well educated. Pope Gregory began his career as an official in the secular government of Rome. When he was thirty he turned to God, used his family property to found monasteries, and became a monk. He lived in his monastery for five years. During this time he learned the stories about St. Benedict that he included in his book, *The Dialogues of St. Gregory*. Gregory's monastic life was interrupted by the invasion of a new barbarian tribe, the Lombards, who ravaged Italy and nearly attacked Rome. The Pope asked Gregory, an experienced administrator, to help manage Church property in this crisis. Then the Pope sent Gregory to Constantinople as his representative for seven years. Afterward Gregory wanted to return to his monastery, but the Pope still needed his assistance. In 590 Gregory was chosen to be Pope.

Gregory inherited many problems with his new office. The most urgent ones were caused by war and natural disasters. The few remaining Byzantine forces were concentrated in Ravenna, north of Rome and on the other side of Italy. They could not prevent the Lombards from taking control of the rest of the country. Cities still recovering from the wars of Justinian were sacked again. Italy was devastated by famines, floods, and plagues. Gregory said that there was no one left in the countryside and scarcely anyone in the towns. Many survivors of the wars lost their farms or businesses and made a living by begging or stealing.

Providing for the poor was Pope Gregory's first priority. The Church had extensive land, but it was not very productive. Wars had caused the death of many farmers and their livestock and had disorganized the management of the remaining resources. Gregory reorganized the administration of the land. He found men who were able to farm it, even if they were former slaves or refugees. The Pope replaced incompetent or dishonest administrators. He made all of the administrators take an oath on the tomb of St. Peter that they would administer Church property honestly, and he established a system to check up on them by inspecting their accounts. Gregory, who was well trained in all aspects of land management, gave instructions on improved methods of farming and raising livestock. These changes increased the income from the land belonging to the Church so that the Pope was able to care for the poor.

Since there was no effective civil government in Rome, Gregory was forced to take over many duties normally managed by secular officials. He used some of the revenue from the Church's land to pay the Lombards not to attack Rome, to pay the soldiers who were defending the city, to support refugees, and to repair roads and buildings. Later Popes continued these secular occupations as well as carrying out their spiritual duties.

Gregory was able to heal many of the problems in the Church because he was patient and assumed that he could persuade most people to do what was right. People who did not want to follow his advice were often persuaded by their neighbors or subjects. Gregory was able to arrange for the election of holy, well-educated men as bishops in many dioceses. Unworthy bishops and priests might be removed by Church councils or their bishops, with Gregory's approval. He tried to improve religious life for monks and nuns, and he attempted to repair churches, monasteries, and towns destroyed by wars. He was able to end most of the schisms caused by the Eastern emperors' attempts to influence the Church, and the other schisms were healed by later Popes. He kept in touch with bishops and political leaders all over Europe and Africa so that he might be able to persuade them to live by Christian moral standards. He persuaded some Arian nations to become Catholic. Other barbarian tribes were converted by missionaries or conquered by the Catholic Franks. One of the Pope's most satisfying triumphs was baptizing a group of Lombard leaders into the Church, though it took generations before the whole tribe was converted. Pope Gregory left the Church better than he found it, in spite of the difficulties he faced.

When Gregory was living as a monk, he noticed some English slaves in a market and resolved to go to England as a missionary. Roman Britain had been Christian, but pagan Germanic invaders had nearly exterminated Christianity there. When Gregory became Pope, he sent a monk named Augustine and forty companions to England. These men obediently set out on their mission, but they traveled very slowly. When they reached the west coast of France they heard that the pagan Saxons had murdered some Christians in England, and this discouraged them so much that they sent a message to Gregory asking whether they should continue. When the messenger returned after several months, he said that the Pope had not changed his mind, so they sailed to Britain, expecting to be martyred on their arrival.

The situation was less dangerous than they believed. When they landed, they sent a message to King Ethelbert, a pagan Saxon who had married a Catholic princess and was not opposed to Christianity. He insisted that their first meeting should be held outdoors so that they would not be able to cast any spells on him, but he agreed to let them have a church and preach to anyone who would listen. Eventually Ethelbert was converted and became such a devout Catholic that he is considered a saint. With the support of monks in new monasteries, most of England became Christian. Augustine and his monks were assisted by the gift of miracles, which helped convert many pagans. After his death, he was called St. Augustine of Canterbury.

Pope Gregory had fasted so much as a monk that his health was damaged, and he was often crippled by severe gout and fevers. He continued with his activities as much as possible, especially with Mass, prayers, and religious processions to ask God's help with military invasions and famines. His reputation for holiness increased with his bad health and suffering. Like many other saints, he attracted people to Christianity by a magnetism that cannot be explained by any combination of historical factors. He had been chosen to manage the Church, and he received the grace from God to overcome all obstacles in doing it. He is called Gregory the Great because of his holiness and his tremendous accomplishments in rebuilding the Church.

After the death of Pope St. Gregory, missionary activity continued. Monks from Ireland began founding monasteries in Germany and other lands to convert the pagans. Soon they were joined by monks from England. Those going to Germany went first to Rome, where they were given the insignia of their offices as missionary bishops by the Pope. This made it clear that the Church in Germany was not independent or controlled by secular rulers, but was under the authority of the successors of St. Peter. The missionaries cooperated with Catholic Frankish rulers, who had conquered much of Germany and wanted them to organize and reform the local churches. The level of education in France had declined seriously, and the situation in Germany was even worse. St. Boniface, a missionary bishop and the Pope's representative, said that he found some German monks and priests who read their prayers and said Mass in Latin without understanding what the words meant. He imported scholars from English monasteries to improve the situation. They laid the foundation for a revival of learning and monastic life under the great Frankish king and emperor, Charlemagne.

Discussion Questions

Identify: Pope Gregory the Great, Lombards, St. Augustine of Canterbury

1. Describe the main events of Pope Gregory's life. How did they prepare him for being Pope?
2. Describe social conditions in Italy shortly after the Lombard invasions. What did Gregory do to help end the famine and devastation?
3. Describe missionary activity during Gregory's lifetime.

3. Charlemagne: Protector of the Church

Emperor Charlemagne ruled the combined Frankish, German, Roman, and Catholic society that had developed in France and part of Germany. Charlemagne's father, Pepin III, was the chief official of the Frankish king. These kings had become so incompetent that their kingdom had been ruled by officials for several generations. Charlemagne's father asked the Pope whether it was right that the one who ruled the realm was not the king, and the Pope replied that the one who was actually ruling ought to be the king.

The king's crown symbolized his authority. St. Boniface, the bishop who was the Pope's representative, crowned and anointed Pepin as king of the Franks in 751. This showed that the king had received his authority from God and the Pope, through the hands of the bishop. The coronation increased the king's power and prestige and signified that he was the legitimate ruler of the nation. The anointing of kings was not a sacrament like the anointing given for confirmation or the sacrament of Holy Orders, but it gave a special role and charism to kings. The ceremony of anointing kings when they were crowned reminded them that their power came from God and they should use it as God wished, by ruling according to Christian laws and protecting the Church. For a thousand years, most of Europe was ruled by anointed kings and queens.

Society had changed in many ways since the Franks became Catholics. The distinction between people of Roman and German descent had nearly vanished, and society was united into one nation. However, society had become more fragmented in other ways. The king and his warriors, or knights, no longer fought on foot, but on horseback. This meant that a knight had to own enough land to support a warhorse, grain and hay to feed it, servants to care for it, a suit of armor and weapons, a steward to manage the land while he was away fighting for the king, and farmers to raise crops to feed his family and servants. Knights were given estates with enough land to support all of these people and animals by their feudal lord, the king or local duke. The knights swore an oath of homage, vowing to fight for the king or duke in return for the land and protection. This system was called *feudalism*, and in most of Europe it lasted until the end of the Middle Ages.

Knights and dukes were in control of administering justice on their property. They judged who was guilty and enforced the penalty. The system made it relatively easy for knights to acquire land and property. The free people who farmed the land often lost their ownership and their right to leave the estate and became serfs, completely dependent on the knight who was the lord of the manor. Knights were restrained by kings and the Church from committing too many crimes, but over the years they gradually gained tighter control over the land.

People often gave land to the Church. However, in the feudal system the main requirement for holding land was the ability to defend it and to fight for the king in war. This was a dilemma, since monks and priests who controlled land were not allowed to bear arms and usually had no military training. Church officials usually had to give some of the income from their land to local knights to provide military service to the king. Bishops, abbots, and abbesses had to swear oaths of homage to kings or dukes when they took possession of their dioceses or monasteries and the associated lands. They often received the insignia of their benefices from these leaders, as did other feudal rulers. Church property was the subject of frequent lawsuits, and land given to the Church often returned to the control of secular rulers after a few generations.

King Pepin's son was Charlemagne, which means Charles the Great. He was one of the most famous kings in history and became a model for future Christian rulers. He was so energetic that he could fight or hunt all day, feast all evening, and be up before dawn the next day to attend Mass and do business. He was always kind to his mother and his brother. He had three wives, because the first two died young, and he had many children. He built his palace near hot springs so that he and his household could take baths and swim in the winter, and he gave his dependents good clothes and plenty of food. His sons and daughters were all taught to read and write and were given a good education. Then the boys went on to learn horsemanship and knighthood, and the girls learned weaving and the other arts practiced by upper-class women. He enjoyed the company of his children so much that he kept all of them with him whenever possible. He also enjoyed banquets with his knights, though he disliked heavy drinking and kept his athletic figure and his health most of his life.

Kings at this time usually acquired and kept their power by winning wars. Charlemagne and his knights were frequently attacked, and they also fought wars to defend the Pope from the Lombards and other enemies. As did earlier Frankish Kings, Charlemagne fought many battles against pagan German tribes and extended Frankish control north and east in Germany. He also fought invaders from Spain.

A battle Charlemagne and his knights fought in 778 at Roncevalles, in southern France, became the basis for *The Song of Roland*, the legendary story of a great Frankish knight who held off attacking Muslim Arab knights for hours with a few companions. Roland killed many enemies, then died a glorious death. He was honored by all of his companions and by Charlemagne, the great king. The story inspired Christian knights for hundreds of years and illustrates the ideals of chivalry for readers today. Feudal society had major drawbacks, but its leaders followed a code of honor that required so much bravery and loyalty that many Christians today have difficulty comprehending it. The oath of homage sworn by a knight to his feudal lord meant that the knight was required to give his life in battle for his lord if necessary. Knights sometimes followed their lords into burning siege towers, knowing that they would almost certainly be burned to death. Knights obeyed their lords in attacks on castles even if it meant that they would be thrown off the walls, be crushed by rocks, have boiling oil poured into their armor, or be captured and spend years chained to the walls of dark dungeons. The knights who won glory in these battles certainly deserved it.

Charlemagne enjoyed listening to music and seeing works of art, sculpture, weaving, and jewelry. He built a beautiful church at Aachen, which still can be visited today. He attended morning and evening prayers and Mass every day. The prayers were sung by choirs of monks, and Mass was chanted by the priest and included impressive ceremonies, music, incense, and beautiful vestments. The church was adorned with Italian marble, carved wood, expensive statues, silver lamps and candles, stained glass, paintings, and tapestries. The king enjoyed theological debates and kept informed on religious controversies in the Byzantine and Western Churches.

Charlemagne became king of the Franks in 768. Since Charlemagne did so much for the Church in Germany, protected the Pope from enemies, and supported him in theological disputes against the Byzantine emperors, Pope Leo III crowned Charlemagne as emperor in the year 800. The coronation and title formalized the relationship of support and protection between them and gave Charlemagne special recognition as the greatest ruler since the end of Western Rome. In many ways Charlemagne was more than that. He was the first great medieval monarch, and his rule signified the formation of a new society.

The years between A.D. 800 and 1000 were some of the most warlike in history. Charlemagne's successors continued his policy of conquering pagan tribes in Germany and encouraging the inhabitants to become Christians. Most conquered Germans were willing to join the Church. Pagan religions had no sanctions against people who became Christians, and pagans usually thought that if their gods could not protect them, there was no reason to worship them. During those years, Europe suffered from frequent raids by Vikings and Norsemen, pagan Germanic warriors from Scandinavia who traveled by boat to attack towns and monasteries, steal valuables, capture slaves, and then return home. However, missionaries converted the Scandinavian countries between A.D. 800 and 1000. They were helped by several Danish and Norwegian kings, who became Christians and then converted most of their leading nobles. It took many years for these countries to become thoroughly Christian, but eventually the Scandinavians gave up making unprovoked attacks. Instead, the Scandinavian warriors worked for kings who hired them. The kings rewarded the Scandinavians with land, money, and honor if they were good fighters, so they gained more than they had in their earlier raids. These uncultured, warlike years resulted in Western Europe becoming Christian and set the stage for a new development of civilization and culture later in the Middle Ages.

Discussion Questions

Identify: St. Boniface, Charlemagne, *The Song of Roland*

1. What was the significance of King Pepin being crowned and anointed king by St. Boniface?
2. Describe feudal society and knights in the time of Charlemagne. How did the changes in warfare since the time of Clovis cause society to change?
3. What effect did the changes in society have on the Church?
4. Describe Charlemagne and the main events of his life.

4. The Iconoclast and *Filioque* Controversies

Between A.D. 700 and 800, two errors became major problems. The first was called the *Iconoclast*, or image-breaking, *controversy.* The second was called the *Filioque*, or the "and the Son", dispute. These disputes caused further stress to the relationship between the Roman and the Byzantine parts of the Church, but their peaceful resolution showed that the Eastern Church was still united with the Western Church under the authority of the Pope, in spite of the efforts of Eastern emperors to control the Church.

Historians suggest that the Iconoclast controversy was the result of influence on the Byzantine empire from Muslims, Jews, and a few minor Christian sects. These religions forbid the use of religious art. The Byzantine emperor believed the arguments of some theologians who said that many Christians were so attached to pictures of Christ and the saints that they were breaking God's commandment not to worship idols. In about 730, these theologians and a few bishops persuaded the emperor to remove the statues and paintings from churches. After riots by the people of Constantinople had been put down with imperial armies, the emperor began forcing all of the Eastern bishops to take the statues and images out of their churches. Most bishops agreed rather than face imprisonment or worse punishment.

A few Catholics venerated pictures and statues excessively, but most of them simply liked the beautiful images and found them helpful in understanding their Christian faith. Statues reminded people of the power of God and the virtues of the saints and encouraged Christians to pray. Images were useful tools for religious education, since they depicted scenes from the life of Christ and the history of the Church. In addition to these arguments in favor of using images, tradition had sanctioned them, and most Catholics had learned that changing traditions often resulted in major errors in the faith. The Iconoclast emperors used their absolute authority to force their religious views on a hostile population.

The most effective resistance to the Iconoclasts came from monks. St. John Damascene and a few other monastic leaders spoke out against the emperor's use of force to change Catholic worship. St. John argued that people derived a great deal of benefit from visual aids such as statues. The monks appealed to the Pope. He supported the monks by condemning the Iconoclasts. When this had no effect, he excommunicated the patriarch of Constantinople, who had been appointed because he was willing to enforce the emperor's unorthodox plans. Excommunications were used by Popes, bishops, and patriarchs as a last resort in major theological disputes. The Pope's response infuriated the emperor so much that he sent a fleet of ships to attack Rome. The ships sank in a huge storm, and the emperor was unable to raise money for another fleet. The emperor died in 740, but his successors carried on the dispute. Another Iconoclast emperor arrested many monks and abbots who opposed him, ordered their tongues and right hands cut off, and sent them to die in exile. Eastern bishops and Popes had good reason to fear the Byzantine emperors.

Eventually the Iconoclast emperors were succeeded by the empress Irene, who ruled for many years as regent for her son. She deposed many Iconoclast bishops and promoted the traditional Catholic practice of having pictures and statues in churches. With the Pope's agreement she called a council, which met in Nicea. This council defined the proper veneration of saints, who are holy only because of God's gifts, and the adoration we should give to God, who is the source of everything good. This council, called the Second Council of Nicea or the Seventh Ecumenical Council, is the last ecumenical council accepted by the Eastern Orthodox Church.

After Empress Irene had given up power, the Iconoclasts continued their efforts. It eventually became so obvious that

the movement had been forced on the Church by unorthodox emperors that it was abandoned. Eastern churches re-
installed statues and paintings, to the delight of most
Christians. The definitions of the Seventh Ecumenical Council should have been useful in the West, where excessive or
superstitious veneration of saints was not uncommon. However, Charlemagne's bishops mistranslated some of the decrees, which were written in Greek. They thought that the
council had authorized the adoration of images, which would
have been heretical. Charlemagne ordered them to write their
objections to the Pope and the Eastern emperor. The Pope
attempted to explain the truth, but Charlemagne and his bishops were not willing to hear it. The controversy increased
the distrust of Western bishops and rulers for Byzantine emperors and the Eastern Church.

The *Filioque* controversy began hundreds of years before
Charlemagne's time. When the Church Fathers were defining the Trinity, they believed that the Holy Spirit proceeded
from both the Father and the Son, but they did not insert
that into the Nicene Creed. Subordinationists or semi-
Arians, who did not believe Christ was fully divine, thought
that the Holy Spirit was sent by God the Father alone. Even
though later Eastern theologians believed God the Son was
fully divine, they were not certain whether the Holy Spirit
proceeded from him or only from God the Father. The
Nicene Creed stated, "We believe in the Holy Spirit, the
Lord, the Giver of life, who proceeds from the Father." It
seemed obvious that the Holy Spirit proceeds from both,
since Jesus is fully God and equal with the Father, but by this
time most Greek theologians were reluctant to modify any
definition of orthodox doctrine.

Charlemagne and his bishops were convinced that they
had as much authority as the Greek theologians, and they

thought that the Creed should say, "We believe in the Holy Spirit, the Lord, the Giver of life, who proceeds from the Father *and the Son*" (Filioque). The Pope believed the addition was correct, but he did not want to insert it officially into the Creed until the Eastern Church could be persuaded to accept it. Nevertheless, the addition was recited in the churches in Charlemagne's kingdom. The Pope did not add it to creeds recited in Roman churches until many years later, when a split with the Byzantine Church over other questions seemed imminent. The Pope was more anxious to preserve Church unity than to insist on the point. Charlemagne and his bishops were more concerned with their authority, and with defending a doctrine they thought was important, than with unity. The Roman Catholic and Eastern Orthodox Churches still recite slightly different creeds today, though they have essentially the same belief about the Holy Spirit.

In spite of the two controversies the Eastern and Western branches of the Church were still formally united, but it was a precarious union. Some government leaders and other influences repeatedly threatened to separate them. Charlemagne's interventions in the disputes indicated that he was following in the footsteps of other Christian emperors. He used his armies to protect Popes and their territory in Italy, but the *Filioque* controversy showed Popes that a strong Christian emperor in Germany might turn into a greater threat than the Byzantine emperor.

Discussion Questions

Identify: Iconoclast, St. John Damascene, Seventh Ecumenical Council, *Filioque*, Venerable Bede

1. Describe the main events of the Iconoclast controversy.
2. Describe the main events of the *Filioque* controversy.
3. What role did the Eastern emperors and Charlemagne have in these controversies?
4. How did St. Benedict Biscop and Venerable Bede help build up the Church?

Featured Saint: Bede

Bede was an English monk who entered the Benedictine monastery of St. Peter and Paul at Wearmouth and Jarrow in 682, when he was only seven years old. Vocations at such a young age were not uncommon at that time. Monasteries took in abandoned children, orphans, and young people given away by their parents, and many of them remained as monks or nuns all their lives. Benedictine monasteries and convents also accepted older vocations such as retired knights or widows who were willing to obey the rule and the abbot or abbess. Later monastic life became more specialized, and monastic communities stopped accepting children.

Many English monks become missionaries in Germany, but Bede stayed in his monastery, except for a few visits to friends in neighboring monasteries. He devoted his life to monastic prayer and to his work of teaching and writing historical books and commentaries on the Bible. His biblical commentaries were so learned and orthodox that they have been very influential. He was the only English theologian to be given the title "Doctor of the Church". His historical books, especially *The Ecclesiastical History of the English People*, were so accurate and readable that they are still popular today among ordinary readers, particularly in England. He was loved in his own monastery because of his tranquil, happy personality; his charity and love for his fellow monks; and his deep prayer life. Bede is a saint, but he is usually called Venerable Bede, a unique title that shows respect for his knowledge and goodness.

Bede's scriptural studies were possible because an earlier monk, St. Benedict Biscop, had made four trips to the continent and to Rome. St. Benedict's main goal was to learn more about religious life, but he brought back books, religious art, relics, and noted teachers. He asked the Pope to send experts in the Greek language, stained glass windows, building, and music. The Pope sent the most accomplished and experienced men available. On one trip the saint accompanied the Pope's newly appointed archbishop of Canterbury to England. This was the first foreign bishop since St. Augustine of Canterbury, but he was able to resolve the disputes dividing English Catholics and to increase their unity with the rest of the Church. Monks taught by St. Benedict Biscop and the experts he brought were sent to other monasteries. Because of them, English monks were some of the best educated people in Europe. St. Benedict Biscop had learned how to keep monasteries well regulated without being excessively strict and kind without being indulgent. England was relatively peaceful at this time, and Bede was the most famous scholar in a golden age of monastic life.

Most of our knowledge about the early English Church comes from Bede. Fortunately, he was a critical thinker and a careful writer. He tried to obtain accurate information for his histories by interviewing people who had been participants in or eyewitnesses to the events he described or who had gained their information from reliable sources. This was particularly important with his stories of miracles. Some early biographies of saints included stories that were unreliable, exaggerated, or completely fictitious. If Bede included such stories, he stated where he had heard them and whether there was any other proof for them. He was equally careful with his biblical commentaries. When explaining a verse, he gave the opinions of other theologians and Apostolic Fathers, then gave the reasons for his explanation. His books are still quoted in modern biblical commentaries.

Why was Bede so important? His books and the students he taught contributed to the life and unity of the Church. His commentaries were orthodox and knowledgeable. When monastic bishops from England became missionaries, they had the same faith, scholarly background, and language as bishops from Rome or Constantinople. It is important that Christians know the truth about Christ and the Church, and Bede was careful that English Catholics received the truth free from unreliable legends or errors.

7

Christendom

Featured Saint: Francis of Assisi

CHAPTER 7

Christendom

1. Medieval Society

After the Viking raids ended, Europe became more peaceful, and Catholic ideals gained a stronger influence on European culture. Kings and knights learned that they could serve God by fighting for him in the Crusades or by ruling justly at home, and middle-class people entered the Church as monks, nuns, priests, and bishops. Many people from all classes of society were canonized as saints. The medieval period produced many great thinkers such as Thomas Aquinas, beautiful cathedrals, and new devotions to the Blessed Virgin Mary. It saw the development of literature in national languages instead of Latin and elaborate ideals of courtly love. New institutions were established, including systems of administration, religious orders, dedicated groups of lay people, universities, towns, and new methods of trade and finance. Christian values were not always practiced, but they were discussed and attempted by European society as a whole. The idea of Christendom, a multinational and unified society of Christians, has never been closer to being realized. The centuries between A.D. 1000 and A.D. 1300 were some of the most creative and innovative years in history.

During the Middle Ages, the son of a knight had two basic career options. He could become a knight, which would take at least seven years of hard physical training, or he could work for the Church. The daughter of a knight could either marry a knight or become a nun. Knights could not make a living in business, the arts, or other occupations. They were limited to managing their estates, serving the king or other nobles as fighters, or traveling to fight in tournaments. Knights who inherited their fathers' estates had a good living, but in the later Middle Ages estates were not divided among the children. The oldest son inherited most of the property, and younger sons had to gain their own land by marrying women who had inherited estates or by working for other knights. If there were no sons, the oldest daughter usually inherited the property. Noble women who had no chance of inheriting property or making a good marriage usually entered convents.

The ideal of courtly love helped women live more pleasant and useful lives. According to popular songs and stories, written in national or vernacular languages, knights were expected to treat all noble women with courtesy and respect. Many knights chose a noble woman for a patroness and fought in tournaments or did other deeds in her honor. Women often managed their estates, especially when their husbands were away at war or attending the king's court. Although married women were expected to obey their husbands, many women were very influential in society. Widows usually kept some property. A few women—such as the Countess of Tuscany, who supported Pope Gregory VII, and Queen Mathilda of England—ruled large estates or kingdoms by themselves.

People living in towns did not usually belong to the noble class. They frequently worked in commerce, building, or manufacturing. Towns were given charters, guarantees of freedom, by the king and had their own laws and government. Kings collected taxes from the towns, but they were essentially independent.

Lending money was usually managed by Jews who lived in towns, because Christians in the Middle Ages were forbidden to charge interest on loans. This prohibition had originated to prevent injustice. (Since modern finance is so different from earlier systems, Christians today are allowed to charge interest, but not to charge unjust rates.) Jews were normally prohibited from owning land or belonging to trade associations in the Middle Ages, but their financial role was essential to society. Some of the friction between Jews and Christians was based on the fact that some Christians thought Jewish bankers were getting wealthy at the expense of Christians.

There were few slaves in medieval society. The serfs were the lowest class of people. Serfs were not slaves, since they could not be bought or sold apart from the land they farmed, but they were not free, since they could not quit, leave, or marry outside of the estate where they worked without the owner's permission. Whoever had possession of an estate also had possession of the labor of the serfs attached to that estate. Normally serfs had to work on the land belonging to the owner of the estate three or four days a week and could work on their own crops the rest of the time. People became serfs either by being born to parents who were serfs or by voluntarily putting themselves under the protection of a knight as a serf in return for security and a job. Serfs who escaped from their estates could become free by living in a town for a year, if they could avoid being captured by their owners. Free people who did not own any property could do farm work or a variety of other jobs.

Few people in the Middle Ages questioned the fact that people inherited obligations, such as serfdom, and privileges, such as noble status, from their parents. It seemed as natural as inheriting property or physical characteristics. A few devout Christian rulers, such as the later canonized King

Louis IX of France, freed their serfs. King Louis also tried to correct some of the injustice and harshness of medieval society by establishing and enforcing fair laws. However, most rulers were not very concerned with correcting injustice, though they usually tried to punish lawbreakers.

Even though feudal society was harsh, it ensured that most people were able to earn a living and were trained in their occupations by their families or relatives. Everyone was limited by the fact that there was little wealth in society at that time. Medieval agriculture was so inefficient that it took at least ten agricultural workers to produce enough food to support one person in another occupation, and farming required experience, training, and long hours of hard physical labor. Most jobs in the Middle Ages required so many years of training or apprenticeship that changing jobs was difficult even if an individual could evade the rigid class structure.

Though society had separate classes of people, it was unified by their common Christian faith and moral code. Everyone was expected to follow Christian laws, except for a few people, such as the Jews, who were exempt and had their own laws. Wealthy people were expected to care for the poor, workers were expected to make an honest contribution to society, and rulers were expected to be just and merciful. Medieval society was harsh, poor, and warlike, but it had a unity and security in its religion and customs that are unknown to modern American society.

The Church was integrated thoroughly into society. People from all different classes contributed to the Church, by joining convents and monasteries; by contributing money or work; or by their prayers, self-denial, and works of charity. The most revealing expression of medieval society can be found in the great cathedrals, such as Notre Dame of Paris. These huge stone churches were built in a style called

Gothic. They had many arches; sculptured pillars; banners; paintings; and statues of God the Father, Jesus, Mary, saints, angels, demons, ordinary people, animals, and monsters called *gargoyles.* The interiors were lighted by lamps, candles, and stained glass windows. The effect of height, space, light, color, and vast beauty gave the most magnificent background ever devised to Catholic worship. Gothic cathedrals were more impressive than anything else built at that time. They were a permanent witness to the transcendent faith of medieval Christians, and they have inspired generations of Catholics. The cathedrals were financed by contributions from kings, knights, businessmen, craft and trade organizations, and many other groups. Everyone from the poorest beggar to the king was free to enter the cathedrals and to worship there. The medieval Church was the most civilized, unified, and just part of feudal society.

Discussion Questions

Identify: Christendom, nobles, serfs, St. Louis IX

1. Describe the obligations and restrictions of the noble class, people who lived in towns, and serfs.
2. What could devout Christian rulers do to make society more thoroughly Christian?
3. How do the cathedrals reflect Christian ideas and society in the Middle Ages?

2. The Medieval Church

Frankish emperors after Charlemagne and other feudal leaders claimed the right to appoint bishops and other religious leaders, who had to swear oaths of homage to them for their Church offices and land. This was called *lay investiture*, and the practice was very common. According to monastic rules, abbots and abbesses were supposed to be elected by the members of their monasteries, but they were often appointed by powerful lay people. Sometimes elections were held, but they could be influenced by knights, dukes, or kings. Even if the elections were free, Church leaders often had to do homage to feudal lords. The abbots, abbesses, bishops, and priests who were appointed by lay rulers in the early Middle Ages were often younger sons, unmarried daughters, or loyal vassals who needed a reward. Some of them collected the revenue from their Church property without being ordained or living as monks or nuns. The ordained bishops often led scandalous lives. With such poor leaders, their monks, nuns, and priests sometimes lived worse lives than lay people. Ordinary Catholics with evil or uncaring bishops and priests saw few reasons to obey God's laws themselves. The situation was very bad for society and for the Church.

In 1073 a new Pope came to power and took the name Gregory VII. He belonged to a group of reformers who were trying to free the Church from the control of secular rulers. The reformers insisted that abbots and abbesses ought to be elected by their monks and nuns or chosen by the Pope if the elections were disputed. Bishops should be chosen by the Pope or at least have his authorization to take office. Church leaders should not swear oaths of homage to secular rulers for their spiritual offices. Lay investiture had caused so many problems that some feudal leaders were willing to change, even if they lost their opportunity to support poor relatives on Church property. Recent Popes had tried to persuade kings and dukes to appoint good bishops and to allow free elections, but Gregory VII resolved to tackle the problem at the root. He and a council of bishops decided that in the future, bishops would not be allowed to take office unless they had been approved by the Pope, and disputed elections in monasteries would be judged by Church courts in Rome. Gregory knew that many rulers would do everything they could to stop his reforms, but he was determined to free the Church from their power.

The German emperor, Henry IV, refused to obey the council. He argued that emperors had appointed many good bishops in the past. He might have argued that since lay control had been increasing for many years, this showed that the Holy Spirit was guiding the Church in that direction. However, neither argument was correct. Regardless of whether Henry appointed good or bad bishops, he was acting wrongly. Lay control over the Church had been increasing, but this was not because of God's guidance. It was because lay control, which was wrong to start with, was becoming more common. Many evils in Church life became very widespread before people organized to reform the Church.

Without consulting the Pope, Henry IV appointed his own candidate as bishop in an important diocese. Gregory VII excommunicated the new bishop and Henry. This meant that Christians were forbidden to associate with them, and the excommunication cut them off from the Church, and the sacraments, since they had already cut themselves off by rejecting the authority of the Pope. Gregory went further than that. Feudal society was held together by oaths of homage, and Christ gave Popes and bishops the authority to dissolve oaths. Gregory announced to all of Henry's vassals that he had dispensed them from their oaths of allegiance and they were free to rebel. As Gregory expected, Henry's dissatisfied dukes immediately began organizing a rebellion against him. Henry suddenly found himself in an unprecedented and dangerous situation.

The emperor knew that the Pope was a bishop first and a politician second and thought of a way to save himself. Gregory was staying with his supporters in a castle in northern Italy. Henry took a dangerous winter trip through the Alps and begged Gregory's forgiveness. He promised to stop appointing bishops and to make any other changes the Pope wanted. Gregory was forced to accept his promises and forgive him. With the excommunication lifted, the emperor was able to regain the allegiance of his rebellious nobles.

When Henry was established firmly on his throne, he forced his bishops to excommunicate the Pope, then forced the election of another bishop as Pope. This was a common tactic emperors used to fight Popes. These bishops, called *antipopes*, were not accepted by anyone except the emperor's supporters, but they confused the situation for Catholics. Henry soon gathered his forces and attacked Gregory. The Pope's supporters and armies were defeated, and he was forced to flee from Rome. Many medieval Popes had to go into exile, but Gregory, by now an old man, did not find it easy. When he was on his deathbed he told a friend, in a paraphrased quote from the Psalms, that he had always loved good and hated evil, and that was why he was dying in exile. Gregory VII was one of the few Popes of the Middle Ages to be canonized as a saint.

Gregory's efforts were eventually successful. Many years after his death, most kings signed an agreement saying that Popes had the final authority to decide who would be ordained as bishops or appointed to other Church offices. Lay investiture was no longer allowed, though kings still were influential in selecting bishops.

Catholics today usually give little thought to the fact that the Church is not controlled by secular rulers and claims the right to judge society. Historically, this was a remarkable achievement. It often seemed as though secular rulers would take control of the Church, or enemies would destroy her. In God's providence, political situations changed or reformers took power, and the Church retained her freedom. God never promised to protect the Church from trials, but he promised that the powers of hell would not prevail against her. Catholics can see from the history of the Church that God has kept his promise.

When the Church was free from secular control after the investiture controversy, Christian spirituality became more intense. In order to improve parish life and to help parish priests fulfill their spiritual mission, the Western Church reinforced her rule that all priests and deacons be celibate. Before then it was considered admirable for parish priests to be celibate, but the custom of ordaining married men had been tolerated in some countries because of the laxity caused by lay investiture and frequent wars. Becoming a priest was a spiritual commitment. Requiring men who were candidates for ordination to be celibate helped prevent them from becoming priests unless they had a strong faith and a true vocation from God. Men who wanted to become priests only so that they could collect money from the Church were not likely to agree to be celibate. Priests in religious orders were always expected to be celibate as part of their religious vocation.

After the investiture controversy was settled, several new Benedictine religious orders were founded. Some were groups of hermits, but the most influential order was the Cistercians, founded by St. Bernard. The Cistercians lived in monastic communities and were very ascetical. St. Bernard spoke so eloquently about the love of God, the Blessed Virgin Mary, and monastic life that his monasteries were flooded with vocations. Parents refused to let their children listen to him for fear that they would run away to become monks or nuns. Most of the new Benedictine orders flourished throughout the Middle Ages and still exist today.

St. Dominic and St. Francis founded two entirely new religious orders about A.D. 1200. The members of earlier communities owned no property as individuals, but they worked to support themselves on the property owned by the community. These lands might be very extensive. Dominican and Franciscan communities lived their vows of poverty by having very little or no community property. Members made a living by begging and traveling on foot to preach to poor people in small villages. Later some of them became teachers, missionaries, and theologians. St. Dominic established a more structured community than St. Francis, but his preachers were nearly as poor as the Franciscans. He founded an order of nuns to pray for the Church and to teach women. The Dominicans and the Franciscans both had thousands of members by 1250.

St. Francis founded a community for lay people, called the Third Order Franciscans, so that everyone could share in Franciscan spiritual activities. This division of the order accepted married or single lay men and women. These gave their lives to God by prayer, self-denial, and doing good works, but they continued with their usual occupations and married lives. Members did not take monastic vows. The Dominicans and many other religious orders also established Third Orders that are still popular today.

As the Church became more independent from secular rulers, she developed new administrative systems. The Church always had her own law courts to judge disputes, and these became more powerful. They were based partly on religious tradition and partly on judicial traditions from the Roman

Empire. Church courts were usually more merciful than secular courts at the time, but they used some of the same procedures. In a few cases, such as accusations of witchcraft and
heresy, special courts were allowed to use judicial torture,
which was also used in secular courts. This was the beginning of the Inquisition, but it was established infrequently or
not at all in most nations. The Church today has condemned coercion in belief and torture of any sort. Medieval
Church administrators, who were chosen by God from feudal society, were often blind to its faults.

St. Dominic founded his order to preach to the Albigensians, a heretical religious group that closely resembled the
Manichees of St. Augustine's time and was centered in southern France. Their leaders were very hostile to Catholics and
criticized the wealth and self-indulgence of Catholic priests
and bishops. They converted many people, including some
nobles, and confiscated Catholic churches and monasteries.
Eventually the group came to an end because Catholic knights
attacked the Albigensians and forced them to return Catholic property, the Dominicans converted many, and the rest
were scattered or silenced by the Inquisition. The success of
this heretical group shows that many people were very dissatisfied with the abuses and wealth in the Church and that
the poverty practiced by new religious orders was essential
to Catholic life.

Several other changes took place in the Church. The most
noticeable was a greater devotion to Mary. During the Middle Ages, an increasing number of churches and monasteries
were dedicated to her. The Rosary, which consists of prayers
and meditations on the lives of Christ and Mary, was adopted
by Christians in all classes of society. Some knights dedicated
themselves to Mary, and many religious orders placed themselves under her protection. Theologians debated Mary's role

in God's plan of salvation, and mystics proclaimed the power of her intercession. None of these devotions was entirely new, and they did not obscure devotion to Christ, but they became more popular in the Middle Ages.

Discussion Questions

Identify: lay investiture, Gregory VII, St. Dominic, Third Order Franciscans, Albigensians

1. Describe the issues, events, and outcome of the investiture controversy. Why was it important for the Church?
2. Describe the Cistercians, Franciscans, and Dominicans. What are Third Orders?

3. The Crusades and the Eastern Schism

The Crusades were wars fought by Christian knights who attacked Muslims in the Holy Land in order to defend Christian pilgrims. The Crusades were a response to the military conquest of Christian lands by Arab invaders. Palestine was controlled by Muslims after 636. For hundreds of years Muslims allowed Christian pilgrims to continue visiting the holy places where Christ had lived. The spiritual benefits of these pilgrimages were very important. Medieval pilgrims learned about Christ's life on earth, and they often returned home with a greater love for him and a closer relationship to God. People suffering from persistent illnesses, sinful lifestyles, unhappy marriages, or feuds could go on a pilgrimage as a special way of asking for God's help and atoning for their sins. Often they returned with a changed outlook, new strength to face their problems, and improved health. Many travelers visited shrines in their own countries, such as Santiago de Compostella in Spain, or the tombs of St. Peter and St. Paul in Rome, but as economic conditions improved, more people took the long voyage to Jerusalem.

In 1073 Palestine was conquered by the Turks, a new group of Muslims. They persecuted Christian pilgrims severely. Western Christians regarded this as a declaration of war. In 1095, Pope Urban II preached at a great gathering of knights in France. He told them about the atrocities the Turks had inflicted on Christian pilgrims and asked for a military expedition to take control of Palestine so that pilgrims could travel there. Many knights promised to fight for the Holy Land. After the Pope sent an appeal to the other Christian nations, several kings and many more knights joined the expedition. They were called *Crusaders* because they wore a cloth cross (*crux* in Latin) attached to their garments.

The First Crusade was the most successful. Crusaders defeated the Turks in Jerusalem and several other cities and set up Christian kingdoms. This Crusade inspired more religious devotion and had less contamination from evil motives than later Crusades. For example, the knight who ruled Jerusalem refused to be crowned king. He said that he would not wear a crown of gold in the city where his Savior wore a crown of thorns and took the title Defender of the Holy Sepulchre. Some modern people are cynical about the Crusades, but the Crusaders had no doubts that they were fighting in a just war.

After the Holy Land was conquered by Christians, many knights remained there to defend it from the Turks. Other knights came to serve God by defending the places where Jesus had lived so that Christians could visit them. These knights founded several religious orders, such as the Templars, which were loosely based on the Rule of St. Benedict.

They attended Mass regularly, recited a number of prayers, and worked as guards and soldiers to protect Christians. Other knights came from less worthy motives, such as a desire to escape from their enemies or their creditors. The kingdom of Jerusalem lasted for fewer than a hundred years; then it was reconquered by the Muslims. Many other Crusades were launched and battles fought, but Jerusalem was ruled by Muslims until modern times. Most of the new rulers allowed Christians to visit the Holy Land.

The relations between the Roman and Byzantine parts of the Church became more hostile because of the Crusades. After several hundred years of disputes, the patriarch of Constantinople separated the Greek Church from her relationship with Rome in 1054. No one expected this schism to last longer than the earlier ones, but the two Churches were never united for more than a few decades after that. Recent Popes and patriarchs have both apologized for this ancient misunderstanding, and many modern Christians hope and pray for the reunification of the Church.

One reason that early Popes encouraged the Crusades was that they hoped Western military assistance would promote peaceful relations with the Byzantine Church. Popes always insisted that the leaders of the Crusades should respect the wishes of Byzantine leaders. Some Crusaders followed their advice, but many kings and dukes were more interested in looting cities than in establishing Christian unity. The Fourth Crusade, in 1203, was a disaster. The Crusaders never reached the Holy Land or attacked any Muslims. They hired ships from the Italian city of Venice for transportation, but they had to promise to conquer a town that was hostile to Venice as payment. The town was located near Constantinople, which competed with Venice for commercial domination in the Mediterranean. When the Crusaders were near the town, the Venetian representative persuaded them to help a fugitive Byzantine prince overthrow the Eastern emperor. The Pope's legates were unable to stop them. During this war, the Crusaders defeated the Byzantine emperor and sacked Constantinople. Eastern Christians knew that the Pope was not responsible, but they trusted Western Christians even less after that.

The schism with the Eastern Church affected a number of new Christian lands. Russia and many Slavic nations in Eastern Europe had been converted before 1200 by missionaries from the Byzantine Empire. Mass, the other sacraments, and the Bible were translated into Russian or Slavonic and were administered according to the Byzantine Rite. The new churches followed the Byzantine model of control by secular Christian rulers, and the Russian Church had its own patriarch. These differences did not detract greatly from Church unity before the schism, and some of the missionaries are recognized as saints by both Roman Catholics and Eastern Orthodox Churches. However, most of the Eastern churches eventually followed the Byzantine Church into schism. When Muslims and other invaders conquered more territory in the East, these churches became cut off from the rest of the Christian world and developed separately. They continued using the original translations of the Bible and liturgy even after changes in the languages prevented most people from understanding them, and their theologians were relatively uninfluenced by the increasing clarity of Roman Catholic theology. The churches survived because of their emphasis on tradition and the support of Christian rulers, but they had few resources to resist the attacks of hostile political leaders.

The Crusades had some beneficial effects on medieval society. Knights who lived in the Holy Land learned to respect

and understand their Muslim enemies, and the Muslims
learned more about Christianity. At this time, Muslim scientists were some of the best in the world because they had
continued studying along the same lines as Greek philosophers before the decline of the Byzantine Empire. Western
Christian philosophers obtained many Greek scientific manu-
scripts with Arabic commentaries and continued their philosophical and scientific investigations. After Arab science came
to an end, the impetus for scientific research was preserved
only in Western universities. The Crusades encouraged trade
with the East and stimulated the economy in most Western
countries. The wars halted Muslim attacks on Europe for
several centuries. Crusader ideals helped Christian kings and
knights focus their energy on external enemies, instead of
tearing Europe apart with wars and feuds. Thus, even though
the Crusades were not able to keep the Holy Land free for
Christians, they had some positive results.

Discussion Questions

Identify: First Crusade, 1054, Fourth Crusade

1. What were some reasons that people went on pilgrimages
   and Crusades?
2. What could the people organizing the Fourth Crusade have
   done to prevent such a bad outcome?

4. Christian Philosophy and Science

Philosophy is the love of wisdom, the desire to know and to
understand. Greek philosophers before Christ thought about
nature and man to learn why men exist and behave as they

do. They developed their ideas into philosophies, sets of beliefs or assumptions about the universe. Christ did not establish a philosophical system, but Christianity includes a number of beliefs that can be incorporated into a philosophy. Most pagan Greeks believed that there were ideals, or truths, that existed apart from the material world. The world reflected these truths and became better as it reflected them more perfectly. This philosophy agreed very well with Christianity, since Christians believe that God is the source of all goodness. Evil entered the world when people turned away from God and stopped reflecting his goodness. With God's grace they can turn back to God and, with God's help, become good. Like many early Greek philosophers, Christians believe in immaterial qualities, such as truth, and in spirits, such as angels.

Some philosophies are contrary to Christianity. Christians cannot accept any philosophy that says that there is no truth or that it is absolutely impossible for people to know the truth. God is truth, and Christians believe that God revealed himself so that they would know the truth. Christianity is a supernatural religion, so Christians could not accept the philosophy of some ancient Greek materialists, who said that nothing exists except matter. Augustine and other early Christian writers studied many pagan philosophies to find their relationship with Christianity and explained Christianity with the richness of pagan philosophical languages. Arab and Greek scientists continued thinking about the world and raised new questions. By the Middle Ages, Christians needed a new philosophical synthesis.

Aristotle, a famous Greek philosopher who lived about 300 B.C., was different from most early philosophers. He believed in immaterial qualities such as goodness and truth, but he taught his students to observe visible things such as plants, animals, and stars to learn about their invisible qualities. This approach seems obvious to modern people, but it was not obvious to philosophers before the Middle Ages. Aristotle's teaching, which was developed more fully by medieval Christian philosophers, led to modern science. Christian thinkers assumed that God created the universe in an orderly manner. They began doing experiments to observe the results and discover the invisible laws that governed the material world.

At this time European society was changing. The large bureaucracies needed by kings, nobles, and the Church required many educated administrators. Monastic schools were no longer sufficient, and students began gathering in a few large towns, such as Paris and Oxford, to study in universities. These new schools attracted students from many nations, so the lectures and most of the conversations were conducted in Latin, the universal language of educated people. They developed Scholastic philosophy, which used logic to compare the writings of different experts in order to resolve their contradictions and find the truth. Teachers were fairly independent, and they began investigating every aspect of knowledge. The most convenient source of knowledge at this time was the writings of Aristotle, who had recorded observations on many subjects and had summarized ancient Greek knowledge. Professors in Paris obtained Aristotle's books from Arab and Byzantine scholars and translated them into Latin. Some books included materialistic theories from Arab philosophers. Many Christian professors adopted these theories and became so materialistic that they denied Christian doctrines, including the immortality of human souls and the Real Presence of Christ in the Eucharist. Church authorities quickly responded, but they were not certain how to refute the new errors, since many teachers thought that Aristotle was more authoritative than the Sacred

Scriptures. Fortunately, other professors were able to show that Aristotle did not contradict Christianity.

The most famous professor was St. Thomas Aquinas, who was born about 1225 and was the son of an Italian noble. His parents wanted him to become a feudal lord, or at least a wealthy Benedictine abbot, but Aquinas insisted on joining the poor Dominicans. His family locked him up in a tower to make him change his mind, but they finally had to let him do as he wanted. After he became a Dominican he studied in Paris, where he was nicknamed "the dumb ox" by his classmates because he rarely spoke. His teachers soon noticed that he understood and remembered everything they said. When he began teaching it was evident that he was one of the few men who understood the Greek and Arab philosophers well enough to see where they contradicted Christianity. Using the philosophers' own logic, he showed their errors when their teaching implied that Christian beliefs were mistaken.

St. Thomas and St. Albertus Magnus, an expert on Aristotelian science, attended several local Church councils. They persuaded Church officials to allow the study of Aristotle, and later they convinced most of their fellow professors that Aristotle did not contradict Christian beliefs in immortality and the Real Presence of Christ in the Eucharist. Like most earlier theologians, St. Thomas reasoned that since God created both the universe and Christianity, true science could not contradict Christian revelation. This faith made the Catholic religion more positive toward science than some other religions were. However, St. Thomas did not think that Catholics should abandon their beliefs because of scientific discoveries that appeared to contradict those beliefs. Such contradictions indicated that more evidence was needed so that Christians could understand the world and Christianity better. As did other medieval scholars, St. Thomas accepted some of Aristotle's scientific errors, but his positive attitude toward research allowed later scientists to correct these errors.

The philosophy of St. Thomas had a beneficial effect on theology. Catholics believe that God revealed himself, but that Christians guided by the Holy Spirit gradually move toward a better understanding of God's revelation as doctrines develop. The teaching on purgatory is a good example. Jews before Christ believed that the dead could be helped by sacrifices, and Christians have always said prayers and Masses for the dead, but the belief in purgatory was explained in more detail by Christian theologians in the Middle Ages. One way to determine whether a minor change in doctrine is a development or an error is by using logic to consider its relationship with earlier definitions of the doctrine. If the new variation flows logically from old definitions and does not contradict them or anything in the Sacred Scriptures, it may be a genuine development. If it contradicts earlier official definitions or the constant teaching of the Church, it is an error, unless earlier definitions were misunderstood in popular belief or the teaching was not universal or constant. The writings of St. Thomas about the faith, the sacraments, and Christian apologetics are still some of the best books ever written on these subjects. Thomistic theologians had clear explanations of Christian doctrines and the sacraments and good logical tools for further discussions of doctrines.

St. Thomas Aquinas was the author of several beautiful hymns about the Eucharist that were used on the newly established feast of Corpus Christi, the Body of Christ. This feast helped repair the damage done by a few heretical theologians who denied the Real Presence of Christ in the Eucharist. Aquinas loved Christ very much and gained a reputation for holiness in spite of looking very well fed and being rather absentminded. He died at the age of fifty, but he stopped writing theological books before that. St. Thomas had an experience of meeting Christ in prayer that was so profound that he felt unable to write any more because he thought anything he could possibly say about God would fall far short of God's real glory. God rewarded the saint very richly for leaving everything to serve him as a Dominican and for his faithfulness to his vocation. His life and his books summarized the best characteristics of the Middle Ages and marked one of the high points of faith in the Church.

Discussion Questions

Identify: Scholastic philosophy, St. Thomas Aquinas, Feast of Corpus Christi, St. Francis, St. Clare

1. Why was St. Thomas Aquinas important?
2. What Christian beliefs led to the development of modern science?
3. How did the life of St. Francis influence the Church?

Featured Saint: Francis of Assisi

St. Francis was the son of a wealthy cloth merchant in Assisi, Italy. He was more interested in parties than in getting an education or learning his father's trade, and when he was around twenty, in 1202, he set out with some friends to fight for the Pope. However, he had traveled only a short distance when he became ill. He seemed to hear a voice telling him to turn back. Francis returned home alone and found that his life had changed completely. He began praying and giving away many of his possessions to the poor.

One day he met a man suffering from leprosy who asked Francis for money. St. Francis gave the man what he had and kissed him, because he did not want to turn away from any of God's creatures. After he had gone on a little farther, he looked back, but the leper had vanished. St. Francis realized that he had given the money to Christ. After that he often visited a hospital to care for lepers, who were the outcasts of society because the disease was contagious and deadly.

When Francis was praying in front of a crucifix, he heard Christ tell him to rebuild his Church. Francis thought Christ meant the old church he was praying in, so he sold some of his father's goods to get money for repairs. However, the bishop told Francis to return the money. He did this and even gave his father back his own clothes. Francis' father disowned him, and Francis left home for good. Living as a hermit for a time, he then began to repair the church. Soon he was begging for stone and mortar and repairing it by hand. His friends thought he was crazy, and he continued with his occupations alone for several years. He wore an old, worn-out garment that someone gave him and lived by begging. However, he was very happy because he knew that he was following Christ.

Several companions joined him, and eventually he organized them into a religious order. St. Francis based his rule on the Gospel texts about complete poverty and trust in God. He and the first Franciscans resolved that the community should not own any property. They chose genuine poverty because they wanted to imitate Christ, who had no property and very few possessions. Their order was so poor that when they asked Pope Innocent III to approve their constitutions, he refused at first, because he did not think that anyone could live in such strict poverty. He changed his mind because he had a dream in which he saw St. Francis holding up the walls of the Lateran, the Pope's church in Rome. After the order was approved, many people joined it. St. Francis established the Third Order Franciscans for lay people. He helped his friend St. Clare found an order of Franciscan nuns called the Poor Clares. They were as poor as the brothers and spent most of their time praying, but they usually stayed in their convents instead of going outside to beg. The Franciscan brothers, or friars, traveled to many European countries. Francis also sent them to non-Christian countries to preach to the Muslims and the Crusaders.

Francis gave up control over the Franciscans. After he returned from a missionary journey, he found that the friars had changed the rule and were no longer living in complete poverty. This was a great spiritual trial, but Francis finally realized that any Franciscans who wanted to imitate Christ could still do so. He continued with his life of fasting and prayer. One Lent he stayed in a completely isolated hut on a deserted mountain called Alvernia. While he was there, he received an intense vision of the Cross. After the vision, he found that the wounds of Christ had been imprinted in his hands, feet, and side. (These wounds, called the *stigmata*, have been received by a few other holy men and women since that time.) Francis died a few years later, in 1226.

St. Francis and his brothers established new Catholic devotions and a new spirituality. They joyfully embraced poverty and showed great humility and simplicity, with a love for all God's creatures. Francis was devoted to the baby Jesus, and at Christmas he put a statue of a baby with straw in a manger, as we do today, so that everyone could adore the Christ Child. Franciscans since his time have always cared for the holy places in Jerusalem, to assist pilgrims and to suffer the danger of being martyred by the Muslims. In spite of his constant fasting, Francis was kind and gentle to everyone. His poverty, simple trust in God, and holy life converted many enemies of the faith and indifferent Catholics and earned him a reputation as the most Christlike man who ever lived. His Franciscan brothers understood that when Christ told St. Francis to rebuild his Church, Christ meant that the Franciscans would renew the whole Church.

8

Exile, Plague, and Following Christ

Featured Saint: Catherine of Siena

CHAPTER 8

Exile, Plague, and Following Christ

1. Problems in the Late Medieval Church

By A.D. 1300 it had become evident that the Church needed
to be reformed again because of political conflicts between
bishops, Popes, and feudal leaders. St. Gregory VII had made
it clear that the Church had authority over secular rulers in
feudal society. His successors became so involved with political disputes that they sometimes overlooked their role as
shepherds of the people of God. The investiture controversy
was a victorious battle for the Church, but later wars between Popes, kings, and emperors were very destructive for
everyone. Innocent III, who died in 1216, was one of the
most successful Popes by medieval standards, but he was not
canonized, and his rule set the stage for many later problems.
For example, his relationship with the king of England was
marked with constant struggles.

King John was probably the most unpopular king in English history. He lost a major war with the king of France
and had to give up territory in France that the English kings
had owned for at least sixty years. The king ignored traditional English liberties and feudal customs and used illegal
tactics to raise money. His rule was harsh and unjust. King
John also fought against the Pope over the appointments of
bishops and other issues. Pope Innocent excommunicated

King John and placed England under an interdict. That meant that until the interdict was lifted, the English Church was not allowed to have any Masses or other sacraments, except for people in danger of death. The popular anger because of the interdict forced King John to stop meddling in Church affairs, but many Catholics thought that the Pope was mistaken in depriving nearly everyone in England of the sacraments for several years. The English nobles and bishops, led by the archbishop of Canterbury, forced King John to sign an agreement called the Magna Carta, or Great Charter, in which he promised to abide by traditional English laws and stop committing evil or unjust deeds. The Magna Carta was beneficial for England, but the interdict and excommunications damaged people's trust in the Pope. After Innocent III, Church leaders were much weaker in relation to secular rulers.

The unity of the Church in the Middle Ages was incomplete. Even though nearly everyone in Europe was Catholic, many people received Holy Communion and confession so infrequently that the Church established a rule requiring all Catholics to receive both sacraments at least once a year. Ignorance of the faith and superstition were not uncommon. Many parish priests were badly educated, knowing only enough Latin to say Mass and having little theological training. Though they were not allowed to marry, some established long-term relationships with women and had children, which destroyed their relationship with God and their ability to witness to the faith. People in small towns could learn about their faith from visiting Franciscan or Dominican preachers, but there were not enough of them to form a well-educated Christian population.

The ideal of Church unity was misinterpreted to justify hostility toward non-Catholics. Jews were not allowed to participate in many civic activities. They were not coerced into becoming Christians, since theologians realized that forced conversions were invalid and sacrilegious. However, Jews had so many legal restrictions in some countries that their lives were very difficult. Some nations expelled them in spite of their usefulness to community life. Eventually many Jews moved to Germany, Poland, and Russia, where they were able to live more securely. The laws against Jews in the Middle Ages were not established by the Church, but Christian rulers were responsible. The intolerance toward Jews was one of the darkest aspects of the Middle Ages.

Catholics who renounced their faith by joining heretical churches or practicing witchcraft were subject to severe penalties, including death by being burned at stake. Many individuals disapproved of the harsh laws against people who joined unorthodox churches, but modern Catholic ideals of religious toleration did not develop for hundreds of years. These ideals were completely contrary to most medieval theories of government. This situation shows that secular political theories at that time were not entirely aligned with the gospel of Christ, even though the theories had been developed by Christians. As always, Christian society needed reform and renewal.

The influence of Popes depended on the character of individual Pontiffs. Popes were no longer elected by the people of Rome. For several hundred years, they had been elected by the College of Cardinals, a group usually composed of bishops and archbishops who were appointed by Popes to elect succeeding Popes. This system was established because elections by the people of Rome were so violent and bitter that they resulted in the death or exile of several Popes. In medieval times, there were usually fifteen to twenty-five cardinals, and more than half were normally Italian. This did not mean that they were united. Italy was divided into a number of independent kingdoms or cities that were frequently at war with each other.

The Popes ruled the Papal States, composed of land in central Italy that had been given to the Bishop of Rome by secular rulers in the past. Many Popes came from influential Italian families, though some men from other nations in Europe were elected. They had to guard against attacks by foreign enemies and by the people of Rome, who were often extremely hostile to Popes. With so many political difficulties, weak or worldly Popes were tempted to neglect the care of the Church and to focus on helping their relatives and friends. The practice of appointing one's relatives to Church offices was called *nepotism*. Some of these appointees were conscientious and holy, but since many were seeking secular power and money, nepotism was frequently condemned by reformers.

Religious life was damaged by disputes. Many reformed Benedictine religious orders, which had begun by being very poor and ascetical, accumulated so much wealth that they needed to be reformed again. This was also true of the orders of knights founded during the Crusades. They lost their original purpose when the Crusades ended, but they had received so many donations of land that they were very wealthy. Some used their property for good purposes, but people began to envy them. The Franciscans were being torn apart over the question of whether the order should own any property. Those who were opposed to owning anything believed that religious should imitate Jesus, who owned nothing when he lived on earth. They strongly differed with the Dominicans, who agreed that Christ was very poor but did not believe that he owned nothing. The Pope sided with the Dominicans, and the German emperor sided with the poor Franciscans, since emperors at this time usually disagreed with

Popes in any dispute. The participants accused each other of heresy and other crimes. The conflict damaged the reputations of everyone involved and gained little for religious life or the Church.

University professors began opposing philosophical doubts to faith. St. Thomas Aquinas and earlier theologians had synthesized faith, logic, and science. Some later scholars began promoting theories that were contrary to logic. Others experimented with alchemy, astrology, optics, astronomy, medicine, and other types of learning. Eventually some of these experiments led to modern science, but at the time they often led to accusations of sorcery by ignorant critics. Theologians in the late Middle Ages engaged in complicated abstract debates that sometimes concluded in philosophical discouragement and doubts that human beings could know anything. These doubts went against Catholic teaching, but some people who were having difficulties with their faith because of the changing medieval world accepted the idea. The Church needed another Thomas Aquinas, but did not find one.

In 1300 the king of France, Philip IV, was one of the strongest kings in Europe. He was the grandson of the French king St. Louis IX, but he did nothing to imitate his grandfather's respect for the Church. Philip began feuding with Pope Boniface VIII over the limits of secular authority. French agents kidnapped the Pope and mistreated him for several weeks. He died a short time later, and the next Pope was much more cooperative with France.

King Philip needed money, and he decided to obtain it from the extensive property of the Knights Templar, a religious order for Crusaders based in France. He began by arranging for false accusations that some of the members had denied Christ and had committed heresy or sacrilegious acts. Once the accusations had been made, he arranged to have the monastic knights tried in courts under his control and to be tortured. Most of the Templars confessed to the charges. The king confiscated the property of the order in France in 1307. Some knights who said that they were guilty were released, but many knights died in prison or were executed. About fifty of the leaders who had confessed under torture retracted their confessions later, and Philip had them executed by being burned at the stake. The Pope and bishops protested, but there was nothing they could do legally once the unscrupulous French king gained control of the investigation. The Knights Templar were suppressed in other countries, but members outside of France usually joined other religious orders. The injustice of the trial, executions, and suppression of the Knights Templar show that the practice of Christian ideals in the Middle Ages was imperfect.

In 1309 Philip persuaded the Pope to take up residence in Avignon, in the eastern part of France. (This was possible because the bishop of a city did not have to live in his city, and some medieval bishops visited their dioceses only occasionally.) There were a few practical advantages to the move. Living in France would give the Bishop of Rome protection against the German emperor, the Pope's enemies in Italy, and the people of Rome, who were sometimes very hostile to the Popes. Nevertheless, it was clear that the Pope had moved to Avignon because he was influenced by the French king. The move was a severe blow to the prestige of the successors of St. Peter. It was followed within a few years by a number of major disasters to Europe.

Discussion Questions

Identify: Magna Carta, College of Cardinals, Papal States, King Philip IV of France, Knights Templar, Avignon

1. Describe several problems that showed that the unity and Christian idealism of medieval Christian society was incomplete.
2. Describe the relations between King Philip IV of France and Boniface VIII.
3. How did King Philip suppress the Knights Templar? What did he gain from this?

2. Plague and War

Philip IV was the last strong French king for several hundred years. His successor ruled for ten years, then died without leaving an heir. The succession passed to another branch of the French royal family. However, the king of England, Edward III, claimed the French throne, since he was the direct heir through his mother. In 1339 Edward invaded France. The war over the succession lasted about a hundred years and is logically called the Hundred Years' War. Most of France was devastated, and much of it was conquered by England.

The war immediately showed that the supremacy of knights in battle was ending. It began with the merchants and businessmen of Flanders defeating an army of French knights. When the English invaded, they used a new weapon, an early type of cannon. These cannons could destroy castles, smash the machines used in sieges, and crush people and horses. Later attacks showed that improved crossbows and English longbows could shoot arrows that pierced armor. Men learned that a charge of armored knights on horseback could be stopped by foot soldiers with heavy pikes, strong spears with one end resting on the ground. The horses usually refused to impale themselves on the pikes. No amount of knightly courage, skill, or chivalry ensured victory in battles against enemies armed with these weapons. The feudal aristocracy found that their fighting skills were obsolete.

With the Pope in France, the balance of power in the rest of Europe shifted, but this did not bring peace. Most countries experienced power struggles, battles, or wars. This turmoil preceded one of the world's greatest disasters.

In 1347 the Great Plague struck Europe. The bacteria that caused the bubonic plague was spread primarily by fleas, and the people who caught the disease almost always died within a few days. The plague was carried by rats on ships and by travelers to every part of Europe. Once someone in a town was infected, it was likely that more than half of the population would catch it, and most of them would die. The only escape was to leave town immediately, if possible. Many monasteries, convents, and villages were completely destroyed or had only one or two inhabitants left out of several hundred. Europe lost more than a quarter of its population in a few years. Since the disease was so contagious, many people abandoned plague victims rather than risk catching the disease by caring for them. Conscientious priests, monks, and nuns were severely affected. Priests heard the confessions of the dying and religious cared for the sick, so they were exposed more frequently to the bacteria that caused the plague. Wars temporarily stopped, since all the nations were affected. As soon as the plague had abated, the survivors took up their quarrels again.

After the plague passed, society began to adjust to the reduced population. There were so few farmers left that many villages and farms on inferior land were abandoned and became overgrown with forests. The surviving nobles were unable to find enough people to work for them and cultivate their crops. Nobles were forced to negotiate new agreements more favorable to their serfs to prevent them from leaving to work on other estates, and they often hired free workers, who were paid higher wages than before. However, since so many people had died, the remaining nobles and businessmen inherited more property. Convents and monasteries with few survivors combined with others. People grew accustomed to their losses and went on.

Europe suffered from the psychological trauma for many years, partly because the plague did not vanish. There was never again such a widespread attack, but the plague recurred from time to time throughout the next three hundred years. The people who survived and their descendants were more likely to be immune to the disease, so fewer people died with each succeeding outbreak. Nevertheless, people were still terrified of the plague.

Many people turned to God in prayer. Community prayers might take the form of penitential processions to show sorrow for sin and beg God's mercy, frequent confession and attendance at Mass, and prayer services. Individual devotions included long vigils, severe self-denial, private prayers and meditation, and works of charity intended to please God. People expected the end of the world and the Second Coming of Christ. Since so many priests and nuns had died, lay people were forced to take more responsibility for their religious lives. Third Orders and other lay groups became more influential than before. Some people responded to the plague by anger against God, looting, robbery, or sacrilege. They often looked for someone to blame, which resulted in an increase of trials for witchcraft and hostility against non-Christians. Church officials usually discouraged such blame and advised people to repent for their own sins, but there does not seem to have been much improvement in behavior.

The Hundred Years' War between France and England continued after the plague abated. English knights conquered more and more territory, and the French kings were unable to defeat them. France was torn by rebellions of peasants, or poor farmers, against nobles, attacks by the townspeople of Flanders, and a severe lack of money. By 1428 the French king, Charles VII, had lost so many battles and so much territory that he was willing to recognize the English king as his heir. The situation changed because of one of the most unusual women in history, Joan of Arc, a peasant girl from the village of Domrémy.

Joan was a devout girl. She lived an ascetical life of fasting and prayer while working on her father's farm. When she was about seventeen, she traveled to the French court and asked to speak to the king, saying that she had a message for him from St. Michael the Archangel and several saints. King Charles agreed to see her, but he changed clothes with one of his friends, who was introduced as the king. Joan was not fooled. She walked to the side, where the king was standing in ordinary clothes with a group of noblemen, and told him that God did not want him to give up, but that she would lead them to victory. The king was impressed, and he agreed to fight. Joan put on armor and rode a warhorse, and she directed the French knights in a victorious battle against the English.

A short time later, Joan was captured and sold by her captors, the Burgundians, to the English. The English accused her of being a witch and brought charges against her in an English ecclesiastical court. The English priests and bishops who questioned her said that they found no evidence of witchcraft or heresy, and they refused to use torture. Nevertheless she was condemned to be executed. She appealed to the Pope, but English officials did not allow the appeal. Joan had enabled the French to defeat the English, and they were determined to execute her. She did not expect to die, since the saints who spoke to her assured her that she would win a great victory on May 30, 1431. That was the day she was burned at stake. Her victory was her faithfulness to God in spite of the unjust verdict and condemnation. French rulers appealed the verdict after her death, and it was reversed in an ecclesiastical court of appeals. Joan of Arc was canonized in modern times because of her virtuous life, not because she believed that she heard the voices of the saints. Today she is honored as one of the patron saints of France.

The French quickly pushed the English out of France, and England was torn apart by a civil war. Both countries were so drained by the Hundred Years' War that it took them decades to recover. Europe was entering the Renaissance, an era that encompassed the decline of feudalism and the birth of a new culture. Modern people can look back and see the positive aspects of the change, but people living at the time could see little except social turmoil, corruption in the government and the Church, frequent wars, disease, and new weapons of destruction.

Discussion Questions

Identify: Hundred Years' War, Great Plague, St. Joan of Arc

1. What were the causes of the Hundred Years' War?
2. How did new weapons reduce the influence of nobles and knights?
3. What changes did the plague make in European life?
4. Describe the life and death of St. Joan of Arc.

3. The Avignon Popes and the Conciliar Crisis

The Popes lived in Avignon from 1309 to 1377. During this time, the king of France had a great deal of influence on

appointments and other Church affairs. All of the Popes and
most of the cardinals were French. In spite of the Hundred
Years' War and the weakness of later French kings, Popes
preferred living in Avignon to moving back to Italy. In 1377
St. Catherine of Siena persuaded Pope Gregory XI to return
to Rome. By this time the city had declined in population
and importance because of the revenue lost from the Church.
Romans were delighted to have the Pope back and gave him
a royal welcome. Nearly everyone in the Church thought
that the Pope should live in Rome.

However, trouble from the French cardinals was still ahead.
Gregory XI died a few months later, and the cardinals met
in Rome to elect a new Pope. They were surrounded by a
mob of Romans, who demanded that they elect an Italian
Pope who would be willing to live in Rome. The cardinals
elected Urban VI. However, most of the cardinals were not
satisfied with their choice. They left Rome and then elected
a French "Pope", who took the name Clement VII. He and
his successors in Avignon are now numbered among the antipopes, men who falsely claimed to be popes. These were
usually supported by powerful kings or emperors. The dis-
senting cardinals claimed that the first election was invalid
because they had been coerced by the people of Rome. The
cardinals may have expected their first choice, Urban VI, to
abdicate peacefully, but he knew that his election was valid.
He refused to recognize the new election and established a
residence in Rome. The French claimant, Clement VII, accepted the argument that the first election was invalid and
ruled from Avignon. He was recognized by the French and
their allies, and the first Pope was recognized by the rest of
Europe. Since no one knew whether the cardinals had really
been coerced except the people who were there, and these
people disagreed, it was difficult to be certain who was the

true Bishop of Rome. Catholics believe that there can only be one Pope, but neither side would admit that the other man was the true successor of St. Peter.

This division, often called the Great Western Schism, was completely unnecessary. The cardinals could have avoided it by supporting their first choice, but they preferred living in comfort with a French claimant in Avignon to protecting Church unity. Their irresponsible actions illustrated the evil effects of allowing the French king to dominate the Popes and cardinals. The Church desperately needed reform. God protected his Church by keeping the French claimant from teaching anything contrary to faith and morals, but it was a terrible situation. The Catholics who recognized the Roman Pope accepted the people he appointed, and the ones who followed the French claimant obeyed his decisions. Some religious orders sought the approval of both men or split into two separate orders. Many Catholics stopped believing that a Pope had any special authority from God. Both men appointed cardinals, and when each died, his cardinals held a new papal election. It began to look as though the schism would continue indefinitely.

After thirty years of negotiation and debate, Christians united in calling for a council, which met in 1409. Nearly all of the cardinals from Avignon and Rome gathered in Pisa, Italy, together with hundreds of bishops, theologians, and representatives from Christian rulers. Neither the Pope nor the claimant had much popular support. This council, acting on its own authority, which it claimed to receive from God, deposed both the Pope and the French claimant and elected another "Pope" (anti-pope Alexander V). The Roman Pope and the Avignon claimant refused to give up their offices, since the council had no authority on its own, and the new claimant elected by the council soon lost his popular support. He was deposed by another council, which met at Constance, in the German empire, in 1414. The opening decrees of this council were very hostile to Popes in general. Some theologians proposed that the Church should be governed by general councils, similar to the national parliaments in some nations, rather than by Popes. In 1415, after the Council of Constance had been in session for several months, the Roman Pope, Gregory XII, sent a message formally convoking the council and announcing his own resignation. This made the council legitimate.

The last Avignon anti-pope was deposed by the Council of Constance in July 1417. The Church had not had an effective Pope for two years, since by this time almost no one obeyed the Avignon claimant. The council made many decisions usually reserved to other Church authorities, such as judging legal cases and heresy trials and appointing bishops. These activities took so much time that many delegates protested. Some theologians pointed out that the Popes had shown more interest in genuine Church reform than most local bishops, who would have complete control over their dioceses if there were no Pope. In spite of the theologians who wanted the Church governed by general councils, the council decided that the cardinals and some national delegates should elect a new Pope. This Pope took the name Martin V. Since the whole council, which had been formally convened by Pope Gregory XII, and all of the cardinals had agreed on the procedure for the election, it was clear that the new Pope was the true successor of St. Peter. However, there were other questions that were not resolved for many years.

Martin V took over the leadership of the council. He combined a list of demands from the earlier sessions of the council and suggestions from the bishops into seven decrees. They were designed to end some common financial and administrative abuses in the Church. For example, anyone who paid money for a religious office was automatically excommunicated and deprived of the office, and no Church taxes could be collected without the consent of the bishops from the nations that were going to be taxed. Martin V signed these decrees, but he never signed other decrees that proclaimed the authority of councils to govern the Church. The decrees that the Pope did not sign did not become part of the official teaching of the Church, though they indicated the wishes of some Christians. The call for general councils instead of Popes to govern the Church is called the *conciliar movement*. Councils were held at frequent intervals for twenty years after the Council of Constance, but some of their actions were very irresponsible. Most Christians realized that frequent councils were not the right solution for the problems affecting the Church.

The conciliar movement threatened to destroy a chance for unity with the Byzantine Church. Attacked by new Muslim enemies, the emperor in Constantinople encouraged the Eastern Orthodox church to unite itself with the Roman Catholic Church in the hope of gaining military assistance. The Pope referred the question to a council he had convened that was meeting in Basle. However, the council delegates were so hostile to the Pope that they refused to adjourn in order to choose a meeting place suitable for the Eastern Christians. The Pope finally persuaded a minority of delegates to meet in Florence, Italy, with the Greeks. The Roman Catholic and Greek Orthodox delegates worked out an agreement settling their doctrinal and administrative differences. The Council of Florence was an early triumph for ecumenical dialogue. The Pope, the council, the Greek delegates, and the Eastern emperor formally signed the decrees.

The Greek bishops and emperor formally accepted the authority of the Pope, and the Churches were united. However, the union was only temporary. The armies sent by the Pope and the kings of Hungary, Albania, and a few other nations were defeated by the more numerous Turks, and the Greek bishops retracted their agreement to the new union. A few months later, in 1453, Constantinople was conquered by Muslims. It was never recaptured by Christians.

What can modern Catholics learn from the Great Western Schism and the conciliar movement? One unpleasant truth is that conditions in the Church can become so confusing that holy people with good intentions are unable to agree on a course of action. Another is that, although the Pope cannot err in his solemn teachings on faith and morals, Catholics cannot take it for granted that all members of the Church hierarchy will be able to act in the best interests of Christianity. Catholics must demand high standards of integrity from priests, theologians, bishops, and Popes in order to avoid the dangers of corruption, sin, and schism. God used council delegates and secular rulers to bring the Church back to unity in that emergency situation, but the council decrees calling for parliamentary government in the Church were never ratified. Desperate situations sometimes call for desperate remedies, but the same remedies applied in ordinary times could be deadly, or at least detrimental to Church unity.

Discussion Questions

Identify: Council of Constance, Martin V, conciliar movement, Council of Florence

1. How did the Great Schism begin and continue?
2. How did the councils and Popes end the schism?

3. Why were some decrees of the Council of Constance not accepted as the official teaching of the Church?
4. How was the Eastern Church temporarily reunited to the Roman Catholic Church?

4. *The Imitation of Christ*

By 1400 social conditions had changed greatly. Nobles were still expected to be loyal fighters, but kings relied increasingly on mercenary armies and administrators chosen from the middle class of businessmen and Church officials. People in the bottom class of society had more freedom and were better paid, because labor was scarce and they were able to insist on better working conditions. Peasant rebellions and city uprisings showed that kings and knights were no longer able to control society. The rebellions were suppressed, but society never regained its earlier inflexibility.

Serious hostility against the Church had developed. In addition to the scandal of the Great Schism of the West, some Church leaders were criticized because of their luxurious or immoral lives. The Church had the legal authority to demand tithes and other taxes, and many people thought that bishops were using the money to commit sins instead of helping the poor or preaching the gospel. Church leaders who led good lives were respected, but people often regarded them as exceptions in a widespread decline of moral standards.

The hostility was inflamed by several heretical groups, the Lollards in England and the Hussites, followers of John Huss, in Bohemia. Both groups suggested several reforms that were really needed, such as translating the Bible into modern languages and using the wealth of the Church to help the poor. They also adopted beliefs that were completely unorthodox.

Neither sect believed that Christ established a hierarchy for his Church or that the sacraments were true or necessary. Their members believed that the Church was invisible and was composed only of the people predestined by God for heaven, so they refused to listen to Church authorities. Both groups frightened secular leaders because they encouraged rebellion and hatred against nobles. The Council of Constance tried John Huss for heresy, condemned him, and ordered him to be burned. The Lollards and Hussites were defeated by English and Bohemian armies, but they were not forgotten. A hundred years later their beliefs were revived in the Protestant Reformation.

The years from 1300 to 1450 were not entirely filled with troubles. Although Catholic life suffered a series of scandals, many devout Catholics learned to live lives of close union with Christ in spite of their questions and fears and to make the best possible choices in difficult circumstances instead of giving up. During these years, Catholic traditions and spirituality gained a new dimension of love and faithfulness to Christ.

Upper- and middle-class lay men and women were often well educated or at least learned how to read and write in their own languages. Literary classics were written that have been influential ever since. These included some spiritual books. The best known among these is *The Imitation of Christ*. It was written by a priest in a religious order, but it was quickly adopted by lay people. This book has become very popular because of the close relationship with Jesus it describes. The book contains a dialogue of a soul with itself; with Christ; and with its doubts, fears, and temptations. It describes inspirations from Jesus and the great consolations and joy in serving him and gives advice about dealing with spiritual darkness and trials. It is traditionally Catholic in the way that the author recommends using the sacraments, the example of the saints, and the advice of good priests. It develops Catholic tradition by highlighting the importance of the soul's own prayer and inspirations from God. Many canonized saints have considered it the best spiritual book ever written, but it is equally influential among ordinary Catholics struggling with difficulties and wishing to be closer to Christ.

Bibles were translated into many languages. The books were expensive, even after printing was developed in 1453, but they were widely read. Lay people also used prayer books similar to those used in religious orders. They contained Psalms, biblical readings, selections from the Apostolic Fathers, and prayers for the feast days of Jesus, Mary, and the angels and saints. Prayer books were frequently expensive and illustrated with beautiful pictures and decorations, but more affordable versions were also available. Other religious books included biographies of saints, writings by monastic authors such as St. Bernard, books written by Dominicans and Franciscans for lay Christians, and Third Order literature.

Christian mysticism is the hidden, mysterious life of union of the devout Christian soul with God. During these years, many books were written about union with God in contemplation and love. Some spiritual books were composed by mystics such as St. Bridget of Sweden and St. Catherine of Siena, who wrote down the revelations they had received in prayer. These books were reviewed by the authors' spiritual directors and other knowledgeable priests, so Catholics had some assurance that the revelations were not caused by self-deception or delusions from the devil. Most books, such as *Mirror of Eternal Salvation* by the Flemish mystic John van Ruysbroeck, were written in a more ordinary manner. They taught readers how to love and obey God, how to meditate, and how to avoid the temptations and difficulties they encountered in their search for God. Mysticism and contemplative prayer seem to have flourished in the late Middle Ages. Many holy priests were available to help lay people, even in the worst days of corruption and schism. In addition, lay groups such as Third Orders and other communities helped members live devout lives without falling into self-deception and error.

Many books mentioned the trials of the Church, deaths from disease and war, lack of certainty in intellectual affairs, and the hazards of treacherous friends and attacks from enemies. The best books taught their readers how to use all of these trials to learn that God was their only friend, security, and guide. Suffering could be beneficial because people could use it to become united with God by turning to him with their whole hearts. However, some people refused to trust God and fell into disbelief or error. The problems that brought many people closer to God caused others to turn away from him in anger and frustration.

Discussion Questions

Identify: Hussites, Christian mysticism, *Imitation of Christ*, St. Catherine of Siena, acts of penance

1. Why were so many Catholics hostile to the hierarchy of the Church at this time?
2. What spiritual books were popular in the late Middle Ages?
3. How did devout Catholics cope with the problems in the Church?

Featured Saint: Catherine of Siena

St. Catherine was born into a very large family in Siena, Italy, in 1347. Her father was a cloth dyer, and her mother was occupied with the care of the twenty-four children. Catherine was a very cheerful little girl. When she was six, she had a vision in which she saw Jesus in heaven with several saints. She followed him completely after that and began spending many hours in prayer and solitude. When she played with other children, she usually persuaded them to join her in prayers or other religious activities. Her family became worried about her, particularly when they found that she did not intend to marry. They gave her tremendous amounts of housework in the hope that she would forget her good resolutions, but she did all the work cheerfully and spent the nights praying.

Catherine wanted to join the Third Order Dominicans so that she could share in the spirituality of the Dominicans but live at home and help the poor and sick. Most of the Third Order Dominicans were older women and widows. They were reluctant to have such an unusual girl join them, but they finally accepted her. She began wearing the Dominican habit, which was customary for Third Order members at that time, and increased her prayers, fasting, and other acts of penance. (Acts of penance are works of charity, prayers, or sufferings that one voluntarily undertakes to gain graces for oneself and for others or to atone for sins.) Catherine spent several years as a hermit in a small room in her parents' house, eating and drinking practically nothing. During this time she had many visions and inspirations from God, but she also had severe temptations. After two years Jesus appeared to her and told her that she should leave her hermitage and go back to her other works of charity.

As a Third Order Dominican, St. Catherine went to confession to the Dominican priests in the city. One of them was Raymund of Capua, who became the superior of the Dominicans. After his death he was declared Blessed, which is the last step before a person is canonized as a saint. He became Catherine's spiritual director, which meant that she followed his advice, told him all of her temptations and spiritual experiences, and prayed for him. He guided her and helped her in every way that he could. Later he wrote her biography. At first he doubted that she was really close to God, since her visions and life were so extraordinary, but several things reassured him. First were her virtuous life and obvious goodness. Her prayers cured him of the plague after he had been given up for dead. He was still in doubt and prayed to Jesus to guide him. When he was talking to her, he saw her face vanish and found that he was looking at Jesus. After her ordinary appearance returned and he got over the shock, he realized that this meant that her life was inspired and motivated by Jesus, so that her works were the works of Christ. His support helped her to avoid the criticism and disbelief of other Catholics and protected her from slanders by her enemies. Later he witnessed many of her miracles.

Raymund of Capua was not Catherine's only friend. Many priests and lay people in Siena enjoyed her company. They gathered in an informal group to follow her advice and learn about the spiritual life. God gave her the gift of reading souls, and she was able to help people with temptations and other trials. On many occasions she wrote letters to people with advice about problems that had just arisen and that she could not possibly have heard about. Her followers learned to love God and serve him in everything. Many of them became priests, monks, or nuns, and the others served God as lay people with their prayers and good works.

Since Catherine had gained a reputation for holiness, she was asked to speak to groups of people, and she converted so many of them that it took three priests to hear all of the confessions. She wrote several books, including her *Dialogues*, and hundreds of letters. Rulers sometimes asked her to join delegations to negotiate peace treaties. Once she went to Avignon with Raymund for diplomatic negotiations between Pope Gregory XI and some Italian cities. She took the opportunity to ask the Pope to return to Rome and reminded him that he had taken a private vow to live in Rome if he was elected Pope. This revelation astonished him, since he had never told anyone about the vow. After her persuasions and prayers, he agreed to return to Rome.

In spite of these activities, Catherine continued with her prayers, fasting, and mystical life. She was so unhappy about the state of the Church that she offered her life to God to obtain more graces for the conversion of sinners. She was frequently united to God so closely that she was unaware of anything else and appeared to be in a trance. These experiences filled her with joy. In times of spiritual darkness she felt as though all of the trials of the Church had been caused by her sins, even though these amounted to nothing more than a lack of enthusiasm for doing good and distractions in prayers. Neither her spiritual ecstacies nor her spiritual trials interfered with her good works. However, her health was very poor, and she died in 1380.

St. Catherine was canonized in 1461, and she was declared a Doctor of the Church in 1970 because of her excellent spiritual books. Catholics are not obliged to believe that each revelation and vision was dictated by Jesus, but her books contain nothing contrary to faith and morals and can be helpful to Christians. Her life was so ascetical that it would be impossible to imitate it without extraordinary help from God. St. Catherine was given the support, strength, and advice she needed to carry out the mission God gave her. Catholics who read about her life can find assurance that if God asks something unusual or difficult, he provides the grace and assistance to do it.

9

The Church in the Renaissance
and the Reformation

Featured Saint: Thomas More

CHAPTER 9

The Church in the Renaissance and the Reformation

1. The Renaissance

The Renaissance was an era of change between about 1400 and 1600. The word *renaissance*, which means "rebirth", was used because many Renaissance artists and writers were inspired by recently recovered ancient Greek and Roman ideals. They created a new culture based on the beauty of pagan sculpture, painting, and literature. During the Middle Ages, art was unworldly. Representations of human beings were depicted with heavy garments and slightly out of proportion, looking taller and more slender than real people. The effect was beautiful but unrealistic. Renaissance art was realistic and, some say, even more beautiful. The focus of Renaissance art and literature was man. Artists and writers used careful observation to depict people accurately and attractively. Their new outlook is often called *Renaissance Humanism* or *Christian Humanism*, because they studied people without forgetting their relationship with God. The Renaissance began in Italy before 1400 and spread to the rest of Europe later.

Since Renaissance writers followed classical Greek and Roman models, Christian Humanism encouraged careful

scholarship. People searched monasteries for old manu-
scripts and found many texts that had been lost for nearly a
thousand years. Some important documents had only one
remaining copy in a small monastic library until Renaissance historians found it and printed many copies. To distinguish between genuine discoveries and forgeries, scholars
compared paper, parchment, grammar, and styles of writing from different nations and eras. They assigned dates to
many disputed texts and discovered that some Christian books
had been written later and by different authors than previ-
ously believed. For example, a treatise on the Virgin Mary
believed to be from St. Augustine was actually written hundreds of years later by an unknown author, and a famous
book on mysticism attributed to a disciple of St. Paul was
actually composed about A.D. 500. Humanists began com-
paring stories about saints and proved that some of the
most remarkable miracle stories were unknown until hundreds of years after the deaths of the saints. This meant that
these stories were more liable to be inauthentic. Other
miracle stories were attested by many contemporary writers, which meant that there was good evidence that they
were true.

Scholars obtained Hebrew texts of the Old Testament and
compared them with different Christian texts. They found
that copyists had been extremely careful not to change anything, even in passages that were very demanding, unclear,
or difficult to reconcile with other parts of Christianity. The
Bible was held in reverence more than any other book. News
of advances in biblical scholarship and new scientific discoveries quickly traveled across Europe, so that a professor in
Oxford, England, could learn about the theories of Coper-
nicus in Eastern Europe a few months after he developed
them.

Church art and music from the Renaissance were some of the finest ever created. Their beauty helps people remember that God made man and the world and that they are good. High-quality religious paintings made it easy for Renaissance Christians to visualize themselves as part of religious scenes from the Bible. The art and literature of that era provided a fascination that modern religious art seldom achieves. For example, Dante's *Divine Comedy*, written in the beginning of the Renaissance in Italy, tells the story of a man who is given a guided tour from the bottom level of hell, through purgatory, to the highest summit of heaven. Dante assigned famous local people appropriate places in the next world, depending on their good or evil deeds in this life. His book helped readers understand the teachings of Christianity. Religious paintings and sculptures sometimes depicted the artist's patrons or local citizens inserted into New Testament scenes. These techniques attracted attention and discussion and made Christian beliefs seem vivid and compelling.

The Renaissance was an exciting time for the Church. Popes, bishops, and priests were as immersed in the culture as the rest of society. Monasteries and churches were made beautiful by new architecture and sculpture. Christian learning advanced tremendously. In theological debates, scholars who spoke Greek, Latin, and Hebrew could refer to the Bible and the Apostolic Fathers using accurate texts in the original languages. Knowledge of Christianity penetrated every level of Western society, since people who had money and knew how to read were able to buy Christian books and learn about the faith. Religious orders, theological schools, and positions in the Church were well supplied with applicants.

In Renaissance society, individual ability was so important that social barriers were more relaxed than they had been since the early Middle Ages. The increases in trade and new types of manufacturing meant that all of society was becoming more prosperous. Middle-class and noble men and women on the whole were well educated. Wealthy people from any background were expected to be patrons of art and literature, to keep informed about politics, and to play important roles in society. Most people in the Renaissance had more opportunities to enjoy beautiful things, listen to music, read books, travel, and live comfortable lives than their ancestors in the Middle Ages.

Italian bankers and merchants from other countries became very influential in politics. The Medici family in Florence, Italy, grew so wealthy and powerful through banking and trade that they dominated city government, produced several Popes, and married one daughter to the king of France. The Medicis were famous patrons of writers, artists, and the Church, which they enriched by donations of beautiful paintings and sculptures. Other associations of merchants became powerful enough to influence the outcomes of wars, the selection of national rulers, and the appointment of important Church officials.

Renaissance political leaders were different from medieval leaders. Kings had income from their own estates, but they increasingly needed additional money. During the Renaissance monarchs had frequently to ask for financial assistance from churches, towns, and businessmen. In many nations these organizations voted on taxes in national parliaments. If they did not wish to assist the king or queen, they did not vote that ruler any money. Monarchs still had feudal supporters such as dukes, barons, and knights, but these leaders became more independent in the Renaissance. They were nearly as likely to betray their kings by fighting for their enemies as to assist them in war. This meant that kings in the early

Renaissance were weaker than they had been in the medieval era.

Rulers usually found it difficult to raise effective armies. They still needed knights, horses, and pack animals, but they also needed cannons and other artillery, troops of foot soldiers with pikes and guns, experts in new methods of besieging castles, food and hay, and enough men and wagons to transport everything. Kings usually had to hire mercenary armies to help their own troops fight their enemies. Unemployed soldiers joined together in bands under strong leaders and fought for kings or anyone else who could pay them. Some leaders of mercenary armies became very powerful. A few married Italian heiresses and ruled as dukes, even though their family backgrounds were completely unknown.

The Popes owned the Papal States in Central Italy, and they were forced to defend them from greedy neighbors in the same way as other Italian rulers defended their own lands. They formed alliances with European kings and Italian cities or hired mercenary troops. Income from the Papal States helped pay for the expenses of Church administration, but Popes were often forced to raise money by other methods to hire armies or to finance special projects. The need for money led Popes and bishops to approve some questionable means of raising money. This was one of the most important causes of the Protestant Reformation.

Discussion Questions

Identify: Renaissance, Dante, *Divine Comedy*

1.   Describe Renaissance art and literature.
2.   What is Christian Humanism?

3. What did Humanists learn about ancient Christian texts, miracle stories, and the Bible?

4. Describe some social, political, and military changes during the Renaissance.

2. Problems in the Church

Christ established his Church to lead people to God. Priests, bishops, and Popes received the sacrament of holy orders so that they could administer the sacraments, help individuals and society obey God's laws, set a good example in Christian living, and follow Christ themselves in a special way. All Catholics had the obligation to imitate Christ, help the Church, and encourage other Christians. The Church needed to be visibly holy, so that unbelievers could look at her and see that she reflected God's life and love.

The Renaissance Church fulfilled many of these responsibilities. Most bishops and priests administered the sacraments, or at least delegated other priests to preach, say Mass, and hear confessions. Christians were able to learn the teaching of Christ from Catholic books and holy priests, monks, and nuns. Lay people knew that they were responsible for living devout Christian lives and spreading the faith. Many Renaissance Catholics were filled with love for God and other people.

Modern Catholics have become newly aware that the Church needs to use art, liturgy, and architecture appropriate to each culture. Renaissance Catholics, like their medieval ancestors, never lost sight of this need. The Church used the best secular art forms, Renaissance scholarship, and new methods of studying old texts to teach the Catholic faith. Christian art and learning were so well done that they improved Renaissance cultural standards. Inevitably, there were problems. Christian leaders often spent too much Church money on decorations and too little on their other responsibilities. Nevertheless, the Church in the Renaissance fulfilled her goal of teaching Christ's message with appropriate art and liturgy and administering the sacraments.

In spite of these achievements, the Church in the Renaissance did not fulfill other tasks given to her by Christ. Her most obvious problem was a constant financial crisis. Popes and bishops needed money for Church administration, the military defense of the Papal States, and caring for the poor. Financial demands were exaggerated because some Church leaders thought that they should live in the same style as secular rulers. Many of them lived comfortable lives in luxurious palaces and sponsored expensive works of art, literature, and architecture. There were good arguments in favor of such a style of life. Renaissance art commissioned by Popes and bishops has been responsible for many conversions to the Catholic faith over the centuries, and it still inspires people today. Popes who appeared to be poor were likely to be attacked by their enemies, and bishops often felt that impressing rivals with their wealth increased their safety and effectiveness. However, Christ was poor. Bishops who were extremely wealthy and used their money selfishly did not set a good example for Christians. In addition, the desire for money led some Church leaders to use questionable or evil financial tactics.

Church taxes were collected from parishes, monasteries, or bishops. Although these taxes were legal, they were a poor method of raising money, because they made people dislike Church administrators. The sale of indulgences was a more serious abuse. An indulgence is the remission by the Church of the temporal punishment due to sin after the eternal punishment and guilt of sin has been removed. An indulgence can be used for the benefit of someone who has died if that person is still being purified in purgatory, or for one's own soul if one has sincerely given up sin, made a good confession, and received Holy Communion. Christ gave St. Peter the power to bind and loose, so Popes have the authority to judge which prayers or charitable works may be done to receive indulgences.

In the Renaissance, Church officials reasoned that since giving money to the Church could be a charitable work, financial contributions could gain indulgences, which would help relieve the sufferings of people's relatives in purgatory. This was not entirely correct, since the person making the gift and the person who had died needed to have good spiritual intentions in order for the indulgence to do any good. Also, giving money in exchange for receiving an indulgence could degenerate into "selling" indulgences, which could have a bad influence on people's spiritual lives. Some people may have thought that they could commit as many crimes as they wished because their relatives would buy indulgences for them after they were dead. In spite of these drawbacks, "selling" indulgences became fairly common in some parts of the Church, especially in Germany. The Church in Germany was more desperately in need of reform than any other part of the Church. The German church had never regained its integrity after the deaths in the hierarchy during the plague, and the faith of German Catholics had been damaged by the German emperors' frequent conflicts with the Pope.

Some bishops were so greedy for money that they persuaded the Pope to appoint them to more than one diocese. They collected the revenue from each diocese and appointed subordinate bishops, who were paid a small fraction of their income, to care for these dioceses and administer the sacraments. Some bishops never visited their dioceses. The practice of bishops ruling a number of dioceses was called *pluralism*, though the word is used more often to indicate divergent theological systems. Catholics who saw large sums of money leaving their dioceses to support absent bishops were very angry. Many people believed that bishops obtained multiple offices in return for making payments to the Pope. The Council of Constance (1414–1418) had outlawed *simony*, the practice of buying and selling Church offices, and it has always been regarded as one of the worst sins a person could commit. Nevertheless, it seems to have been common in the Renaissance.

The Church had other problems. Many people believed that important Church leaders were living immoral lives by having illicit relationships with women or even by having their enemies poisoned. Several Popes openly acknowledged their illegitimate children and spent much of their time promoting their children's careers. Christians became discouraged about the possibility of reforming the hierarchy. They assumed that immoral Popes would appoint immoral cardinals, who would then elect more immoral Popes, who would continue to sell offices and commit other sins. There were some requests for another council, but since the laws enacted by the Council of Constance against simony and immoral behavior were not being enforced, it seemed unlikely that a new council would accomplish anything.

Moral standards in the Renaissance were reflected in *The Prince*, one of the most famous books on political theory ever written. The author was an Italian named Niccolò Machiavelli. He said that if political leaders wished to be successful, they should be willing to break oaths and kill all of their enemies, since they would always find people willing to trust them. They should control their friends and allies by giving them what they wanted, whether it was money, power, honor, a good marriage, vengeance on their enemies, or the opportunity to do good. According to Machiavelli, such a prince would be supported by all of his friends, and his enemies would all be dead, so he would be able to rule in peace. One of Machiavelli's favorite princes was Cesare Borgia, the illegitimate son of Pope Alexander VI. Cesare was famous for his treachery and cruelty. He was a successful ruler, but Alexander VI died before Cesare was able to consolidate his conquests. Machiavelli's book contained some good practical advice, but it became infamous because of the unscrupulous conduct it recommended. The political and social chaos in Renaissance Italy showed that treachery and murder might bring temporary peace, but society could not survive for long unless it was based on ethical behavior.

The early Renaissance was a time of contradictions. It produced some of the world's greatest religious artists and saints and the worst Church leaders in history. Many Christians turned away from the world in frustration and put their hope in God. Others stopped obeying God and fought vicious battles for worldly success. Most Christians compromised, and nearly all of them proved their basic faith by asking for the sacraments before they died. The Renaissance was one of the most creative and interesting periods in world history.

Discussion Questions

Identify: simony, pluralism regarding Church offices, *The Prince*, Alexander VI

1. How did the Renaissance Church succeed in fulfilling the mission Christ gave her? How did she fall short of Christ's ideals?

2. What arguments can be used to justify a wealthy lifestyle for Popes and bishops? What arguments are used against such a lifestyle?
3. What does *The Prince* imply about the morals of Renaissance leaders, including Church leaders?

3. The Church in Spain

Most nations during the Renaissance were disturbed by scandals of simony, the pluralism of bishops controlling many offices, and immorality among Church leaders. Spain was the only country in Europe that reformed its Church before 1500. This improvement protected the country from religious wars and allowed it to direct its energy to conquering and colonizing the New World. Since the Spanish Church converted millions of unbelievers, its reform was very important in world history. This reform could not have taken place without the help of Ferdinand and Isabella, the king and queen of Spain. However, their tactics for strengthening the Church included some coercive practices that were seldom imitated by other rulers and have been condemned by the Church in modern times.

Spain was Catholic at the end of the Roman Empire, but it was conquered by Arian barbarians after that. Its Christian rulers were defeated by Muslims before A.D. 800. During the Crusades, knights from France and northern Spain began attacking the Spanish Muslims. Each new generation of Christians pushed them farther south. By 1450 Portugal and all of Spain except the southern part, the kingdom of Granada, had been reconquered. Christian Spain was divided into two kingdoms, Aragon and Castile. There were many cities with wealthy businessmen and large communities of Jews, and the country was fairly prosperous.

The kingdom of Aragon was stable after 1450, but the kingdom of Castile was torn by a dispute over the succession. The young king, Henry IV, married a beautiful Portuguese princess, but she had no children for eight years. During this time, the king made himself unpopular by giving away land and money that should have been used to pay for the government, appointing dishonest officials in return for bribes, and hiring a guard of Muslim soldiers. Most people believed that the king was immoral and perverted. Eventually the queen had a daughter, but scarcely anyone believed that the king was her father. Since Henry did not bother to enforce the laws, bandits roamed the countryside, making trade and business very difficult. Many people in Castile began looking for a better king.

Henry's half brother and sister offered hope for an improved government. A group of Church leaders and nobles rebelled against King Henry and proclaimed Henry's brother king, but he died a few months later. The rebels then asked his sister, Isabella, whether she would let them crown her queen of Castile. She refused because Henry was the lawful king. She said that if she joined a revolution against him, her subjects might rebel against her. The rebellious nobles were forced to make peace with Henry, who was too weak to deprive them of their titles and possessions.

Even though Isabella had refused to join the rebellion, Henry thought that she was dangerous to him. He decided to prevent her from causing trouble by forcing her to marry one of his companions. The man he chose was one of the most immoral men in Spain and twenty-seven years older than Isabella. She and her friends fasted and prayed for three days, asking God to save her from this marriage, and the man unexpectedly died. After this Isabella trusted God in everything. Nevertheless she did not give Henry time to make another choice. She sent her chaplain, a loyal friend, to negotiate with several potential husbands in other countries. He told her that Ferdinand, the heir to the throne of Aragon, was about her age and wanted to marry her. Another friend, Archbishop Carrillo of Toledo, helped her escape from her brother. Archbishop Carrillo traveled with her to Aragon and said the nuptial Mass for her and Ferdinand, who had spent the summer fighting battles to defend his father's kingdom. He was seventeen years old, and she was eighteen.

Henry was furious, but there was nothing he could do. When he died a few years later, most people in Castile acknowledged Isabella as queen of Castile, rather than the daughter of Henry's wife. Isabella and Ferdinand spent many years traveling around their kingdoms and fighting. They suppressed several rebellions and invasions, punished illegal deeds and violence, and recaptured the royal property that Henry had given away. They had few resources at first except for Ferdinand's troops from Aragon, a few loyal allies, and their courage and determination. Isabella frequently spoke to parliaments or groups of nobles and persuaded them to enact her laws, vote money to finance wars, or support her with their troops. On several occasions she traveled to rebellious towns with a small escort and argued with the leaders until they promised to stop fighting against her. Eventually the nobles and Church leaders in Castile obeyed Isabella because they believed that she was the lawful queen and they trusted her judgment and character. Ferdinand frequently left her in Castile while he fought battles in Aragon. In spite of these absences, the couple were united until Isabella's death. The two nations merged in 1479.

Since Isabella was a devout Catholic, she decided to reform the Church in Castile. Spain was ruled by the descendants of the knights who expelled the Muslims, and most Spaniards thought that it was very important to believe and practice the true Catholic faith. Some bishops and priests were well educated, conscientious, and holy. Others lived luxurious lives, neglected their dioceses or parishes, and spent their time on secular occupations such as hunting, scientific research, collecting large fortunes, or scheming for political power. There were no heresies after the Muslims destroyed the Arians when they conquered the land, but the country had a unique problem. Some Jewish converts to Christianity had continued practicing the Jewish religion secretly, and they attended Mass and received the sacraments without any faith. Some of them became priests and bishops because these positions provided a comfortable living. Many Jews became sincere Christians, and others remained openly Jewish instead of pretending to convert.

The most important problem was the common belief that insincere Jewish converts were saying invalid Masses and committing other sacrileges. This belief caused serious hostility against Christian Jews. Isabella decided that the best way to deal with the problem was to turn it over to Church courts. She asked a Dominican named Torquemada to organize these courts, and she and Ferdinand gained special permission from Rome to establish the Inquisition in Spain and to control it themselves. The Inquisition did not have jurisdiction over Jews who had not become Catholics. Inquisitors looked for evidence of Jewish worship among converts. Unlike Philip IV in his trials of the Templars, the Inquisitors used torture only occasionally, when independent evidence of sacrilege or other crimes was present. Nevertheless, many converted Jews were judged guilty and were given fines or other penalties. Others were declared innocent. Later, Ferdinand and

Isabella demanded that Spanish Jews and Muslims become Christians or leave Spain. Most of the remaining Jews left. These measures enabled Isabella and Ferdinand to strengthen their control over Castile, but their injustice in banishing all non-Christians has never been forgotten.

Some people judged guilty by the Spanish Inquisition went to Rome and were acquitted in ecclesiastical courts of appeal. The Pope remonstrated with Ferdinand and Isabella, but he did not feel strong enough to revoke their control over the Inquisition. Since Christians in Spain thought that problems regarding Jews were being solved legally, unlawful violence against Jews subsided. Even though the Spanish Inquisition fulfilled Isabella's expectations, it was not imitated in other countries. Many people realized that the threat of legal penalties should not be used to enforce unity in religious belief, and even the people who believed in coercion began to see that it was nearly impossible to manage the Inquisition in a just manner. Modern Catholics can trust that there will never be another Inquisition. Coercion in religion was condemned by the Second Vatican Council, and many Popes have spoken out against it.

Isabella asked the Pope to appoint Church leaders who were holy and capable. She passed over her old friend Archbishop Carrillo of Toledo and persuaded the Pope to appoint a more ethical candidate as the cardinal of Spain. The archbishop was so hurt and angry that he joined Isabella's enemies in a short rebellion against her. Later she suggested a famous Renaissance humanist, Cardinal Ximines de Cisneros. Under his leadership, the Church was thoroughly reformed. He improved the education and morals of priests and bishops by founding new schools and insisting on high standards, and he persuaded religious orders to follow their rules and serve God in peace.

Isabella and Ferdinand continued the old crusade against the Muslim kingdom of Granada and destroyed it in 1492. This conquest gave them control of the whole Spanish peninsula except for the kingdom of Portugal. That year they financed Christopher Columbus in a voyage of discovery in the Atlantic Ocean. Columbus believed that he could find the East Indies by journeying west, but instead he found a continent that was unknown to Europeans. Spanish adventurers quickly followed him, searching for gold. They were accompanied by priests and missionaries. Explorers soon discovered the wealthy Aztec nation in Mexico. Cortez and a small group of soldiers offered to help free several Native American tribes from their Aztec rulers. With the assistance of their Indian allies, Cortez and his men defeated the Aztecs and set up a Spanish kingdom in Mexico. By 1530 Spain was becoming one of the wealthiest and most powerful countries in Europe. Its united monarchy, the lack of religious disputes, and the huge quantities of gold imported from the New World gave it an advantage over other nations that lasted for nearly a hundred years.

The Spanish Church was strong and healthy. However, its reforms were guided by the king and queen, who used some tactics that were considered excessive then and have been condemned in modern times. After the Protestant Reformation, fear of the Inquisition and the memory of the expulsion of the Jews contributed to four hundred years of misunderstanding and hatred between religions. It was clear to many leaders during the Renaissance that the Spanish model was not the right way to reform the Church.

Discussion Questions

Identify: Isabella, Ferdinand, Spanish Inquisition, Cardinal Cisneros, Granada, Aztecs, Cortez

1. Describe the early life and marriage of Isabella of Castile.
2. Describe the reign of Ferdinand and Isabella. What were their main accomplishments?
3. How did Isabella resolve the problems of moral laxity and low standards among Church leaders?
4. Why was the Inquisition more powerful and fearsome in Spain than in other countries?

4. Martin Luther

Martin Luther was history's most famous and successful rebel against the Roman Catholic Church. However, he had no intention of disagreeing with Catholic doctrines at first. He was born in 1483 in Germany. Luther was preparing to become a lawyer when his life was changed by a violent thunderstorm. A bolt of lightning struck the ground beside him and terrified him so much that he vowed to enter a religious order. He became an Augustinian priest and a university professor. However, this did not bring him peace. He seems to have been seriously disturbed by scruples, which caused him to feel guilty about everything he did. He went to confession very frequently and prayed, fasted, and did other penances, but nothing helped. His superiors told him to relax and stop worrying, but he was convinced that God would have no mercy on him. Since he had given his life to God and expected no reward, he was miserable.

A religious experience brought Luther peace. He was reading St. Paul's Letter to the Romans and noticed the words, "He who through faith is righteous shall live" (Rom 1:17). He understood that since faith was so important, his guilt was unimportant. If he had stopped with that experience he might have remained a Catholic, but he went on to conclude that faith was all that mattered for salvation. This view is known as justification by faith alone. He thought this meant that the Church hierarchy, doing good works, and most of the sacraments in the Catholic Church were not necessary. Holding tightly to the text that had given him peace, he placed less emphasis on several other Bible verses. These included Jesus' words "If you love me, you will keep my commandments" (Jn 14:15) and the letter of St. James, which said, "Faith by itself, if it has no works, is dead" (Jas 2:17).

Luther began to criticize Church doctrines. His break with the Church occurred because of a campaign to sell indulgences in Germany. Many Catholics were unhappy with the campaign. Good spiritual dispositions were necessary for indulgences to be effective, and the priests who "sold" them sometimes made unjustified promises to the people who donated money to get indulgences. Luther was completely opposed to indulgences. Since he thought that nothing was necessary for salvation except faith, he concluded that there was no need for indulgences. In addition, he did not believe that the hierarchy had any authority to speak for God. In 1517 Luther condensed his beliefs into a proclamation and nailed it to the door of the church at Wittenberg as an invitation to debate. This proclamation has become known as the Ninety-Five Theses.

The Dominicans who were sponsoring the "sale" of indulgences took up the quarrel, and the debate showed that Luther had rejected many Catholic doctrines. He wrote three long pamphlets that urged German leaders to stop obeying the Pope and explained his other unorthodox beliefs. The Pope excommunicated him. Luther refused to modify his views, and the German emperor, Charles V, ordered Luther's arrest for heresy. However, another German leader protected Luther by hiding him in his castle. Germany was subdivided into more than a hundred small states, and each subordinate ruler had complete authority in his own land. Luther's protector always remained a Catholic, but he hoped to reduce the power of the Pope, and he was too sympathetic to some of Luther's views to let him be arrested. This attitude was very common among rulers at the beginning of the Reformation.

Luther modified his views and policies throughout his life. At first he accepted only the Bible as a guide in religious faith, and he believed that the Holy Spirit would show the correct interpretation of the Bible to each person who read it devoutly. Later he modified this belief because many of his followers disagreed with his interpretations. He saw that if everyone interpreted the Bible as he pleased, the result would be anarchy, and he thought that anarchy was unacceptable. Martin Luther eventually formed a church under the authority of secular rulers. It had an established body of doctrine that included many traditional Christian beliefs, but rejected others. Modern Lutherans do not necessarily agree with all of Luther's views.

Luther's ideas about human nature and grace were different from traditional Catholic beliefs. Catholics believe that human beings have both good and bad inclinations inherited from our first parents. With the help of God's grace given through the sacraments and our good works, prayers, and faith, we can become truly holy and pleasing to God. Luther believed human beings were so badly damaged by original sin that they could not do anything good. They could never be justified in God's sight and would always be evil. He thought that we are saved through faith in Christ, who hides our sins under the cloak of his sacrifice and virtues. According to Luther, our own sacrifices and efforts are worthless for salvation, though they can be helpful for the prosperity of the world. Faith is the only thing that saves us.

Luther did not believe that religious vows, self-denial, and celibacy for priests and nuns were beneficial. He said that priests should marry and that religious orders should be suppressed. Lutheran rulers often confiscated the land and possessions of religious orders and churches in their nation, and priests who became Lutherans could marry. Since Luther did not believe that the Eucharist was a representation of Christ's sacrifice, his church did not have priests to offer sacrifice. Lutheran clergymen were called *ministers*. They had a ceremony similar to the Eucharist and believed that the consecrated bread and wine included the presence of Christ in some manner, but they did not have Mass. Lay people who became Lutherans had no obligation to listen to Catholic teaching. They were expected to obey the Bible, as they felt that the Holy Spirit led them and as Luther directed them.

Martin Luther rejected Catholic doctrines and most sacraments, founded his own church, and converted the majority of people in many parts of Germany to his teaching. Since Luther did not reject the sacrament of baptism and retained most of the orthodox beliefs about the nature of God, Lutherans were still Christians, but the damage done to the unity of Christ's followers was incalculable. After Luther successfully rebelled against Rome, many other leaders formed non-Catholic churches. Since all of them protested against Catholicism, their churches were called Protestant churches. The rapid success of Protestant teachings eventually forced Popes and bishops to realize that they had to reform their own lives and the Catholic Church.

Discussion Questions

Identify: Martin Luther, indulgence, Henry VIII, St. Thomas More, Bishop Fisher

1. Describe the Catholic and early Lutheran ideas about human nature and grace. (Modern Lutherans do not necessarily agree with all of Martin Luther's ideas.)
2. How did Luther's experiences influence his theological ideas?
3. Describe St. Thomas More's life (see below). What Catholic doctrine did he refuse to deny?

Featured Saint: Thomas More

St. Thomas More, born in England in 1478, was one of the most brilliant Renaissance Humanists. He received his early education in an elementary religious school, in the household of the archbishop of Canterbury, at Oxford University, and finally in law school. More became a lawyer and entered Parliament. He was the friend of some of the most influential Humanists of the age and kept in touch with them throughout his professional career. His family life was happy, and his young wife thought that he was an excellent husband because he was always kind to her. They had three daughters and a son. The children were all well educated, especially the oldest daughter, Meg. She was a brilliant scholar in Greek and Latin, which were considered essential among Humanists.

As a young man, Thomas More spent four years with the Carthusians, one of the strictest religious orders in England. He decided that he did not have a religious vocation, but he continued some ascetical practices throughout his life. As a lawyer and judge, he was absolutely fair and never accepted bribes, one of the curses of Renaissance life. He advanced in his profession and attracted the notice of King Henry VIII. He eventually became chancellor, one of the highest positions in the English government.

Henry VIII wanted to divorce his first wife, Catherine of Aragon, and to marry Anne Boleyn. Henry was in love with Anne and wanted her children to be legitimate so that he would have a son to succeed him as king of England. He was convinced that Catherine would never have a son, though they had a daughter, Mary. Cardinal Wolsey, the primate of England, tried to persuade the Pope to annul the king's first marriage. The Pope refused because the marriage was valid and could not be annulled. Henry believed that the Pope, Clement VII, refused to annul his marriage to Catherine because Clement had been defeated in war and the Papal States were dominated by Catherine's nephew, the German emperor, Charles V. King Henry decided to reject the authority of the Pope. Thomas More resigned his office, since he could not support the king in this action. He returned to private life with his family. He had very little income, but he hoped to live in peace.

The king divorced Catherine and married Anne Boleyn. He drew up an Act of Succession, which required his subjects to take an oath to recognize his marriage to Anne as a true marriage and his children by her as heirs to the English throne, and to reject the authority of the Pope. Only one bishop, John Fisher, and one prominent government official, Thomas More, refused to sign the act. Both were put in prison.

More wrote many books as a Christian Humanist, but one of his best books was the spiritual book he wrote in prison, *A Dialogue of Comfort Against Tribulation*. He was happy to suffer for God at first. His daughter, Meg, was visiting him when his former companions, the Carthusian monks, were carried by his window in carts to be executed for refusing to accept the Act of Succession. The monks were cheerful and happy. More said that if he had been more ascetical and detached from the world, he might be as cheerful as the Carthusians. He became discouraged because his friends and family tried to persuade him to be reconciled with the king, and his health became very poor. However, he never signed the Act of Succession.

Henry VIII was determined that Thomas More and Bishop Fisher would cooperate with him or suffer the death penalty. They were kept in prison for a year and a half, under increasingly harsh conditions. The Pope made Bishop Fisher a cardinal, to honor him and protect him from the king, but Henry continued with his plans. One of the king's ministers, acting on his orders, arranged for a witness to testify falsely that he had heard Thomas More and Bishop Fisher make treasonous statements against the king. King Henry demanded their execution. As More was escorted to the scaffold, his strength and good spirits returned, and he was even able to joke with the executioner. He was beheaded in 1535. His death, as well as the death of Bishop Fisher, was treated as an outrage by Humanists all over Europe, but it had the effect the king wanted. Few people in England at the time dared to refuse Henry's demands. Later Catholics were more courageous. Thomas More and Bishop Fisher were venerated as saints by English Catholics and were canonized in 1935.

10

Catholic Reform and the Council of Trent

CHAPTER 10

Catholic Reform and the
Council of Trent

1. Early Catholic Reforms

Many influential Catholics who were unhappy about abuses in the Church did not become Protestants. They tried to reform the Church by living good lives and following Christ themselves. Some reformed their own dioceses or parishes, preached the gospel in their own religious orders, founded new religious orders, or lived exemplary Catholic lives as lay people. They were not able to prevent early Protestants from leaving the Church. However, they helped other Catholics live better lives and trained the theologians, missionaries, and saints who enabled the Catholic Church to survive and flourish after the Council of Trent.

Many Renaissance Humanists criticized or satirized the Church to motivate religious leaders to reform their lives. The best known Christian Humanist was Erasmus. He was born in Rotterdam in the Netherlands at about the same time that St. Thomas More was born in England. Erasmus was educated by a lay association called the *Brothers of the Common Life*, then entered a monastery. Later, he left the monastery and received a dispensation from his vows as a monk. He was a brilliant writer and conversationalist. He spent the rest of his life staying with wealthy rulers, writing books, and visiting Humanists such as his friend Thomas More. In one of his books, *The Praise of Folly*, he satirized Christian leaders who praised people for bad or worthless qualities and ignored true wisdom and goodness. Protestant leaders hoped that Renaissance Humanists would join them, but most Humanists remained Catholic. Writing satires about religious leaders was not the same as leaving the Church. When Protestants began rejecting the Catholic faith, Erasmus wrote a retraction of his most bitter criticisms. Humanists wanted the Church improved, not destroyed.

Julius II, who was elected Pope in 1503, promised to call an ecumenical council to discuss Church reform. It was the fifth council to meet in the Lateran, the Pope's church in Rome. This council lasted from 1512 to 1517. Pope Leo X, who ruled from 1513 to 1521, guided the end of the council. The Fifth Lateran Council clarified several disputed doctrines, but it did not effectively reform the Church. The decrees that were enacted against the evils in Church life contained so many loopholes that they did nothing to stop the abuses. The council's ineffectiveness was very harmful, because it convinced many future Protestants that the Church would never reform herself. The council helped later Catholics by teaching them that laws full of loopholes and exceptions were useless. Bishops and the Pope had to have strong incentives and effective laws to stop crimes committed by bishops, priests, people in religious orders, and ordinary Catholics. The Council of Trent, which met thirty years later, enacted decrees that required Church leaders to impose appropriate sanctions on wrongdoers in the Church.

Pope Hadrian IV and Pope Clement VII, who reigned from 1521 to 1534, did little to improve Church life. They excommunicated Protestant leaders, but the Protestants ignored the excommunications since they did not believe that Popes had any authority from God. Protestants became very hostile to the papacy. Martin Luther often referred to the Pope as the Antichrist, or used other, more insulting terms, in his pamphlets against the Catholic Church.

Several new religious orders were founded between 1500 and 1560. The most influential groups were associations of priests such as the Oratorians, the Theatines, and the Jesuits. The Oratorians were an association founded by St. Philip Neri to help priests live good lives and carry out their sacred ministry in a holy manner. St. Philip was very cheerful and trusted God in everything. He was able to inspire his followers to love God and to trust that God would help them in every difficulty. Protestants believed that human beings could not be holy and pleasing to God, but Philip Neri showed priests that by trusting God, they could become like Jesus and please God in everything. Priests who found it difficult to imitate Jesus could learn to do better by imitating St. Philip Neri or joining his Oratorians.

The Theatines were founded by St. Cajetan and Cardinal Caraffa, who later became Pope Paul IV. Unlike the Oratorians, who formed a loose association, the Theatines were a religious order of priests. Several other orders of priests were founded at about the same time to train priests in theology and help them live virtuous lives. The most influential new religious order was the Society of Jesus, or the Jesuits, founded by a Spanish former soldier named Ignatius of Loyola. The Jesuits were completely devoted to Christ, and they taught the Catholic faith wherever they were sent by the Pope. Jesuit theologians were some of the best educated men in Europe. However, they were best known for their love of Christ, their obedience to the Pope, and their missionary activities. Many Jesuits have become canonized saints and martyrs.

Older religious orders were reformed or split apart into strictly reformed and unreformed groups. The best known of these reformed orders is probably the Discalced Carmelites, established in Spain by St. Teresa of Avila and St. John of the Cross. The Franciscans, Dominicans, and Benedictine orders were also reformed. These orders had been so badly damaged by the plague, schisms, and wars that their rules had been relaxed in order to prevent them from becoming extinct. In the orders that split, even the unreformed parts began living more ascetical lives than they had before 1500.

Catholic rulers, particularly the German emperor Charles V, tried to persuade Protestants to return to the Church. Charles sponsored a number of debates with Protestants, but these debates accomplished very little. The German Church was full of scandals, which had nearly destroyed the Catholic faith in many areas. Some people still believed the teachings of John Huss, the heretic who had been condemned and executed a century earlier. Protestant beliefs spread very quickly in Germany and parts of Switzerland. While Charles V was sponsoring debates and compromises, Protestant preachers were converting many dissatisfied Catholics, including priests, bishops, and secular rulers.

Early Protestants asked for religious toleration, but when they took control of a country, they usually outlawed other religions. In most countries the religion adopted by the ruler became the state religion. In a few countries people were able to prevent rulers from taking power unless they followed the religion of the majority of the population, but in most countries people had the choice of accepting the religion of the ruler, leaving the country, or suffering persecution, exile, imprisonment, or death. Rulers who allowed religious dissent were often attacked in religious wars and rebellions. Intolerant rulers often prevented religious wars. At the end of his life, Emperor Charles V advised his son, King Philip II of Spain, to suppress dissent ruthlessly. The emperor had decided that toleration and compromise caused endless trouble and gained nothing.

Discussion Questions

Identify: Erasmus, Fifth Lateran Council, St. Philip Neri, Jesuits, Charles V

1. What was the attitude of most Renaissance Humanists to scandals in the Church?
2. What were the long-term effects of the Fifth Lateran Council on the Church?
3. What was the early attitude of Charles V to the Protestant movement? What was his attitude at the end of his life?
4. Describe the Oratorians, Theatines, and Jesuits.

2. New Protestant Churches

Martin Luther founded what would later become the Lutheran church because he rejected the Pope's authority. Luther proclaimed the principle that any devout person can read the Bible and interpret it correctly, with the help of the Holy Spirit and without the help of the Church. Luther accepted many early Christian traditions, such as the doctrines about the Trinity defined by early ecumenical councils. Later Protestants read the Bible on their own and came to their own conclusions. Some of them rejected Luther's views and established new Protestant churches.

One early result of Luther's preaching in Germany was a massive peasant rebellion against the nobles who ruled them.

Like the followers of John Huss a hundred years earlier, Lutheran peasants thought that the most important abuses in Christian society were committed by greedy nobles who left their workers scarcely enough to live on. Lutheran nobles joined forces with Catholic nobles to suppress the rebellion. Thousands of peasants were killed in battle or executed, and many of the survivors eventually returned to the Catholic Church. To prevent social chaos, Luther put his church under the control of Lutheran rulers.

Another result of Luther's attack on the Catholic Church was the formation, or revival, of the Anabaptists. This sect, a distant relative of modern Baptists, denied more traditional Christian doctrines than did Luther. The Anabaptists did not believe in infant baptism, and a few of them practiced polygamy or shared community property and wives. Early Lutherans joined forces with Catholics to arrest and execute a number of Anabaptist leaders, since their beliefs led to anarchy. The sect survived in a less radical form.

Luther did not conclude that, since his principle of individual interpretation of the Bible led to many contradictory beliefs, he was mistaken. He believed that his own interpretation of the Bible was correct and that the beliefs of the Pope, many early Catholic writers, and the other Protestants were wrong. Most Protestant leaders were equally certain of their own beliefs, even when they disagreed with Luther. This disagreement led to fundamental doctrinal differences among Protestant churches.

An early Protestant from Switzerland named Zwingli completely denied that the Body and Blood of Christ became present in the Eucharist, saying that it was only a memory or commemoration of Christ's death, though Christ might be present spiritually in the hearts of those celebrating the Eucharist. He suggested that when Christ said "this is my body" at the Last Supper, he was pointing at himself. This reasoning did not convince Luther and most other early Protestants, who disagreed with the Catholic teaching but believed that Christ was really in the Eucharist in some manner. Zwingli and his followers led attacks on Catholic churches to smash the altars, tabernacles, and statues of saints, since he did not believe in the sacraments or the intercessory power of saints. Zwingli was killed in a religious war against Catholics, but Swiss Protestants soon found another leader, John Calvin.

Calvin set up a Protestant religious state in Geneva, Switzerland. Calvinist elders, one type of Protestant leader, had the duty to report behavior regarded as ungodly, such as adultery and dancing, to secular authorities, who administered punishment. Calvinists did not have ordained priests. Each congregation was expected to choose a minister, who would preach the word of God to them. Under Calvin's influence, the government sponsored trials, imprisonments, and executions for Catholics and Protestants who disagreed with his views and for people committing many other crimes.

John Calvin believed in "predestination". According to his theology, God predestined some people for heaven and others for hell, and there was nothing people could do to change their destiny. Since he believed that people predestined for heaven behaved in a virtuous manner, Calvinists tried to live good lives to show that they were predestined for heaven. Calvin believed that God often rewarded virtue with material prosperity, so Calvinists often believed that the poor were sinners who were predestined for hell. After Calvin's success in some parts of Switzerland, Calvinist missionaries converted most of the people in Scotland, where they were called *Presbyterians*. The Pilgrims who fled to the United States from England and the Netherlands were

Calvinists called *Puritans* or *Congregationalists*. French Calvinists, who became numerous in a few parts of France, were called *Huguenots*. Modern Calvinists usually modify their founder's beliefs, since the absolute predestination of some people to hell, regardless of anything they do, is difficult to reconcile with God's mercy.

Calvin, Luther, and the other early Protestants rejected Catholic beliefs about the effects of God's grace on people's souls. The Apostolic Fathers and later Catholics believed that God became man so that man might become like God. Even though we have been weakened by the sin inherited from Adam, we have good qualities. With the help of God's grace, we can become holy and pleasing to God. We will be like God and united with God in heaven. Early Protestants believed that human beings were completely bad because of original sin and could not do anything good. Some modern Protestants have returned to a more Catholic idea of grace. Others have gone to the opposite extreme and believe that nearly everyone is good and will be saved, regardless of how many sins they commit and whether they have faith in Christ. This view is contrary to Catholic and early Protestant beliefs.

Protestant and Catholic Churches had completely different views on the nature of the Church and the need for Church unity. Catholics believe that Christ established a visible Church on earth. Christ is the head of the Church, but she is governed by his representatives, the hierarchy of priests, bishops, and the Pope. Christ wants all Christians to have the same faith and belong to the same Church. Since everyone is expected to believe in the true faith, Church leaders have the obligation to teach the truth, reconcile their differences, and prevent heresy and schism.

Protestants thought that Christ did not found a visible Church on earth (at least not as Catholics understood it) or establish a hierarchy. The first Protestants broke away from the Catholics for several reasons. They thought that Catholic beliefs were wrong, that human beings were so sinful that no one could live a virtuous Catholic life, or that Catholics were so sinful and hypocritical that virtuous people had to leave the Church to escape contamination. Protestants did not see much need to reconcile their beliefs with those of the Catholic Church or other Protestants. They continued splitting apart over doctrinal or personal differences and forming new churches. A few of them stopped claiming to know the truth, but made the opposite error and denied that anyone can know the truth about God. There are many Protestant denominations today.

Luther hoped that he would be able to convert Jews to his new religion, but he soon reverted to intolerance against them. Calvinists thought that the Jews, like many other people, were not predestined for heaven. Different Protestant groups worked out different relations with Jews, but none of them offered real toleration for hundreds of years. Catholic countries were also intolerant, though the degree varied with different Catholic rulers. In most European nations, Jews were forbidden to hold positions in the government or to own extensive lands, and they often had to live in small sections of the towns and wear distinctive clothes. These restrictions were gradually lifted in many countries after 1700.

Many Muslims were the enemies of Christians. During the Renaissance, Europe was faced with constant wars against Muslim Turks, who were eager to invade Italy, Spain, and the countries in Eastern Europe. Muslim Turks did conquer some parts of Eastern Europe during the Renaissance. Emperor Charles V frequently signed peace treaties with Lutheran princes because he was so busy fighting the Turks that he was unable to deal effectively with the Protestants.

Discussion Questions

Identify: Anabaptists, Zwingli, John Calvin, Presbyterians, Congregationalists, absolute predestination

1. Why were there so many different Protestant churches?
2. Describe Protestant and Catholic views on Church unity.

3. The Council of Trent

Pope Paul III was elected in 1534. He began preparing for an ecumenical council by appointing bishops who had reformed their own dioceses or religious orders to be cardinals. They planned for the council and negotiated with secular leaders. Many German rulers were Protestants, and the ones who were Catholic were committed to compromise and discussion. Martin Luther and other Protestant leaders had been asking for a council since 1517. However, when the Pope called for a council, Protestants did everything they could to delay it, because they wanted a different type of council. Some civil authorities made unacceptable demands for control over it. The council finally gathered at the city of Trent in 1545.

The first sessions of the Council of Trent set up the order of procedure. The topics to be discussed were proposed by the Pope's legates and drawn up in documents for discussion by groups of theologians. The whole assembly debated the proposals, which were voted on by the bishops and cardinals. The format reduced the business of reforming the Church to manageable segments and gave bishops the opportunity to accept, reject, discuss, and modify proposals. Even though Protestants were excluded from the Council of Trent, their views were represented because a few Catholic bishops had adopted some Protestant views, and others were uncertain about basic Catholic doctrines. Many Catholic theologians, especially the Jesuits, had obtained copies of Protestant books and studied them thoroughly, since they hoped to persuade Protestants to return to the Catholic Church. Decrees affecting Church abuses and discipline were voted on by some bishops who had committed the offenses that were condemned.

The council was interrupted by the reign of Pope Paul IV, formerly Cardinal Caraffa. He had witnessed the Lateran Council thirty years earlier and doubted that an ecumenical council would really reform the Church. During his reign he made every possible effort to enforce existing Church laws instead of reconvening the council. This made him very unpopular, but he ended many abuses. For example, many bishops and cardinals left Rome to avoid his disciplinary laws and visited their dioceses, often for the first time. After he died, the next Pope reconvened the Council of Trent.

The council had two basic tasks. One was to enact decrees that would end the crimes committed by Church leaders. The other was to define and reaffirm Catholic beliefs, so that Catholics and Protestants would know exactly what the Catholic Church taught about disputed doctrines. Even though Catholic teaching had been consistent, there had been some development of doctrine since apostolic times, and Church teaching on many subjects was not summarized anywhere in a concise and authoritative fashion. St. Thomas Aquinas and other theologians had written summaries of the Catholic faith, but none of them was completely authoritative, and their summaries often filled ten to fifteen volumes. Theologians had to read many books in Latin before they could understand what the Church taught on a few controversial subjects, such as predestination. Some bishops and priests, and most Catholics, did not know enough Latin to read long theological texts.

Many theologians at the council, especially the Jesuits, had spent decades studying the writings of the Bible, the Apostolic Fathers, and later Catholic authors. These theologians had a profound knowledge of Church teachings on every subject. The Jesuits showed so much love of Jesus and loyalty to the Church that most of the bishops attending the council were impressed by their holiness and knowledge. Even so, the documents proposed by Jesuit theologians at the Pope's request were debated and revised before they were passed. The decrees restated traditional beliefs clearly and established disciplinary laws that guided the Church for the next four hundred years.

The disciplinary decrees ended a number of abuses by bishops such as controlling more than one diocese, living outside of their diocese, buying and selling religious offices (simony), collecting the revenue from their diocese without being ordained, and similar crimes. Bishops or priests who committed immoral acts, simony, or other serious offenses were automatically suspended and deprived of their offices. The Council also laid down strict laws regarding the admission of candidates for the priesthood. Priests who were ordained had to have the theological knowledge, training, and stability to live a virtuous life. If these decrees had been in effect earlier they would have excluded most of the immoral Renaissance priests, bishops, and Popes and many men who became Protestant leaders after being ordained or holding offices in the Catholic Church.

The council required that each bishop establish a seminary in his diocese to train priests. This decree was difficult to implement at first, since many dioceses had very little income, and there were not enough trained theologians to act as professors. The situation changed when the new religious orders of priests gained more vocations. Soon many seminaries were staffed by Jesuits or Theatines, and later by French Vincentians or Sulpicians. Since the professors had taken vows of poverty and were willing to live and teach in small, inexpensive buildings, more bishops were able to establish seminaries. The influence of these holy professors on the priests they trained was one of the most important results of the Council of Trent. There were still scandals among Church leaders, but they were much less frequent and were regarded as exceptions in Catholic life.

Since parish priests were expected to live virtuous lives, they set a good example for ordinary Catholics. Immorality in society seems to have gradually declined. Behavior that would have been laughed off in the early Renaissance was regarded as intolerable several hundred years later, and the worst crimes among Church leaders were completely suppressed. Church leaders had learned that tolerating evil behavior did nothing to reform criminals and encouraged others to imitate them. The only way to reform the Church was to punish Church leaders for their evil deeds by depriving them of their Church offices and to insist on good behavior as a prerequisite for ordination. Church leaders were not usually saints, but after the Council of Trent, people who were living openly immoral lives were not allowed to hold offices in the Church.

The decrees of the council on Church teaching did not establish any new doctrines, but they reaffirmed or explained the doctrines taught by earlier Catholics. For instance, each sacrament was defined clearly, and its manner of administration and effects were laid out in detail. Since all sacraments, including the sacrament of Holy Orders, were instituted by Christ, the Church hierarchy was clearly an essential part of Christ's Church. These decrees showed the errors of Protestants who rejected the sacraments and refused to admit that the hierarchy had any authority from God. The council also passed dogmatic decrees defining Catholic beliefs about grace, predestination, the need for unity, and the nature of the Church. The decrees clearly stated that people who held different views had cut themselves off from the Church, and that was a serious sin. Of course, this applied only to people who knew the correct Catholic teaching and deliberately rejected it. Later Protestants who had no opportunity of knowing Catholic teaching were in a different situation. They were deprived of most of the sacraments and the benefits of being a Catholic, but they could be saved if they obeyed Christ to the best of their ability.

The Council of Trent met from 1545 to 1547, 1551 to 1552, and 1561 to 1563. The sessions were interrupted by several wars, the deaths of several Popes, and the reign of Pope Paul IV. The eighteen-year interval between the beginning and end of the council may have created a better opportunity for genuine reform. There were more bishops, cardinals, and religious orders dedicated to Catholic reform in 1563 than in 1545. Catholic rulers had less hope that diplomatic or military efforts would restore Church unity, and most of them supported the council reforms after the decrees were passed.

After the Council of Trent, theologians wrote the *Roman Catechism*, which was approved by the Pope, St. Pius V, in 1566. The book included a short summary of everything Catholics needed to know about their faith. It was easier to read and more complete than the *Decrees of the Council of Trent*, and it became the basis of most later Catechisms for priests or lay people. The *Roman Catechism* was one of the most useful teaching aids during the Catholic Reformation.

By this time Protestant leaders had established firm control in many countries. Most rulers believed that they had the right to choose the religion their people would follow. Rulers could exile or execute anyone teaching unapproved religious beliefs. In many Protestant countries, ordinary people maintained their Catholic faith for several generations, but eventually most of the population conformed to the main religion in most countries. (Ireland, which remained Catholic in spite of domination by Protestant England, was the most notable exception.) The conversion of one ruler often meant that the entire country would eventually follow a new religion. Religious differences increased the bitterness of disputed successions and feuds over land or power. The next hundred years witnessed religious persecution and religious wars in many countries. In the end Protestants controlled independent sections of Germany, Switzerland, Holland, and Eastern Europe and all of Scotland, Scandinavia, and England. Catholics regained control over Poland, Bohemia, parts of Germany, and several other nations after being temporarily displaced by Protestants. The rest of Europe remained Catholic.

The Council of Trent ended religious confusion among Catholics. Protestant and Catholic beliefs were clearly distinguished. The Church hierarchy was effectively reformed, so Protestants who left the Church after the council were forced to reject doctrines or discipline rather than criticize serious abuses. Unfortunately, most Protestants did reject many Catholic doctrines. They remained separated from full unity with the Catholic Church. The split was more serious than the Eastern Schism, since the Greek Orthodox Church retained sacraments and most of the faith that it had received from the Apostles in spite of rejecting the authority of the Pope. Modern improvements in communication and honest dialogue between Catholics and Protestants have increased hopes for full unity among Christians. However, resolving the doctrinal differences will require prayer and conversions as well as charity.

Discussion Questions

Identify: Council of Trent, Pope Paul IV, *Roman Catechism*

1. How did Pope Paul III prepare for the Council of Trent?
2. How were Protestant views represented at the council?
3. What changes were made in Church discipline to end crimes among Church leaders?
4. What influence did the new seminaries for priests have on Catholic life?
5. Why were the Jesuits so influential at the council?

4. The Catholic Church in England

Henry VIII was the king of England from 1509 to 1547. King Henry renounced the authority of the Pope so that he could divorce his first wife and marry Anne Boleyn. After the Act of Supremacy and the execution of Thomas More and Bishop Fisher, Henry confiscated the property of all of the religious orders in England and forced the bishops to give him a huge sum of money, which they raised by selling Church property. In spite of these facts, Henry thought that he was a good Catholic. Some of the bishops he appointed and his closest advisors believed in Protestant doctrines, but Henry insisted that the Church in England retain its traditional liturgy. Most Catholics hoped that the next ruler would return to communion with Rome.

Anne Boleyn, King Henry's second wife, gave birth to a daughter, Elizabeth. Henry was furious, since he already had a daughter and wanted a son. He lost interest in Anne, and she was tried and executed for adultery and treason in 1536. Henry married a third wife, who died shortly after becoming the mother of a son, Edward. Henry married three more wives in quick succession, but he had no more children. When Henry died, his nine-year-old son was crowned as Edward VI.

The regents chosen for Edward were Protestants. They appointed Protestant bishops and advisors. The English Church was required to use semi-Protestant worship services, prayer books, and ordination rites. Many Catholics did not realize that the liturgical changes were important. Most priests and bishops followed the new order of worship during King Edward's short reign rather than lose their jobs or face worse penalties.

Edward died in 1553. According to the revised Act of Succession, the next ruler was Henry's first daughter, Mary Tudor. Her mother was Catherine, the daughter of Ferdinand and Isabella of Spain. Queen Mary attempted to restore the Catholic faith in England. She was supported in this plan by a number of bishops and probably by the majority of the English people. Unfortunately, she made several serious mistakes. The first was her marriage to King Philip II of Spain. The English were afraid of being dominated by fanatical Spaniards and the Spanish Inquisition. King Philip spent some time each year in England. He treated his wife and her subjects with kindness, but his presence increased tensions among English Catholics.

Queen Mary and her representatives persuaded the Pope to drop his demands for the return of Church property. After he had agreed to this, most of the English bishops and priests were reconciled with Rome. They returned to the Catholic liturgy, and England was again part of the Catholic Church. Queen Mary made her second major mistake when she tried to suppress dissent. A few bishops, Protestant ministers, and important laymen refused to return to the Catholic Church. Mary insisted on having them arrested and tried for heresy. Against the advice of her Catholic bishops, several hundred Protestants who refused to renounce their beliefs were burned at the stake, including three of Edward's bishops. This punishment would have been considered severe even in Spain. In England it was regarded as outrageous. Scarcely anyone there had ever been executed for heresy, much less burned at the stake. In spite of Queen Mary's good intentions, her harshness made Catholicism very unpopular.

Queen Mary died in 1558, and her half sister Elizabeth, the daughter of Anne Boleyn, was crowned queen of England. Elizabeth rejected Mary's union with Rome and established the Anglican church, which is called the Episcopal church in the United States. Since her advisors were Protestants who did not believe that Mass was a sacrifice, the ordination ceremony they used excluded the Catholic belief about the priesthood and the sacrament of Holy Orders. Bishops and priests consecrated by means of the new rite were not validly ordained. This was true of all Protestant religions. The only valid sacraments they had were baptism and matrimony, which did not need ordained priests for administration. Losing the other sacraments did not concern Protestants, since they had rejected them or had never learned about them. Anglican bishops established liturgies that were similar to those for confirmation and ordination. They adopted a ceremony called Communion that was similar to Mass, but it excluded the idea of Christ's sacrifice and the

Real Presence of Christ. Sunday worship was usually limited to singing, Bible readings, prayers, and a long sermon. Protestants usually omitted the sacrament of penance completely. Some modern Anglicans and Episcopalians have returned to more Catholic interpretations of their faith.

The Catholic bishops during Elizabeth's reign were much more courageous than they had been under King Henry VIII or King Edward. Only two bishops agreed to her demands. The rest of them, and about four hundred priests, were deposed from their offices. Elizabeth established a new hierarchy of Anglican bishops, and most people in England accepted her church. In 1570 the Pope excommunicated her, since it was clear that she had no intention of returning to the Catholic faith. Elizabeth resolved to suppress the Catholics in England who were loyal to the Pope and also to suppress some radical Protestant sects, such as the Calvinist Puritans, which were undermining royal authority. The queen wanted complete control over her church.

After 1570 there were scarcely any Roman Catholic priests active in England. Parliament passed laws making it treason to obey the Pope or to be a Roman Catholic priest. This meant that priests who were captured by the queen's police could be tortured to force them to reveal the names and hiding places of other priests and could be executed by being hanged, drawn and quartered, or torn apart. In spite of this, Catholic men began traveling to English seminaries in Rome, France, and Spain, where they became parish priests or Jesuits. Catholic women sometimes joined English convents in France. English Jesuits could be sent anywhere in the world, but many of them volunteered to return to England.

Jesuits and parish priests in England were kept hidden by loyal Catholics and were able to say Mass, hear confessions, and teach the faith. Several hundred of them were captured by the English government between 1570 and 1600. Most captured priests were imprisoned for years, tortured, and executed, along with some lay men and women. Ordinary Catholic lay people had to pay such severe fines that they usually became very poor in a few generations. Catholics were excluded from holding public office and from being educated in English universities. Nevertheless, the Catholic faith survived in England. When the harsh anti-Catholic laws were repealed in the 1800s and some Anglicans began converting to the Catholic faith, they were able to join the remnant of the old English Catholic Church, which was still alive in spite of nearly three hundred years of persecution.

Queen Elizabeth was a very successful ruler. She never married, so she never shared her power with anyone except her favorite ministers. When she died the Anglican church was firmly established. Elizabeth had survived several external threats to her government, including an attempted invasion by King Philip II of Spain. She had tightened English control over Ireland and had attempted to suppress the Catholic faith there. Her successor was King James of Scotland, who became James I of England. He continued her religious policies in England, though Scotland had become Presbyterian in 1560. England suffered from many religious upheavals in the future, but the country never returned to the Catholic Church.

Discussion Questions

Identify: Edward VI, Queen Mary of England, Queen Elizabeth of England, St. Ignatius of Loyola

1. What steps did Queen Mary take to restore the Catholic faith in England? Did these actions have the effect she intended?
2. Describe Queen Elizabeth's relationship to the Pope, English Catholics, and Puritans.
3. Describe the life of St. Ignatius (see below).

Featured Saint: Ignatius of Loyola

St. Ignatius was born to a noble family in 1491. He received an indifferent education, became a soldier, and fought in several battles for the king of Spain. After a short, promising military career, his leg was severely injured by a cannonball, and he returned to the family castle at Loyola while it healed. He asked for something to read, hoping for novels or adventure stories, but a book about the life of Jesus and a collection of stories about the saints were the only books available. Ignatius read these books and imagined living like the saints. At other times he thought of a beautiful noblewoman he loved and planned his future career. One day he noticed that after he had been thinking about imitating the saints, he felt happy and peaceful for hours, but after he thought about the woman or his future as a nobleman, he felt unhappy and dissatisfied. Later he realized that peace and happiness with good resolutions are signs of the presence of the Holy Spirit. He decided to give up his career as a soldier and to spend his life following Christ and imitating the saints.

After his leg healed, Ignatius went on pilgrimage to Montserrat, a monastery and shrine dedicated to Mary. He remained in the nearby town of Manresa. He lived sometimes in a shelter for the poor and sometimes in a cave. After a year of peace and joy in his new life, he suddenly experienced such severe scruples and unhappiness that he was tempted to commit suicide. He consulted several priests, but they were unable to help him, since he was convinced that they did not realize how sinful and evil he was. One day he began thinking about his state of mind, and he suddenly saw how the devil had tempted him into fear and despair. After that he refused to listen to temptations, and he was never bothered in the same way again.

Ignatius spent several years making a pilgrimage to the Holy Land. When he returned, he decided that his mission was to help souls. He began by attending a Latin class with young boys. After several years he had learned enough to enter the famous University of Salamanca. Several friends began imitating his simple lifestyle and apostolic activities, but they dropped away. The Spanish Inquisition imprisoned him for a few weeks, thinking that he was a secret Protestant missionary, but they decided that he was innocent and released him. He went alone to the University of Paris to finish his studies. In 1534 he received a degree to teach theology.

Ignatius spent his spare time trying to persuade others to give their lives to God by helping the poor, teaching the Catholic faith, and following Christ. When he graduated, he and six companions took a vow to go to the Holy Land together. In 1541, with the Pope's approval, they pronounced solemn vows and formed themselves into a religious order called the Society of Jesus, often called the Jesuits. They were unusual because they took a fourth vow of obedience to the Pope and because it took seventeen years to be completely trained as a Jesuit. Most religious orders took three vows and had no more than seven years of training.

St. Ignatius developed a system of spiritual exercises that helped people give their lives completely to Jesus. These exercises were meditations based on Scripture, especially on the life of Christ, and they included insights from his own experience resisting temptations and discerning the influence of good or evil spirits. Jesuits were taught to imitate Christ by remaining loyal even if they were tortured or martyred or if they spent their entire lives teaching the same subject in an uncomfortable school in a remote part of the world. Jesuits were very influential in reforming the Church, and *The Spiritual Exercises of St. Ignatius of Loyola* has helped millions of people to learn to love Christ and to live good Catholic lives.

I I

The Church and World Empires

1. Early Missionary Activities in the Spanish and Portuguese Empires
2. St. Francis Xavier and Missionary Work in Asia
3. The Church After the Council of Trent
4. The French Church

Featured Saint: Margaret Mary

CHAPTER 11

The Church and World Empires

1. Early Missionary Activities in the Spanish and Portuguese Empires

Most of the history of the Church before 1450 took place in Europe, in Britain, or in the countries surrounding the Mediterranean Sea. Early Christians carried the gospel to parts of India, Ethiopia, Persia, Mongolia, and perhaps the western part of China. Some of these churches survived, but they did not convert many of their neighbors. By executing or enslaving Christian missionaries, Muslim rulers prevented Christianity from spreading to the East and to Africa. Most evangelization during the Middle Ages took place in Eastern Europe, the Scandinavian countries, Russia, and the rural areas of Europe, where people were ignorant of many Christian doctrines and filled with superstitions.

China, Africa, and most of India and Asia were practically unknown to medieval Christians. Trade goods from China to Europe were carried by caravans and changed hands many times. It would have been extremely difficult for missionaries to accompany the caravans back to China, and scarcely anyone made the attempt. There was no direct transportation to China, Africa, and most of India and Asia before 1500. The little known about the interior of Africa was discovered by Muslims, who colonized the eastern coast of Africa and kidnapped slaves to sell. North and South America were completely unknown to Asians and Europeans.

After 1450 the king of Portugal began sending ships south to explore the west coast of Africa. They discovered little of commercial value, but they established some trading posts and ports. After many years they sailed around South Africa and began exploring the eastern side of the continent. They reached Asian countries that produced spices, silk, and other valuable products. Portuguese traders were able to buy these goods cheaply, ship them back to Europe, and make tremendous profits. They soon established permanent Portuguese colonies along both coasts of Africa and in several Asian nations. Muslim traders were already established in many of these countries.

Franciscan priests accompanied these voyages of exploration. They began missionary work by preaching to the Portuguese sailors, who were usually more interested in making money than in their religion. The Franciscans preached to the natives wherever the Portuguese established bases. European traders usually hired local servants or bought slaves, who often became Christians. Missionaries learned enough from these people about local religions and languages to preach the gospel to the rest of the population.

Missionaries encountered diverse religious systems. Natives in most of Africa and many small islands believed in local gods or various types of spirits. These people were often happy to become Christians. However, Europeans also found Muslims, Hindus, Buddhists, and Chinese Confucians. These religions or philosophies were more sophisticated, and their followers were more difficult to convert to Christianity. There are many stories of lay Catholics converting their business associates. However, most missionary work was done by Franciscans, Dominicans, and Jesuits. The work made better progress when trained theologians learned enough about local religions to explain Christianity in the people's own terms.

Spanish explorers usually traveled west to the New World, but some of them reached Asia. The Spanish and Portuguese rulers agreed to confine their activities to separate spheres of influence. Portugal had access to much of Asia and Brazil in the Americas, and Spain controlled the Philippines in Asia and most of both American continents.

England and France gained control of the United States and Canada and began colonizing them after 1600. French missionaries and settlers converted some Native Americans to the Catholic religion, but the Calvinist Puritans and the other early English settlers were not usually interested in converting their Native American neighbors. Instead they forced the original inhabitants of the land to move further and further west. Many Native Americans were killed by enemies. European diseases such as smallpox and the flu killed millions of Native Americans, who had very little inherited immunity to these diseases.

Portuguese and Spanish explorers operated in different ways. Portuguese settlers colonized Brazil, which had no advanced cultures, but in Asia the Portuguese usually established small settlements with the permission of local rulers. Spanish explorers conquered the Aztec civilization in Mexico and the Incas in Peru and set up colonies in those countries under the authority of the king of Spain. Wherever they went, Spanish conquerors were inclined to try to overthrow local rulers and take control of their countries. However, Catholics did not believe in driving out the inhabitants of newly discovered lands or enslaving or killing them. Popes and religious leaders had to insist many times that the natives must be well treated, since Spanish adventurers wanted as much control as possible over their conquests. A few rulers were excommunicated for enslaving their workers, and this helped prevent the practice from becoming established by law, but in many cases the Native Americans were little better than slaves. Spanish and Portuguese nobles also bought African slaves to work in a few places such as Brazil and Puerto Rico. The Spanish monarchy as well as the Pope forbid slavery, so many Europeans involved in the trade were Protestants, though some Catholics participated.

Eventually slaves gained the free status of local natives. The conquerors tried to convert the people they ruled to Catholicism, but the conquerors usually adopted many aspects of local traditions and culture themselves. The final result of Spanish and Portuguese domination was a variety of Catholic cultures that combined European, native, and some African influences.

The work of evangelizing the Native Americans was helped by a miracle. In 1531, a few years after the Spanish conquerors had defeated the Aztec rulers of Mexico, an Indian Catholic named Juan Diego was returning home from a journey near Mexico City. He suddenly saw a beautiful woman, surrounded by light. She told him to go and ask the bishop of Mexico City to build a shrine for her there. Juan protested that he did not think the bishop would believe him, but he went anyway. The bishop of Mexico City was a devout and holy man. He spoke kindly to Juan, but he did not believe that the Blessed Virgin Mary had actually appeared to him. The bishop said that they could not build a church there at that time. A few days later the woman appeared again to Juan, even though he had gone out of his way to avoid the place where she had first appeared. (He was in a hurry to find a priest to go to his uncle who was dying. She assured him his uncle would live.) He explained that the bishop had not believed him. She told him to go back and ask again, but this time she gave him some roses to take to the bishop. Juan wrapped them in his cloak, a fiber garment called a *tilma*. When he saw the bishop, he repeated his request and opened his cloak. The roses fell out. To his astonishment, the bishop knelt down in front of the cloak, followed by the rest of the Spanish nobles in the room. Imprinted on the cloak was the beautiful picture of the Blessed Virgin known as Our Lady of Guadalupe.

The bishop of Mexico City built the church, which became a shrine of pilgrimage and prayer for the people of Mexico and later, for many North American Catholics. Juan Diego spent the rest of his life caring for the shrine and the pilgrims who traveled there. He was canonized by Pope John Paul II in 2002.

The picture on Juan's tilma showed the Blessed Virgin with features somewhat similar to those of local Native Americans, and her garments, position, and attitude indicated her purity, holiness, power of intercession, and subordination to God. The image helped Native Americans understand the doctrines of Christianity and showed them that the Mother of God loved them and wanted them to become Christians. The miracle helped convert millions of Mexicans to the Catholic faith in a few years, and it remains an inspiration for Catholics today.

Most of the European conquests in America and Asia took place before the Council of Trent. The Spanish and Portuguese churches, which had little need for reform, were well suited to spread the Christian message to new countries, even though Spanish and Portuguese adventurers were usually poor models of Christian behavior. The Catholic Church became firmly established in the newly discovered lands and gained many sincere converts among the Native Americans and Asians.

Discussion Questions

Identify: St. Juan Diego, Our Lady of Guadalupe

1. Describe the relationship between Catholic and Portu-
    guese conquerors, the Church, and Native Americans. What
    was responsible for the deaths of most Native Americans at
    this time?
2. Describe the appearance of Our Lady of Guadalupe to St.
    Juan Diego. How did this miracle help with the conver-
    sion of Mexico?

2. St. Francis Xavier and Missionary Work in Asia

Francis Xavier was one of the original companions of St.
Ignatius of Loyola. He met Ignatius at the University of Paris,
but he was not attracted to Ignatius' life of prayer at first.
However, Ignatius kept reminding Francis of the words of
Christ, "What does it profit a man to gain the whole world
and lose his own soul?" Francis agreed to make the Spiritual
Exercises under the guidance of St. Ignatius. After the month
of meditations, Francis decided to give his life entirely to
God. He earned a degree in theology and became a priest.
In 1540 the Jesuit order was approved. Francis traveled with
a few companions to Portugal and sailed from there in a merchant ship around Africa to Asia to work in the Portuguese
missions.

By this time many Portuguese settlements were well established. The Portuguese town of Goa in India had many
churches and a bishop, but missionary activity was dragging.
Francis began preaching to the Portuguese settlers in India,
but he was not very successful in persuading them to live
good Christian lives. After a short time he went to a rural

area on the coast of India, which was occupied by the lowest class of people in Hindu society. He learned enough of the language to preach and translate the creed and some prayers. Then he began telling the people about Jesus. Since the adults did not listen at first, he spoke to the children.

Once when St. Francis Xavier was traveling through a small town, he learned that a woman there had been in labor for three days and was expected to die. She was being treated with a succession of Hindu religious chants. Accompanied by one of the local leaders, he went to her house and explained the Creed and the Gospels. She said that she believed and wanted to be baptized, so he baptized her. Immediately afterward, she brought forth her child. Because of this unexpected healing, Francis was able to baptize everyone in the village. He soon gained a reputation for working miracles. Sometimes he wrote prayers on pieces of paper. The children he had baptized laid them on sick people, who were frequently healed. He became so famous that he was constantly busy teaching people about Christianity, and he baptized so many people that he could scarcely lift his arm for another baptism. He wrote to St. Ignatius of Loyola and begged him to send more Jesuits, since one man could not possibly instruct all of the Indians who were willing to become Christians.

Francis spent several years in India and converted thousands of people. Newly arrived Jesuits took over his missions, and many Indian communities became solidly Catholic. The Jesuits also attempted to convert Hindus from the upper classes, but this was more difficult. Portuguese influence in India was eventually replaced by English domination, but Catholics are still an influential minority in parts of Indian society.

St. Francis Xavier traveled farther east to remote Portuguese outposts. In each one he preached first to the Europeans, who often needed conversion nearly as much as the non-Christians. A few merchants had established harems, imitating local Muslim customs, and they had stopped practicing their faith. A story tells how St. Francis converted a rich Portuguese trader with a harem of six women. The man invited Francis to dinner frequently, and the Jesuit gradually persuaded the man to give up one woman after another, for various reasons. Finally Francis married the trader to the last woman in a Christian wedding. Francis usually asked to meet the cooks and other servants when he was invited to dinner, so that he could praise their cooking and encourage them to become saints. He instructed children, servants, and slaves, as well as their parents and masters. Even though many Europeans resented his efforts to convert them, most people believed that he was a very holy man. Another Jesuit said that the influence of Francis Xavier was so powerful that the rest of them were simply riding along on his reputation.

Several years later, St. Francis met a man from Japan who had committed murder and was traveling to find relief from his guilty conscience. The man became a Christian and accompanied St. Francis and a few companions back to Japan. They were some of the first Europeans to see the country. Anjiro, or Paul, which was the man's Christian name, interpreted for Francis. Paul visited the local ruler and obtained permission for Francis to preach and make converts. Paul's family and some friends became Christians. St. Francis visited the local Buddhist monasteries to learn about their doctrines and explain Christian beliefs, but the language barrier prevented much success, even with Anjiro's translations. Francis admired the Japanese people for their honesty, fortitude, bravery, sense of honor, and intelligence. He traveled to several other parts of Japan, visited the imperial court, and founded several missions. When more missionaries arrived a few years later, St. Francis left Japan, because he hoped to establish a mission in China.

Later missionaries converted many Japanese to Christianity. However, the government became very hostile to Europeans. Foreign missionaries were expelled or martyred, along with many Japanese Christians, and no Europeans were allowed in Japan for two hundred years. The Japanese Catholics did not abandon their faith. They continued worshiping secretly without priests or any sacraments except baptism and matrimony. When Europeans were again allowed in Japan, they found that the small Japanese Church was still alive. As St. Francis might have predicted, his Japanese converts and their descendants were some of the most determined Christians since the early days of the Church.

St. Francis Xavier died before he reached China, but later Jesuits and Franciscans founded several missions there. Converting well-educated Chinese was very difficult. Chinese scholars and rulers were proud of their ancient traditions and thought they had nothing to learn from outsiders, whom they considered barbarians. A Jesuit named Matteo Ricci traveled to the imperial court and persuaded many Chinese leaders that Christianity was a civilized religion. He learned how to explain Christianity in Chinese terms, and impressed the emperor and his nobles with inventions from Europe. He and his successors baptized a few Christians, but China remained predominantly Confucian.

Jesuits in India, China, and Japan tried to explain Christianity in language that people from these cultures could understand and established liturgies and devotions that included some local customs. These missionaries were so sympathetic to non-Christian traditions that enemies of the Jesuits accused them of adopting native superstitions themselves instead of converting people to Christ. This accusation seems to have been unfounded, but it confused European religious authorities and caused the Jesuits many difficulties. They were able to convert some people, but Christians are still a small minority in these three nations.

The Philippines, dominated by Spain, became the most Christian nation in Asia. Most of the people there became Catholics and formed a coherent Asian Catholic culture. Korea heard of Christianity in a unique way. Koreans read about the religion in imported printed material and sent messengers to learn about the new teaching. The messengers brought back some missionaries, and many Koreans became Catholics. In spite of later persecutions by hostile rulers, the Catholic Church in Korea is very strong today. There are also many Korean Protestants. Southeast Asia, especially Vietnam, has a strong Catholic minority. Most large dioceses in the United States today include some priests, nuns, and lay Catholics from these countries. The future of Christianity will be strongly influenced by large numbers of Asian Catholics.

Discussion Questions

Identify: St. Francis Xavier, Matteo Ricci

1. Describe the missionary activities of St. Francis Xavier in India. What happened to the Church in India after St. Francis left?
2. Why did St. Francis have so many difficulties with the Portuguese traders?
3. Describe the mission of St. Francis in Japan. What happened to the Japanese Church later?
4. Describe the mission of Matteo Ricci in China. Why were the Chinese so hard to convert?

3. The Church After the Council of Trent

For several hundred years before the Council of Trent ended in 1563, the Church was damaged by scandals among her leaders, pressure from secular rulers and changes in society, and attacks from former Catholics who had become Protestants. Catholics in many countries were so confused by these evils that they had difficulty trusting God to guide the Church. After the Council of Trent, reforms were gradually implemented in most nations. The notorious scandals and abuses stopped. Catholics became more secure in their faith because of the Catechism; improvements in the liturgy; and better education for monks, nuns, priests, and bishops. Life in the Church never became simple, since the Church was never free from problems, but Catholics gradually became more trusting and optimistic. Between the Council of Trent and the Second Vatican Council, which ended in 1965, Catholic life developed a depth of morality and self-confidence that surpassed anything known in the Church since the Middle Ages.

The most obvious change was the improvement in the hierarchy. Priests and bishops were educated in theological seminaries and learned how to live good lives, to pray, and to manage their parishes and dioceses. Priests were expected to avoid close friendships with women, which might lead to scandals or immoral relationships. Bishops who learned about immorality among priests had the obligation to remove them. It was soon uncommon to find priests committing major sins or living scandalous lives. Bishops, priests, and nuns were often the best-educated people in the community, so they were respected more than they had been for several hundred years. Catholics could be proud of their leaders.

Before the Council of Trent, bishops had little legal control over Franciscans, Dominicans, and many other religious orders operating in their dioceses. These orders were under the jurisdiction of the Pope and the orders' own superiors, who might not know what local monks and nuns were doing. Bishops usually had to petition Rome or the religious superiors to remove monks who were not living good lives. The petitions might take many years or be ineffective. After the council, bishops had much more legal control. They were able to stop immoral or unorthodox preachers and to prevent scandalous situations in monasteries and convents from becoming serious abuses. Many religious orders reformed themselves, and the rest avoided most of the evil deeds that had sometimes taken place during the Renaissance.

With a reformed, well-trained hierarchy and improvements in religious orders, Catholics could be confident that any priest they approached in confession would be well educated, orthodox, and trustworthy. This led to a school of spirituality in which lay people respected all authority, especially Church authority, much more than they had during the Renaissance. Satires about Church leaders such as *The Praise of Folly* became infrequent. Instead, most people respected and loved their leaders. Devout Catholics were usually content to follow the guidance of priests and religious superiors. While this situation lasted, Catholic life was peaceful and secure, at least in countries where the reforms of the council were well implemented. The situation has changed in recent years, because of changes in the modern world and in the education of priests since Vatican II. Many older Catholics miss the tranquillity instilled into the Church by the reforms of the Council of Trent.

After the Council of Trent, Pope St. Pius V published a standardized missal, which contained the readings and prayers for each Mass of the year, including all of the feast days. The new missal did not make any great changes except to increase uniformity in the liturgies for various saints. To avoid mistranslations, increase unity, and follow tradition, the Mass was said in Latin except in the Eastern Rite Catholic churches. Many people understood some Latin, especially the liturgical prayers that were the same for each Mass. Later missals often had translations into local languages printed beside the Latin. The breviary, which contained the prayers said by monks, nuns, and priests every day, was also revised. Both books remained relatively unchanged until Vatican II, and their beautiful prayers helped shape Catholic life and thought for hundreds of years. People who did not understand Latin learned about the faith from sermons, teaching sisters and brothers, catechisms, devotional books, or Bibles in their own languages. The unified liturgy increased the security of Catholic life. Catholics could attend Mass anywhere in the world, with the exception of the Eastern Rite Catholic churches, and find the same liturgy they had at home.

Security in liturgy and doctrine fostered security in social and moral practices. Catholic countries had an established moral code and traditions about how to follow it. For example, everyone was expected to stay married, though Catholics might live apart from their spouses if theirs was an exceptionally bad marriage. Since a couple had to stay married, they had an incentive to find ways to avoid confrontations with their spouses, children, parents, and relatives. Men and women traditionally had different roles in the family, which reduced argument and gave both spouses opportunities to use their energy and creativity. Both spouses were expected to love each other and their children and to sacrifice themselves for their family's good. Children were expected to respect and obey their parents, help with work in the family, and care for their parents in their old age. These ideals helped foster stable, happy marriages and security and love for the children. Large extended families helped with difficult marriages by negotiating problems, giving financial assistance, and providing refuge. Parish priests gave advice and helped settle problems. In modern times, many Americans have lost these ideals and customs. They often wonder how their ancestors survived without divorce, jobs outside of the family, or psychologists. Traditional Catholics did more than endure the hardships of family life. Ideally, they found strength in God in prayer and the sacraments; made use of many social and religious resources, which have become less important in modern society; and gained love and security from their families in return for their sacrifices and efforts.

Catholic priests were required to be obedient to bishops, bishops to the Pope, and monks and nuns to their religious superiors. Even if a bishop or superior were hostile or eccentric, a subordinate could use various methods to avoid confrontation, live a good life, and do God's will. They usually had authority in their own parishes, dioceses, schools, or work. They were able to carry out their responsibilities even if their leaders were unhelpful. Many canonized saints found God's will by peacefully obeying harsh or erratic superiors. Catholic life gained a new dimension of love and generosity because of the sacrifices sometimes needed to trust God to work through his Church. At that time, the benefits of having a strong hierarchy outweighed the difficulties of putting up with difficult superiors. The Church as a whole was much stronger and healthier than she had been during the Renaissance, when religious leaders in most countries were weaker and more tolerant of abuses.

After Catholic life had improved and the Church hierarchy was reformed, Catholics became more confident in proclaiming their belief that the Catholic Church had been founded by Christ and was the true Church. Most of the countries permanently lost to Catholics were converted by Protestants before the reforms of the Council of Trent took effect. After that Catholics defended their faith with more energy and determination. They tried harder to prevent Protestant rulers from taking control of their countries and to stop anyone who was teaching heretical doctrines. Since Protestants also could be very determined, religious differences often caused violence. The quiet work of individual conversion and the search for God can easily be overlooked in the history of wars, persecutions, and martyrdoms. The fervor that led to religious wars reflected the fervor with which many Christians fought their own sins, loved God, prayed, and helped others.

Discussion Questions

Identify: St. Pius V

1. What factors helped increase the trust and respect of Catholics for the hierarchy?
2. What changes mandated by the Council of Trent helped improve the reputations and behavior of monks and nuns?
3. What benefits did the Church obtain from having a hierarchy with the authority to enforce good behavior and correct teaching among her priests, monks, and nuns?

4. The French Church

The Church in France was called the Gallican Church, from the Latin word for the old province of Gaul in France. This Church had negotiated an unusual relationship with the Popes after their long residence in Avignon and the Great Western Schism, which ended in 1417. The king of France had more authority than any other ruler to direct his Church. French monarchs nominated bishops, and the Pope normally approved them. This meant that the bishops were frequently more loyal to the French king than to the Pope. If the Pope's decrees were not promulgated by the French Parliament or the king, people in France were not legally required to obey them. French kings after the Council of Trent were able to prevent the Pope's decrees and the reforms of the Council from being successfully implemented for many years. The Pope was very limited in his control over the Gallican Church.

French humanists were critical of the Church, but most of them remained Catholics. They promoted Bible reading, prayer, and a reform of devotional life. A few humanists and others became Calvinists and formed study groups and churches. After the Protestant Reformation France was ruled for many years by a succession of regents and kings who spent most of their energy on wars in Italy and Germany. These rulers outlawed Lutheran and Calvinist teachings, but they were reluctant to enforce the laws. A few Protestants were executed, but most of them went into hiding and continued converting people. By 1560 there were many Protestants in France, especially in some of the cities.

After 1560 the unexpected deaths of two French kings in quick succession left France under the control of a regent, Catherine de Medici. She was the mother of the young French king, Charles IX. In order to control France, she was forced to balance the interests of several powerful noble families. The Guises and the dukes of Lorraine were devout Catholics, but Protestant leaders were influential in the kingdom of Navarre, La Rochelle, and other places. Their disputes led to a civil war, which ended with the death in battle or the assassination of several Catholic leaders by Protestants.

Catherine decided that the Protestants were very dangerous and attempted to suppress Protestant worship services. This suppression led to another civil war, and Catherine was forced to sign an agreement permitting Protestant activity in some places. She gained peace by marrying her daughter to a Protestant leader, Henry of Navarre. This marriage infuriated the Catholics. Later Catherine ordered the infamous St. Bartholomew's Day massacre of Protestants to prevent a Protestant uprising. About two thousand Protestants died. After several more civil wars and deaths in the royal family, Henry of Navarre was the only leader with military support and a claim to the French throne. However, the city of Paris refused to surrender to him, and Henry realized that most people in France would never accept a Protestant king. His ministers told him that he could be saved in either church, so he renounced his Protestant beliefs and became a Catholic. He was crowned in Paris in 1593. Even though he was quoted as saying, "Paris is well worth a Mass", his actions as king of France indicate that his decision led to a sincere conversion.

Henry's conversion gave France a strong king, but it did not bring peace. French Protestants, called *Huguenots*, were allowed to continue worshiping in some areas, according to an agreement signed at Nantes. King Henry was assassinated after ruling for sixteen years. Protestants in La Rochelle, a city on the Bay of Biscay, attempted to revolt from France with help from England. After the revolt was suppressed in 1628, French Huguenots lost some political control, but they were still allowed freedom of worship. Richelieu, the powerful French cardinal, refused to revoke the religious toleration of Protestants guaranteed in the Edict of Nantes, saying that it was better to leave the Protestants to God than to attempt to force their conversion. The Edict of Nantes was revoked much later.

Cardinal Richelieu was the chief advisor to the French monarchs from 1624 to 1642. He tried to strengthen the political influence of France in relation to the rest of Europe and to help the king of France control the French nobles, cities, and Church. Reforming the French Church was a low priority with him, though he tried to arrange for the appointment of conscientious bishops. The unscrupulous cardinal formed alliances with either Protestants or Catholics, depending on which seemed most likely to increase the power of France. During the Thirty Years' War (1616–1648) Richelieu allied France with the Protestant King Gustavus of Sweden against the Catholic Habsburg Emperor Ferdinand of Austria. Much of Germany was devastated and Protestant control was consolidated in several areas. Richelieu's political ambitions helped establish the absolute power of later French kings, set the stage for the disastrous French Revolution more than a hundred years later, and prevented the Pope from intervening effectively in serious theological disputes in France.

The decrees of the Council of Trent were not officially promulgated in France until fifty years after the council. French kings were opposed to the decrees because they were afraid that the reformed Church would be more independent. The reforms were finally put into practice by the French bishops, without the permission of the king and Parliament. Many saints, such as Vincent de Paul and Francis de Sales, helped revive Catholic life in France. Religious orders such as the Jesuits attempted to counter Gallican claims to independence by stressing the Pope's primacy. Unfortunately, they encountered severe opposition, both from the king's theologians and from Catholics who were deceived by the new errors of the Jansenists.

French Huguenots believed that God predestined some people to hell and some to heaven, regardless of anything those people could do. The Huguenots believed that this was strict justice and ignored the mercy and love of God. Some French Catholics named Jansenists, led by bishop Cornelius Jansen, also overlooked God's love and mercy. They believed that God required such perfect purity that scarcely anyone could receive Holy Communion without sin or receive a valid absolution in confession. Some Jansenists refused to go to Communion or confession for many years, even though they were living good moral lives. This practice was contrary to the Church law requiring all Catholics to receive the two sacraments at least once a year. The Jansenists promoted a gloomy, fearful spirituality, and devout Jansenists often tried to deny themselves everything they enjoyed. They thought that human desires were so badly corrupted by original sin that they had to be ruthlessly suppressed. Jansen's followers disliked popular devotions to Mary, because these usually reminded people of her love, kindness, and intercession for sinners.

Jansenism was confusing to many Catholics. Many saints practiced strict self-denial because of their love for God, and thinking about God's justice can be very helpful to Catholics. However, saints were joyful, and they usually believed that many people were good. Jansenists were gloomy and thought that everyone committed constant sins, even in their attempts to do good. Many erroneous Jansenist ideas were condemned by the Pope and by most French bishops. Unfortunately, this condemnation did not end the problem. The Jansenists denied that they had meant their doctrines in the same way that the Pope had understood and condemned them.

After more explicit condemnations, they modified their doctrines slightly, but they were still erroneous. Jansenism eventually influenced much of the French Church. The belief never led most Catholics into outright heresy, but it gave some French Catholics and spiritual writers a fearful, negative outlook on life. French missionaries were very active in England, the United States, and Canada, so the harshness of Jansenism influenced these places. However, new French devotions stressing the love and mercy of God were also influential in mission lands.

God raised up saints to remind Catholics that God is love, not strict justice. The best known saint was Margaret Mary, a Visitation nun. She was responsible for establishing the popular devotion to the Sacred Heart of Jesus, a revelation of Christ's love for us. St. Louis Marie de Montfort, a priest who founded several religious orders and established the Consecration to Mary, constantly stressed the love of God and the intercessory power of Mary to help people live good lives. Jesuits always emphasized God's love and mercy more than his condemnation of sin. All of these individuals believed that Catholics should practice self-denial out of love for God, but they differed from the Jansenists in their happy emotional outlook, their trust in God's mercy, and their frequent reception of the sacraments.

Jansenism was countered by another heretical movement called Quietism, which recommended that devout Catholics make no effort in their spiritual lives. Quietists thought that if they relaxed completely, God would control them. They made no effort to practice virtue or resist temptation, so they usually fell into immorality and stopped practicing their faith. This unorthodox belief was quickly condemned and had little influence at the time, although Catholics today are as likely to resemble Quietists as Jansenists. Some modern Catholics believe so strongly in God's mercy that they forget God's justice and make little effort to avoid sin.

French kings after 1650 became more tyrannical. Louis XIV, who died in 1714, suppressed the Edict of Nantes and forced all Huguenots to become Catholics or leave the country. Hundreds of thousands of them moved to French Canada or other nations. Since the French kings were so powerful, French nobles and bishops were unable to force them to rule wisely or justly. This situation eventually led to the French Revolution.

Discussion Questions

Identify: Catherine de Medici, Henry IV of Navarre, Huguenots, Edict of Nantes

1. Describe Jansenism, Quietism, and Gallicanism.
2. Summarize the life of St. Margaret Mary.
3. Catholics believe that obedience to legitimate Church authorities is a sign that a person is close to God. How does the life of St. Margaret Mary illustrate this principle?

Featured Saint: Margaret Mary

St. Margaret Mary Alacoque was born in 1647 in a small town in France. Like many saints, she was a very devout girl. Her father died when she was eight, and she was sent to a convent to be educated. Several years later she became very ill. She returned home and remained an invalid until she was fifteen. When she recovered, she was treated as a servant by the relatives who were managing the household. She tried to attend Mass, Benediction of the Blessed Sacrament, and all of the other religious services in the small parish church several miles away. However, her relatives did not believe that anyone could be so devout and accused her of going there to meet some man. After many years of conflict, Margaret entered the Visitation order, a cloistered contemplative community of nuns.

Life in a strictly cloistered convent, where one spends a lifetime with the same small group of women, is never easy. Margaret's superiors thought that she was slow and careless, and they were reluctant to allow her to take her final vows. God was guiding Margaret's prayer life, and she was unable to meditate in the way the nuns recommended, because God was leading her into contemplative prayer. She was constantly aware of the presence of Jesus and often perceived him suffering, crowned with thorns. This awareness encouraged her to persevere in her vocation, but it made it difficult for her to concentrate on her work.

Several years after Margaret had taken her final vows, she was praying in front of the Blessed Sacrament. Suddenly she saw Christ. He appeared to her many times after that, reminding her of his love for people and telling her about the devotion to his Sacred Heart, which he wanted her to establish. However, Jesus said that she should do nothing without the approval of her superiors. This insistence on obedience is one of the most important characteristics of true revelations from God. Margaret told her superior about the vision from Jesus, but the nun thought Margaret had imagined it all. After that the superior was very harsh to Margaret, who became ill. When she was unexpectedly cured, her superior asked her to write about her spiritual experiences. She showed them to several inexperienced theologians, who believed that the visions were delusions. This made Margaret very unhappy, but she trusted God to solve the difficulty.

God solved it by allowing Saint Claude de la Colombière, a Jesuit, to hear the confessions of the community. This priest believed Margaret, and with the permission of his Jesuit superiors, he began spreading devotion to the Sacred Heart of Jesus. The Visitation nuns adopted the devotion after a few years, though some nuns in Margaret's community continued to think that she was proud, unbalanced, or deluded. The Sacred Heart devotion was eventually approved by theologians and became very popular. Many churches and homes had pictures of the Sacred Heart of Jesus to remind people of God's love and mercy. St. Margaret Mary died in 1690. Though her whole life had been very difficult, when she died she was respected by her community and happy in the knowledge that the love of Jesus would be known wherever the Sacred Heart was pictured. She was canonized in 1920.

12

Christianity, Revolution, and Secularization

Featured Saint: John Vianney

CHAPTER 12

Christianity, Revolution, and Secularization

1. Absolute Monarchies and England

For more than a thousand years, most of Europe was ruled by Christian kings and queens. The ceremony of crowning and anointing monarchs showed their dependence on God and their commitment to rule according to Christian standards. Society was officially Christian. However, some monarchs caused so many problems for the Church that their archbishops must have regretted performing the coronation ceremonies.

Early kings were limited in their power by their feudal vassals, neighboring rulers, and the Church. In the Renaissance they were also limited by parliaments and cities. After 1600 a few rulers gradually became even more restricted in their power. These included the kings of England, the rulers of the Netherlands, and the German emperors. However, most kings consolidated their power so that they controlled their countries more completely. These kings were called *absolute monarchs.* The strongest was the king of France, but rulers of several other countries, such as Spain and Russia, acquired almost despotic control over their nobles, parliaments, subjects, and bishops.

Absolute monarchs had some Christian traditions to back them. Christianity has always taught that all authority comes from God. Even when Christians were governed by pagan Roman emperors who persecuted them, the Church taught that their reigns were permitted by God. However, Christians, using morally acceptable means, could try to change the government in order to obtain better rulers.

Early theologians taught that anointed Christian kings received special guidance and authority from God to rule their countries and protect the churches under their control. A few later theologians, especially in France, exaggerated the secular and religious authority of kings. These theologians believed that no one had the right to restrict the king's power. This theory was called the *divine right of kings*. Theologians and bishops who believed in its exaggerated form were in the minority, but they were influential because their kings publicized their views. Their theories were indirectly opposed to the Pope's primacy in the Church, which was one reason that kings supported them. Most kings did not want anyone, especially the Pope, restraining their behavior. Monarchs used divine right theories as a rationalization for unjust, tyrannical laws intended to strengthen kings. Secular philosophers provided theoretical justification for absolute monarchs by arguing that the absolute power of the state or the king was more important than individual liberties. Extreme divine right theologians thought that kings were empowered by God even if they lived immoral lives. Their theory gave absolute monarchs a positive image without any obvious negative consequences.

There were hidden negative consequences for absolute monarchs. Absolute authority for kings reduced the powers of nobles, national parliaments, and bishops. Even strong, intelligent kings with good ministers made mistakes. Monarchs with limited intelligence often chose incompetent or evil advisors. Their ministers frequently suggested unjust taxes, unwise social and trade restrictions, and contradictory religious policies. The ministers usually became very wealthy, but the rulers became unpopular, and their countries were impoverished. Since the nobles, city representatives, and bishops had lost their power to restrain the kings and their advisors, no one was able to prevent national problems from becoming intolerable.

The first successful revolution of middle- and lower-class people against the power of kings took place in England. English kings had never been as powerful as some other European monarchs. Ever since King John signed the Magna Carta, or Great Charter, in 1215, English kings had been limited by agreements with their bishops, nobles, and Parliament. Kings were forced to respect individual rights, such as the right to a fair trial, and to ask Parliament for taxes. If Parliament did not vote money or pass laws, the kings had little money to run the government. Many members of Parliament were elected from the middle class of merchants, businessmen, and lawyers. After 1550 many of them were influenced by Calvinist Puritan or Presbyterian beliefs. Radical Puritans thought that the authority of kings was strictly limited, so Parliament became even less submissive to English monarchs than it had been in the past.

When Queen Elizabeth died in 1603, King James I took the throne of England. James had little sympathy with Parliament or the nobility, since he wanted absolute control of the nation. He thought that Parliament restricted his power by requiring him to ask the members for money and to follow their laws. He infuriated his nobles by promoting obscure men to important offices. James became unpopular, and the next king, Charles I, was even more unpopular. He disliked Parliament, Puritans, and the common people. His unsuccessful foreign policies caused serious social unrest and economic hardship. Charles antagonized the Anglican church and the Puritans by insisting on a liturgy that resembled Catholic worship. The nobles distrusted him, and many people hated him. They believed that he was ruling illegally and trying to take away their traditional liberties. Many Puritans emigrated to America, but others resolved to fight his innovations. Parliament became so hostile that Charles did not convene it for many years.

King Charles eventually needed money so desperately that he summoned Parliament. It met in 1640. Many radical Puritans and others were determined to restrict the power of the king. A few leaders arrested, and later executed, the unpopular king and several of his ministers. The Puritans thought that the executions were necessary since there was no other way to restrict the king's power without risking his retaliation in the future. Instead of selecting another king, they chose a Puritan leader, Oliver Cromwell, in 1649. He called himself the lord protector and ruled England for about ten years, with the help of a Puritan army. He hoped that his son would succeed him when he died. However, most English people were thoroughly tired of being ruled by the Puritans, who destroyed church buildings, passed unpopular laws, and were considered violent and uncouth.

Charles I had two sons, who were raised in France. The oldest, Charles II, invaded England after Cromwell's death. He had a very small army, but the English were happy to have a king again and welcomed him home. Charles knew that his throne was very precarious and ruled cautiously. When he died without any children, his brother James succeeded him. King James II had become a Catholic, and Catholics were very unpopular in England. James made some serious errors of judgment in appointing ministers and governing the nation. When his wife had a son, which meant that England was likely to be ruled by Catholic kings for many years, James II was deposed and exiled. Parliament chose a Protestant king, William III, in 1688.

It was obvious that the divine right of kings and theories of absolute monarchy did not apply in Britain, since Parliament had overthrown two kings in forty years. The English had developed their traditional liberties into a national policy of representative government, in which people elected representatives to Parliament, which passed laws to govern them, and a constitutional monarchy, in which kings or queens were restrained by written agreements with their people. This arrangement allowed the nation to prosper. Representative government, individual liberties, and freedom from unjust taxation became the most important characteristics of English-speaking societies. However, the English ruthlessly subjugated some nations they conquered, such as Ireland.

Discussion Questions

Identify: Charles I, Puritans, Oliver Cromwell, King James II

1. What were the causes of the English Revolution against Charles I?
2. How was the monarchy restored in England?
3. What were typical characteristics of English-speaking societies?

2. The French Revolution

European monarchs learned about the English Revolution with horror. They realized that national parliaments, traditional liberties, and religious freedom could be extremely dangerous to kings. Most monarchs did everything in their power to increase their absolute control over their countries. The kings of France were the most successful. The French government became more and more autocratic until it was overthrown by the French Revolution.

Most philosophers in Catholic and Protestant countries before 1700 were sympathetic to Christianity and the rule of Christian kings. Later philosophers often undermined or denied faith in established Christian governments and religions. Their new ideas were spread publicly by debate groups, philosophical societies, and widespread groups of friends. More radical versions of the new ideas were spread by secret societies such as the Masons, who formed influential groups in every country in Europe and the Americas. These groups were very hostile to monarchies and religion. Masons worked to gain power in governments and attempted to limit or destroy Christian influence on society.

The hostility against established churches and governments had many causes, such as the damage done by religious wars, the fact that good people could be found in all religions and nations, and the link between Christian monarchies and the Church. Even though most people believed in Christianity, the Church attracted some of the hatred directed at repressive kings and nobles. The best-known Catholic theologians and bishops were the ones appointed by monarchs to justify their absolute power. Intellectuals who disliked kings often lost their religious faith. They thought that the Church supported the government, so they thought that the Church should be destroyed.

Actually, the Church cannot be blamed for supporting repressive Catholic kings. Most monarchs ignored the traditions of the Church and the attempts of Popes and bishops to persuade them to rule justly, to respect traditional liberties in their countries, and to help the poor. The kings of France, influenced by Gallicanism, led the way in opposing the Pope. After 1700 the monarchs in Austria, Spain, and other Catholic countries seldom agreed to anything the Pope suggested without demanding some illicit benefit in return. The bishops they nominated agreed to support them against the Pope, and the Pope was often forced to accept their nominations. In 1773, the absolute monarchs forced the Pope to suppress the Jesuits, who were well known for their support of the Pope. Jesuit priests were incorporated into the diocesan priesthood, where monarchs thought they would have less influence. The order survived in Russia, and it was refounded in Europe fifty years later. At the time, the suppression of the Jesuits seemed to indicate that the Pope would have to accept a whole series of Gallican-style national churches controlled by tyrannical kings and queens.

Some ideas promoted by new philosophical groups and secret societies were similar to the ideas used to justify the English Revolution against King Charles I. In the American Revolution against England, the colonists made some of the same demands as the earlier English rebels. They wanted individual liberty, representative government, and freedom from oppressive taxes and trade laws. The rebellious colonists were supported by the king of France, who sent them money and military assistance because he wanted to reduce English power. European nobles from many countries helped the colonists fight against British oppression. They returned to their homes with new ideas about individual liberty and revolution.

Many people in France were poor. There were so many laws restricting trade and levying taxes that many businessmen were unable to make much profit. They resented the privileges of kings and nobles, who had inherited their wealth without doing anything to earn it. Serfs or peasants were usually very poor and had no hope of improving their condition. Some workers in the cities were even poorer than the peasants, and they often hated everyone in the upper class, which they blamed for their misery. Most people thought that the power of nobles and absolute monarchs was excessive and unjust.

The French government spent large sums of money on foreign wars and had no way to regain it, since taxes were already so heavy that they were strangling trade. French kings and nobles often lived expensive, immoral, idle lives. King Louis XV and Louis XVI had a few good advisors and ministers, but they were unable to reduce their expenses enough to stop going further in debt. Ten years after the American Revolution, the French government was so impoverished that Louis XVI decided to try a desperate expedient. The French Parliament had not met for over 150 years, because the French kings and their ministers had been strong and wealthy enough to govern without it. It was summoned again in 1789.

The French Parliament had three sections: the Church, the nobles, and the commons. King Louis XVI may have thought that the first two groups would prevent the third from causing any trouble, but he was mistaken. Many leaders from the Church and the nobility realized that France needed social reform desperately, and they voted to combine into one National Assembly. They began by passing some beneficial social legislation, such as ending the legal restrictions that separated the different classes.

Radicals took control of the National Assembly, and the levelheaded members were expelled or fled from France. The assembly became dominated by men who hated the Church, the nobles, and the monarchy. These members passed laws that nationalized, or confiscated, Church property. Monks and nuns were forced to leave their convents and monasteries. Their property was sold to pay for government expenditures. Priests and bishops were supposed to be paid government salaries, but they had to swear to obey the revolutionary French government, rather than the Pope, or be deprived of their offices. Since the revolutionary government was anti-Christian, priests who took the oath were excommunicated. Most priests refused to take it. A large number of these left the country, but many were arrested and imprisoned. The nobles lost much of their property. Some of them persuaded the assembly that they supported its reforms, but many nobles fled to England or other countries. The radicals arrested the king and many nobles and bishops.

The National Assembly forced out its less radical members, and the fanatics left in control began executing their real or imagined opponents. King Louis XVI and his queen, Marie Antoinette, were executed in 1793. Many nobles and Church leaders who had supported social reforms were executed because they disagreed with the unjust, anti-Catholic, or vindictive actions of the new leaders. Soon a Reign of Terror was instituted. A guillotine, a machine for beheading large numbers of victims quickly, was set up in the streets of Paris. Thousands of noblemen and noblewomen, priests, monks, nuns, and ordinary people were executed without trials or evidence, on the orders of the assembly leaders. Paris and much of France were near anarchy, and great numbers of people fled from the country. No one knew who might be arrested and executed next.

French provinces where the Church had been well managed and the nobles had behaved with more kindness and self-restraint did not support the National Assembly. Some areas revolted against the central government, but the revolts were suppressed. The radicals became even more violent, and the most ruthless ones executed some of their less fanatical colleagues. The leaders became more anti-Catholic. In 1794 the assembly abolished Catholicism as the national religion and secularized all of the churches. Some churches were destroyed. Sacrilegious worship services to the goddess of reason were held at others, including the Cathedral of Notre Dame in Paris.

These acts were so unpopular that the radicals lost the support of nearly everyone in France. Robespierre, the most unscrupulous leader, was betrayed and executed. The Reign of Terror ended, and the guillotine was removed. A small group of men called the Directory took control, and the country became more stable. Several foreign kings threatened to invade France and restore the monarchy and the nobles. However, French armies attacked and conquered their neighbors, then spread revolutionary social changes and persecuted the Church in the defeated countries. The Directory was soon overthrown by a young general named Napoleon. He had the military strength to enforce stability and the good judgment necessary to unify France. After nearly ten years of chaos and violence, France returned to relative peace.

The French Revolution became the model for many revolutions against European monarchs and colonial governments. Its slogan, "Liberty, Equality, Brotherhood", was attractive to nearly everyone. Unfortunately, most revolutionaries adopted the French program without much modification, including its hostility toward the Church. The persecuted Church began to reflect the sufferings of Jesus and the early Church more than she had for fourteen hundred years.

Discussion Questions

Identify: absolute monarchies, Masons, divine right of kings, National Assembly, Louis XVI, Reign of Terror

1. Explain why some people thought that the Catholic Church was linked to repressive kings.
2. Describe the main events of the French Revolution.
3. Describe the difficulties the French Revolution caused for the Church.
4. Describe the Reign of Terror.
5. Explain the correct Catholic belief about the authority of governments. How does this differ from the theories of radical divine right theologians or secular theories about absolute government?

3. Society and the Church After the Revolution

General Napoleon was less radical than the leaders of the assembly. After he took control of France, he knew that he needed social stability to promote national prosperity and to safeguard his authority. He also needed a title and prestige. Few Europeans wanted to accept a ruler who was not a king, but Napoleon was not related to the royal family of France. He called himself the emperor of France. European monarchs accepted his claims with scepticism, and French radicals accepted the unusual title as proof that Napoleon was not trying to restore the monarchy.

The French Revolution benefited France by ending legal social stratification. Titles of nobility and the hereditary obligations of peasants and other classes were abolished. Most French people welcomed these changes and opposed anything that might restore the old social order. However, the revolution caused many problems. The worst injustice was the execution of thousands of innocent people. Many nobles, ordinary citizens, and Church leaders lost all of their property. Others bought property confiscated from the former owners and opposed any change that might require them to restore it. Devout Catholics wanted union with the Pope and the restoration of normal Catholic life.

Napoleon realized that returning to union with the Pope and restoring Catholic worship would increase social stability. He persuaded the Pope, Pius VII, to drop his claims for the return of Church property, and Napoleon agreed that all priests and bishops in the new French hierarchy must promise to obey the Pope. Napoleon asked the Pope to crown him as emperor of France, but after going through most of the ceremony, Napoleon took the crown and crowned himself. He wanted to show that he had taken power himself and was independent of the Church. Even so, his support of the Catholic religion allowed Church life in France to recover. The reestablished Church was stronger in some ways than she had been before the revolution. Most of the restored hierarchy had been exiled, imprisoned, or persecuted. French Catholics had many new martyrs to inspire them. Bishops and priests with weak faith or poor morals had found secular occupations during the revolution, and the remaining priests were usually devoted to their religion.

Napoleon soon turned against the Pope. The emperor wanted an annulment from his first marriage and more control over the French Church. Pius VII could not agree to either demand. The emperor conquered the Papal States, kidnapped Pope Pius VII, and held him captive for many years. The Pope was not treated badly, but he was isolated. He was not allowed to see visitors without French officials present or to write uncensored letters. Napoleon eventually released the Pope and allowed him to resume his activities in Rome.

The French emperor responded to threats of invasion by attacking hostile countries before they could attack him. He quickly defeated their armies, deposed their rulers, and installed his own relatives to govern them. Napoleon conquered most of Europe, but he was never able to overcome the English navy. He invaded Russia in 1812. Napoleon's usual tactics were not successful against the vast distances and ferocious winter, and he was forced to withdraw after losing most of his army. He was soon defeated by the British and imprisoned on a small island. He died in 1815.

Though Napoleon caused the Pope a great deal of hardship, his actions benefited the Church in many ways. Most of the monarchies in Europe were overthrown, and the danger that they would split the Church into a series of independent national churches vanished. The rulers Napoleon installed usually allowed the Church to continue with her religious activities, though much of her property was confiscated. When Napoleon was defeated and his relatives lost control of their countries, the kings of each country had to negotiate new agreements with their nobles, bishops, and subjects. They were no longer strong enough to force the Pope to agree to their demands.

In many countries Church life was renewed and flourished. However, the Church was faced with the problem of adapting to the new ideals of liberty and a new social order. Catholics today understand that the Church is not against legitimate goals of freedom and just democratic governments, but many European Catholics in the last century were convinced that the Church should support the return of Catholic monarchs. Kings ruled many European countries until the Second World War in 1940, but they were usually limited in their power by constitutional agreements with their no-bles, the Church, and their subjects. The days of absolute monarchies and unquestioned divine right rulers were gone forever.

After the Napoleonic wars ended, Europe continued to experience social and political turmoil. The French govern-ment changed many times. The monarchy was restored for a few years, then overthrown. Several relatives of Napoleon ruled France at different times. In the intervals, various forms of republican or socialist governments took power. Some of these were very hostile to the Church. Other European coun-tries experienced similar changes. In 1848 and in 1870, so-cialist or early types of communist revolutions took place in many European countries, but they usually ended when the rulers adopted some social reforms. These upheavals caused the Church many problems. They often led to persecutions or legal restrictions for the Church, but if Catholic officials opposed revolutionary movements, poor people thought that the Church was biased in favor of the ruling class.

Before the Napoleonic Wars, Mexico, Latin America, and most of South America had been ruled by colonial gover-nors sent from Spain. Revolutionary societies, including se-cret Masonic groups, had been established in these nations. After 1820 the colonial governments in these countries be-gan declaring their independence from Spain, and some coun-tries suffered from a series of violent revolutions. The Spanish colonies had no experience in self-government, no tradi-tions of democracy, and no precedents for a peaceful transi-tion of power between different parties or local rulers. The French model of revolution called for a Napoleon to restore stability and consolidate social changes, but few men in his-tory have had the military genius and good fortune of the French emperor. Many Spanish American revolutionary leaders were overthrown by their rivals before they had a chance to establish peace and prosperity, and others were overcome by adverse economic conditions. A few countries, such as Portuguese Brazil, avoided major revolutions and remained relatively stable and prosperous for many years.

Some of the new governments in former Spanish colonies were very hostile to the Church. Even in countries where the leaders were devout Catholics, poverty and social turmoil often caused religious difficulties. There had never been enough priests and religious to teach the people about their faith. After revolutionary governments took control, the Church was deprived of her property in most countries, which meant that there was no way to train or support priests, nuns, monks, and catechists. In a few countries such as Mexico some of the governments persecuted the Church severely and gave the Church many new martyrs and saints. The Catholic faith survived, but the damage caused by more than a century of poor religious instruction has never been repaired. Many Catholics knew practically nothing about their religion and relapsed into native religious practices, witchcraft, superstition, moral errors, or indifference.

Even though these revolutions caused violence and social turmoil, they ended Spanish colonial government and a social system that had little except peace and security to recommend it. French revolutionary ideals of liberty, equality, and brotherhood are based on Christian principles, though they must be balanced by other Christian principles such as responsibility, justice, and obedience to legitimate authority. Where these ideals are sincerely implemented, society flourishes. However, violent revolutions are not usually effective ways to implement positive social changes. Many revolutions caused tyranny, injustice, hatred, and oppression instead of liberty, equality, and brotherhood.

Discussion Questions

Identify: Pius VII

1. Describe Napoleon's wars, his support and conflict with the Pope, and his defeat.
2. What benefits came from the French Revolution for society?
3. Give a brief description of political changes in Europe after the French Revolution and the defeat of Napoleon.
4. Describe the revolutionary changes in the Spanish colonies in the New World.
5. Why did the revolutions in colonial governments often result in military dictatorships rather than democracies or other forms of government?

4. Pius IX, Leo XIII, and Catholic Spiritual Life

Between 1800 and 1900 the Church in most countries was involved in a series of conflicts to maintain her independence from secular rulers and to prevent materialistic philosophies from destroying the faith of Catholics. Political struggles and social turmoil dominated the headlines. The efforts of heroic Popes, bishops, and priests kept the Church independent, but the efforts of ordinary people to love and serve God kept the Catholic faith alive. These people seldom made the headlines, but their efforts profoundly influenced the character of Catholic life and thought.

Teaching had always been an important aspect of religious life, and many new religious orders of men and women were founded so that Catholic children could receive a Catholic education instead of being forced to attend schools run by governments hostile or indifferent to religion. Other communities were founded to evangelize or help the poor, establish foreign missions, care for orphans, or provide nursing care. In some countries these religious orders were supported by the government, since they provided valuable services to society.

European religious orders were particularly helpful in missionary countries, including the United States, Canada, and Australia, which had many Catholic immigrants and too few native priests to care for them. In European Catholic countries there were enough vocations to send many missionary priests and sisters to foreign lands. Because of these missionaries and the large number of Catholic immigrants, the number of English-speaking Catholics increased dramatically. There were also many conversions to the Catholic faith from English Protestant denominations.

Churches in missionary countries dominated by France, Spain, Portugal, and the Catholic parts of Germany became much stronger. Many countries, such as nations in the interior of Africa and Asia, were evangelized for the first time. Protestant missionary activity also increased during this century, though some of it was directed toward countries that were already Catholic.

Numerous religious orders were beneficial to Catholics, but an unexpected problem developed. In some countries there were so many teaching sisters, brothers, and priests that lay people became careless about passing on the faith themselves. Parents often thought that if they sent their children to Catholic schools, they could neglect their children's religious education. Some priests and sisters may have discouraged parent involvement in religious education, reasoning that lay people had little training and experience in teaching the faith. Ordinary Catholics sometimes forgot that they had an obligation to evangelize their neighbors and expected the religious to care for the Church. However, many new lay associations helped people participate in evangelization, works of charity, and other apostolates. Third Orders and similar groups were still influential, and Catholics who became involved with their parishes usually found many opportunities to use their talents for Christ.

Two great Popes in the last century helped form the modern Church. The first was Pope Pius IX, who ruled from 1846 to 1878. Pius IX was sympathetic to legitimate demands for freedom and justice, but he quickly became unsympathetic to radical social movements, which were sometimes dominated by individuals or secret societies that were violently anti-Catholic. Shortly after he took office, Italian revolutionaries who wanted to form a unified Italian nation attempted to abolish the Pope's control of the Papal States. Pius IX could not agree to their demands. Since the end of the Roman Empire, the Pope had been both a temporal and a spiritual ruler. If the Pope were not the temporal ruler of a sovereign nation, the Papal States, his political influence might be damaged. In addition, the income from this territory supported the government of the Church. In 1870, after several wars, the Pope lost control over the land, but the succeeding Popes refused to give up their claim to it for many years.

In 1929, Pope Pius XI reached an agreement with the Italian Fascist dictator, Mussolini. The Pope agreed to drop his claims to the Papal States, and Mussolini guaranteed the independence of the Vatican State, a nation with less than a square mile of territory. This agreement allowed the Pope to remain independent of the Italian Fascist government. Modern Popes seem to be managing well without the Papal States. Most historic churches in Italy today are owned by the State, which helps finance their repair and allows Catholics to worship in them. The government of the Church is largely financed by donations from Catholics all over the world. Losing most of their land relieved the Popes of a heavy burden and allowed them to concentrate on their spiritual leadership.

In 1864 Pius IX called for an ecumenical council to meet at the Vatican to discuss how to deal with new political movements and philosophical beliefs that were overthrowing traditions and spreading atheism everywhere in Europe. The First Vatican Council met in 1870. It is most famous for clearly defining the doctrine of papal infallibility, which had always been part of the traditional teaching of the Church. However, the council made several other pronouncements. It formally condemned pantheism, materialism, atheism, and the belief that faith does not need to be reconciled with reason. These statements of Catholic faith were needed to counter philosophical movements that revived ancient non-Christian errors or denied that faith needed to be linked to logic.

Pius IX died in 1878. His successor, Leo XIII, realized that the Church needed to provide guidelines outlining Christian responses to new social movements. Europe was still being torn by attempts to overthrow or limit Christian kings and queens and to continue the unification of nations such as Germany and Italy, which had been composed of many different political units. Early types of socialism and communism were developing as responses to the harsh treatment of workers during the early part of the Industrial Revolution. Communism and socialism were originally based on the premises that there is no God, there is no life after death, and therefore Christian laws of morality should be replaced by radical attempts to enrich the poor and to find happiness in this life. Catholics knew that these movements had many errors, but they were not certain about the Christian solution to the problems of European society at this time.

Following the example of some of his predecessors, Pope Leo began writing encyclicals, letters addressed to the whole Church. The most famous was *Rerum Novarum*. In this document Pope Leo explained which characteristics of new social movements were good and which were evil and should be avoided by Catholics. Organizations such as trade unions to protect workers and lay associations of Catholics were good for individuals and beneficial to society, as long as they followed Christian guidelines. However, the Pope condemned some radical social theories. For example, he reminded Catholics that governments may not confiscate private property, even with the goal of helping the poor. This teaching condemned the foundation of many socialist and communist political parties. Catholics were allowed to work for social change as long as they used moral principles, and they were not required to restore deposed monarchs and maintain strict class distinctions. Many Catholics were very reluctant to follow the teachings in Pope Leo's encyclicals. The delay illustrated the fact that Christian principles are not always easy to accept or apply in new situations. Confused Catholics and many others were able to find the solution to new social problems by following the guidance of the Pope.

By 1900 the Church had devised a system of apologetics to deal with new philosophical attacks. She had adapted to a wide variety of new political situations and adjusted to the loss of most of her property. In spite of political and social upheavals, Catholic life continued. Hardship and persecution gave the Church some of her best Popes and dedicated lay Catholics in more than a thousand years. However, the attacks by unbelievers led to the loss of many individuals, who left the Church to follow new philosophical movements or who never received any Catholic training because society in many countries was no longer officially Christian.

Discussion Questions

Identify: Pius IX, Vatican State, Leo XIII, *Rerum Novarum*, John Vianney

1. How did the new religious orders help the Church?
2. What attitude did Pius IX take toward legitimate social complaints? Toward revolutionary changes in society?
3. What doctrinal questions were defined at the First Vatican Council?
4. How did Leo XIII help Catholics deal with new problems in society?
5. Popes are infallible in statements about faith and morals, but they may make erroneous political decisions. What events in this chapter illustrate these characteristics of infallibility?
6. What methods did St. John Vianney use to help people become better Catholics? (See below.) Which of these methods should be imitated by all parish priests? Are there any that should not be imitated by all priests? Why or why not?

Featured Saint: John Vianney

Parish priests have one of the most important vocations in the Church. They are expected to provide the sacraments, religious education, advice, and a good example to their people. The priest is the most visible representative of the Church for most Catholics, so a holy priest is more necessary than almost any other factor for a healthy parish. St. John Vianney is often called the *Curé of Ars*, meaning the pastor of that town's church. He became famous for spiritual gifts such as reading souls in confession, and his life illustrates the revival of Catholic life in France.

John Vianney was born in 1786. During the French Revolution, his parish was led by a priest who had taken the oath to support the National Assembly rather than follow the Pope. This meant that the priest was excommunicated, and good Catholics could not attend his Masses. John's parents took him with them to secret Masses said by an undercover priest who was loyal to Rome. John knew that if the hidden priest had been discovered, he would have been executed, and John realized that the sacraments and union with Rome were extremely important. After Napoleon took power and the French Church was reunited with Rome, John began studying for the priesthood, but he could not learn enough Latin to keep up with the other students. John's classes were delayed for several more years because he was drafted into Napoleon's army; then he missed his deadline to report for duty and had to hide for a year as a deserter. He spent the time studying Latin, but he made little progress. After Napoleon proclaimed an amnesty for deserters, John Vianney returned to the seminary in Lyons. He was never able to pass his exams in spite of tutoring and years of effort. John gained a reputation as the most unlearned and the most devout seminarian in Lyons. His professors were so impressed with his patience and perseverance that they persuaded the bishop to ordain him in spite of his academic failures. In 1815 John became a priest.

St. John was very thin, his face was plain and unattractive, and his clothes were usually worn out. Whenever he had any money, he gave it to charity rather than buying anything for himself. He spent several years as assistant pastor to the priest who was his former tutor; then he was given his own parish in the tiny town of Ars. By this time he was well known for his ascetical life and for his wisdom in hearing confessions. He preached graphic sermons against drunkenness, blasphemy, missing Mass, working on Sunday without any need, and all of the other sins his parishioners committed. He explained the sins clearly so that no one would commit them out of ignorance. John was asked to give several retreats in other parishes, and these were so successful that the bishop offered John a more important parish, which he declined.

People began coming for long distances to go to John for confession, and they reported his miraculous insights. He reminded them of sins they had forgotten, and he mentioned details from the lives of people he had never met. For example, one woman was very concerned about the salvation of her husband, who had committed suicide by jumping off a bridge. Before she said anything to him, the priest told her not to worry about her husband, because he had repented before he died. John Vianney often spent sixteen hours a day hearing confessions. Countless people were converted from their sins or were inspired to give their lives to God because of his advice and prayers. He also worked miracles of healing, which he attributed to the intercession of St. Philomena.

St. John longed for solitude and wished to join a monastery, but he realized that this was not God's will for him. The crowds of people waiting to go to confession left him little time to sleep, and he often ate nothing except a few cooked potatoes for weeks at a time. The rectory was disturbed by extraordinary noises or more violent attacks, which John and many of his guests believed were caused by the devil. He was criticized by some of his fellow priests, who thought that he was too severe in his sermons, too ignorant, too presumptuous, and probably crazy. They denounced him to the bishop, who replied that if John Vianney were mad, the other priests might benefit by some of the same madness.

John Vianney was extraordinary, but France remained Catholic because of the many dedicated priests and lay people who continued practicing their faith after the French Revolution. St. John died in 1859 and was canonized in 1929. Today he is the patron saint of parish priests, and his holy life and fidelity to his vocation provide an inspiration for everyone.

13

The Modern Church

1. The Nature of the Church, and Modern Miracles
2. Modern Errors and Wars
3. The Second Vatican Council
4. The Church After the Second Vatican Council

Featured Saint: Maximilian Kolbe

CHAPTER 13

The Modern Church

1. The Nature of the Church, and Modern Miracles

Two facts should be evident to readers by now. The first fact is that the basic nature of the Church does not change. The Church was founded by Christ, who established the hierarchy of priests, bishops, and the Pope so that people could know the truth about Christ, receive his grace and life in their souls, and do his will. Christ established the sacraments and a new way of life, including prayer, faith, obedience to the Commandments, and doing good works, to save people and to make them holy. God gave each individual a conscience, a mind, and the obligation to find and obey the truth. All Christians are responsible for doing God's will, in whatever external situations God permits. These fundamental aspects of the Church will never change. However, the second fact that should be evident is that the external aspects of the Church and Christian society do change. This change is part of God's plan.

After the Protestant Reformation and the Council of Trent, the Church in Europe and most of the rest of the world suffered severe external trials. She had to respond to attacks by Protestants and pressure from absolute monarchs. After the French Revolution, the Napoleonic wars, and the revolutions throughout Spanish America, Catholics were confronted by indifferent or hostile governments almost every-where. The Church was forced to rely on her own person-nel and resources much more than she had for the past thousand years. In spite of these difficulties, devout Catho-lics appreciated the fact that the Church was an island of stability in a confusing or hostile world. External trials did not destroy the security of faith gained after the Council of Trent. In many ways the trials increased that security. Priests, monks, and nuns might be persecuted in some countries, but most of them were well educated and lived up to their vocations. In countries where the Church was allowed to exist in peace, she usually became stronger and more posi-tive in teaching the message of Christ.

God strengthened the faith of the Church by a number of remarkable events. Miracles and revelations have always ac-companied the lives of the saints, but in modern times these apparitions have increased in number and influence. In the late 1600s St. Margaret Mary's visions of Christ and his Sa-cred Heart reminded people of the love of God. After 1800 a number of famous apparitions occurred. The first was the appearance of the Blessed Virgin Mary to a young nun, St. Catherine Labouré, in France in 1830. St. Catherine told her confessor that Mary had requested that they establish a religious medal, with a picture of the Blessed Virgin and the prayer "O Mary conceived without sin, pray for us who have recourse to thee." Mary did not tell Catherine to tell her religious superior about this, and the confessor was able to get the permission of the bishop without Catherine's role becoming known to the other nuns or the general public until her death in 1876. Many people reported miracles and conversions after wearing the medal and saying the prayer, so the medal was called the "Miraculous Medal". Devotion to the Immaculate Conception of Mary became much more popular. In 1854, after a long preparation by committees of bishops and theologians, Pope Pius IX solemnly defined the doctrine of the Immaculate Conception. This belief had always been present in Catholic life, but the solemn definition and the establishment of a feast raised the doctrine to its present importance in the Church.

In 1858 another apparition occurred, in Lourdes, France. A young girl named Bernadette Soubirous went with several other girls to gather wood by a river. She fell behind, and suddenly a most beautiful woman appeared. Bernadette was so astonished that she could scarcely speak, but she was able to say a Rosary with the woman, who then vanished. This happened several times. The woman directed Bernadette to a hidden spring of water and also told Bernadette that she wanted a church built there. The visions came to the attention of the local priest and bishop, and they told Bernadette to ask the woman who she was. The woman replied, "I am the Immaculate Conception." Bernadette repeated this to the priest, but she did not know what the words meant. The visions ended after a few months, but the church and shrine that were built at Lourdes have been the site of many miraculous healings that have been verified by Catholic and non-Catholic doctors. Thousands of people make pilgrimages there to ask Our Lady of Lourdes for healing, conversion, or other favors from God through the hands of Mary. Most of the pilgrims are not cured physically, but they often receive strength to turn to God and to find peace in accepting his will for them.

A similar incident happened in Fatima, Portugal in 1917. Three children saw the Blessed Virgin Mary in a series of appearances. She spoke to the children about their own lives and asked them and the whole world to pray the Rosary and do penance for the conversion of sinners. She also asked them to pray for the conversion of Russia. This seemed very strange, since Russia at that time was thoroughly Christian. A short time later the Russian monarchy was overthrown, and the nation was controlled by Communists. Christians were severely persecuted, and Russia needed prayers, perhaps more than any other country in Europe.

The children at Fatima were instructed to come back to the same place at the same time every month. Word of the appearances soon spread. The local priest and the bishop were unimpressed, and government officials were extremely hostile. At that time the government of Portugal was very anti-Catholic, and the bishop had spent some time in prison for upholding the Catholic faith. Some government officials thought that the appearances were a trick to promote Catholicism. The children were imprisoned for a short time, and their families were very angry with them because they thought that the young people were imagining the appearances. However, the children faithfully repeated what they had heard. The Blessed Virgin told the children that the last time she would appear she would work a great sign so that everyone would believe. At the predicted time a crowd of about seventy thousand people gathered on the hill where she had been appearing to the children. It was pouring rain. However, the clouds suddenly separated, and the whole crowd saw the sun change color, move around the sky, and dive toward the earth. People were stunned and thought that the world was about to come to an end. This display lasted for a few minutes; then the sun returned to normal. People noticed that their clothes, which had been soaked by the rain, were dry.

The Church has always taught that Catholics are under no obligation to believe in such supernatural experiences. They are called private revelations, and they are not a basic part of the Catholic faith. The Miraculous Medal, Lourdes, and Fatima apparitions were investigated thoroughly by Church officials to rule out the possibility that the visionaries were lying or were subject to hallucinations. The investigations showed that the messages contained nothing contrary to Church teaching. Catholics may believe that the Blessed Virgin appeared, but they do not have to believe it.

These appearances and many others that have been investigated by the Church have had a tremendous effect on Catholic life. Countless people have been converted to a stronger faith in God, love of Christ, and devotion to Mary and the saints. Apparitions of Mary have been reported and verified in many nations, including Japan and India. Many more visions have been reported, investigated by Church officials, and found to have no spiritual significance, since the visionaries were obviously suffering from delusions or excessive imagination. A number of organizations, usually run by lay people, have spread various devotions to the Blessed Virgin Mary and have publicized her messages to pray, obey the Commandments and the Church, and do penance. This is simply the message of Christ repeated for modern people. Whatever one thinks of Marian apparitions, their influence on Catholic life has been very profound. Perhaps modern Catholics, who live in a predominantly materialistic and unbelieving society, need dramatic miracles to remind them of God's presence and power in the world.

Discussion Questions

Identify: Miraculous Medal, Lourdes, Fatima

1. What aspects of the Church will never change? What aspects of the Church have changed in the past and may change in the future?
2. How are the Miraculous Medal, Lourdes, and Fatima apparitions similar? How are they different?
3. At Lourdes and Fatima, how did the appearances, words of Mary, and miracles help people to love, trust, and obey God?
4. Why aren't Catholics required to believe that the Blessed Virgin appeared at Lourdes and Fatima?

2. Modern Errors and Wars

Protestant churches between 1800 and 1950 were damaged by materialistic philosophies more than Catholics were. Professors in many European Protestant seminaries were hired by government officials, who controlled the seminaries. These professors were chosen because of their academic degrees and political opinions, rather than their faith in Christ. They began studying the Bible in much the same way as historians studied other ancient historical documents. The professors downplayed or ignored the Christian belief that the Bible was inspired by God, and they often disbelieved the stories about miracles and the words of Jesus. They thought that the New Testament had been written so many years after Christ that the Gospels were historically unreliable. Modern Protestant and Catholic scholars, who conducted better textual studies and new archaeological research, have proved that the Bible is much more accurate historically than many scholars in the nineteenth century believed and that the New Testament was written a much shorter time after the events it describes than the earlier scholars claimed. The nineteenth-century view undercut Protestant theology and faith, which had been based on the Bible with little reliance on tradition. This view is still being promoted by a few scholars and many popular books and workshops.

Christians who accept the views of the older European Protestant biblical scholars often disregard or refuse to believe in the supernatural aspects of Christianity. Since Christians have always believed in the supernatural and in miracles, the new teachings cannot be called Christian in the traditional sense of the word. The Protestant denominations that were influenced heavily by these beliefs have declined in numbers and faith. The Protestant denominations in this country that are growing most rapidly are the ones that affirm the theological and historical reliability of the Bible.

Catholics were indirectly affected by the anti-supernatural theories of Protestants. Since priests were not usually educated in the same state-controlled schools as Protestants, most of them continued to follow traditional Catholic interpretations of the Bible. However, some Catholic priests and scholars read about the theories of Protestants who did not believe in the historical accuracy of the Bible, and a few adopted the theories themselves. Some of these Catholic professors began teaching doctrines that were similar to the Protestant theories. They said that people cannot know the truth, that no one can be sure what Christ said or meant, that the Church is conditioned by cultural circumstances and can change her doctrines, and that it doesn't matter what one believes. These teachings, called Modernism, were condemned in an encyclical by St. Pius X, who was the first Pope to be canonized in hundreds of years. It should have been obvious that if Modernism were true, there would be little reason to be a Christian, so adopting Modernism was almost equivalent to rejecting the Christian religion. The condemnation by St.

Pius X and a few excommunications ended the direct threat of Modernism to the Catholic Church for about fifty years. However, beliefs similar to Modernism were so widespread in Protestant and secular society that Catholics continued to be affected. It is nearly impossible entirely to ignore the fundamental errors of the society in which one lives.

World War I, from 1914 to 1918, caused severe turmoil in Europe, but the Church was only indirectly affected. Millions of Catholics were caught up in the fighting or the hardships caused by the war. However, the events after the war did more damage to the Church than the war itself.

In 1917 the Russian monarchy was overthrown, and Russia quickly became controlled by Communists. Russia needed an improvement in its government and society, but the Communists were more repressive than the Russian tsars and were unrestrained by Christianity. They persecuted the Russian Orthodox Church and other religions in Russia severely. Under Joseph Stalin, who led the Communists for thirty years and was one of the most ruthless dictators in history, millions of Ukrainian peasants and others starved to death when the Russians took all of their food. Millions more were deported to labor camps or executed. Even though their constitution guaranteed freedom of religion, Communists believed that religion was "the opiate of the people" and did all they could to prevent Christians, Jews, and Muslims from practicing their faith or teaching it to their children and associates.

Germany was so severely damaged by World War I and the reparations imposed by France and England that it suffered from a major economic depression. So many Germans were desperate for work and food that they elected Adolph Hitler, a brilliant, unscrupulous, magnetic speaker with a plan for Germany. Hitler was a Fascist, which means that politically he tried to organize his government on the principle of obedience and loyalty to himself as the leader of the nation. Hitler had been born into a Catholic family, but he had completely rejected his faith. He was a vegetarian and believed in a strange mixture of mystical Aryan racial superiority theories, astrology, and relativistic philosophy. He hated many nationalities, and he thought that the Germans were a superior race and should rule the world. Hitler arranged for the murder of many people in insane asylums or homes for the handicapped, and he persecuted Jews by sending unscrupulous Nazis, members of his semimilitary political party, to burn their synagogues and confiscate their property. The Pope, many Catholic and Protestant leaders, and a few others spoke out against Hitler's erroneous racial theories and evil policies. On Hitler's orders many German religious leaders were harassed, imprisoned, and executed. Hitler took over Austria and Czechoslovakia. England and France did not stop him, in spite of their treaty obligations to these countries, so he went on to invade Poland in 1939. With his modern army of tanks and planes, Hitler defeated the Polish army in a few days. English and French leaders finally declared war, realizing that nothing else would prevent Hitler from conquering all of Europe.

During World War II Hitler enslaved and later executed all of the Jews and gypsies his police could locate. He also ordered the imprisonment and execution of many Catholics, Protestants, and others who tried to help Jews escape or resisted his other immoral policies. It is estimated that about seven million people died in his concentration camps and gas chambers. Many more people in Eastern Europe and Russia were enslaved and forced to work for years in German labor camps with inadequate food and horrible living conditions, where they often died or were murdered. Hitler's Fascist ally, Mussolini, controlled Rome. The tiny Vatican

State was independent, but Pope Pius XII, who was elected in 1939, could easily have been arrested by the Italian dictator. Like Pius XI, the Pope spoke out against Nazi philosophy, murders, and brutality, but he could give little direct help to Catholics or Jews in Germany. In spite of his limitations, he saved the lives of many Jews, primarily by diplomatic efforts or by encouraging Catholics to help them.

Mussolini was overthrown after Italy had been invaded by English and American armies. Germany was defeated in 1945, and Hitler committed suicide. Japan, Germany's ally, surrendered after the United States destroyed two major Japanese cities in the first (and hopefully the last) wartime use of the atomic bomb.

Most of Europe, Russia, China, and Southeast Asia had been devastated by war. In the countries conquered by Hitler or by the Japanese, the Church had been persecuted. After the war Catholic priests and bishops were restored, churches and monasteries were rebuilt, and religious education was resumed. Thousands of new martyrs inspired Christians to love God and do his will in everything. In many countries the war had forced people to turn to God. Vocations were plentiful, and Catholic life flourished.

After World War II Russia took control of many Eastern European nations, including Poland, Czechoslovakia, Yugoslavia, Hungary, East Germany, and Albania. Communists gained political control of the governments in these nations and joined Russia to form the Soviet Union, which was dominated by Russian Communists and led by Stalin. Religion was persecuted in these countries with varying degrees of severity. In Poland the Church was guided by Cardinal Wyszynski, a man with remarkable faith, intelligence, and diplomatic talents. He signed an agreement with the Polish Communist leaders and persuaded them to keep it, in spite of Stalin's attempts to force them to repress the Church more harshly. The Church in Poland was restricted, but it was able to train priests and educate Catholics. It survived Communist persecution and emerged as one of the strongest Churches in Europe. However, in most of the other Communist countries, religion was persecuted more severely. Cardinal Mindszenti of Hungary was tortured severely by Communists in an attempt to force him to break the union of his Church with Rome, and many priests were imprisoned or executed. In Albania the Church nearly ceased to exist.

China became Communist in 1949. Foreign missionaries were expelled. Christians were persecuted, and many bishops were imprisoned. Today, persecution has diminished or ended in many former Communist areas, but the Roman Catholic Church in China is still outlawed by the Communist government. Traditional Chinese religions such as Buddhism have also been repressed. Communism was founded on atheistic principles, and Communist nations never favored religion, though they differed in the degree to which they tolerated or persecuted it.

Throughout the twentieth century the Church in Africa and most of Asia continued to grow. Missionaries encouraged vocations among the new converts, and today most countries have many African or Asian priests, nuns, and bishops. Some of the bishops were appointed cardinals, with the result that an African or an Asian Pope is a distinct possibility in the future. This may seem radical, but the Church has never forgotten that many of the greatest early theologians and martyrs were from Israel, Syria, Egypt, and Africa. The Catholic Church has always been the Universal Church. She was made by God for all nations, and recent missionary activities have allowed her to reflect the universal aspect of her nature more perfectly.

Hitler's evil deeds led to a consensus among political leaders that certain crimes such as genocide, murdering innocent people because of their race or for any other reason, could not be tolerated in civilized societies. This consensus would have been encouraging, except for the fact that Christians have always believed in this principle. Hitler showed the world that a ruthless leader could persuade some modern people to commit evil deeds that were not tolerated in earlier Christian societies.

Discussion Questions

Identify: Pope St. Pius X, Stalin, Mussolini, Hitler, Pius XII

1. How did Protestant theories about the interpretation of the Bible influence Catholics?
2. What is Modernism? Why is it erroneous?
3. Describe Hitler's relations with the Church. What did Pope Pius XI and Pius XII do to help Jews and others persecuted by Hitler?
4. Describe conditions in the Church in countries dominated by Communist governments after World War II.

3. The Second Vatican Council

After the Second World War Catholic theologians resumed their earlier debates. Many theologians believed that the Church needed to reconsider how to accomplish her mission in the twentieth century. Modernism had been condemned, but some Catholics believed that the Church needed to reexamine the Bible and Church traditions in the light of new discoveries by archaeologists and biblical scholars. Modern political and philosophical movements needed to be evaluated so that the Church could present a more unified explanation and defense of the faith. Catholics needed to understand the relationship of the Church to Protestant and non-Christian religions. Some people felt that the liturgy, which had been relatively unchanged since a few years after the Council of Trent and was still in Latin, should offer more options for adaptation to local customs and languages. Religious orders needed to be modernized. For example, some communities still followed ancient customs such as wearing habits made out of many yards of heavy wool, which used to be the cheapest material available but had become expensive, and wearing elaborate starched veils, which were time-consuming and awkward. Deeper problems, such as a lack of charity in some religious orders, tension between priests and bishops, and misunderstanding between Catholics and non-Catholics, also needed to be addressed.

Pope Pius XII wrote encyclicals that offered guidance on the questions that faced Catholics after World War II. One of his most famous encyclicals explained the correct Catholic teaching regarding theories of evolution, but the Pope also wrote influential works on many other subjects, such as the nature of the Church, the liturgy, and Marian doctrines. In 1950 he declared that the ancient belief that Mary was assumed body and soul into heaven was infallible Catholic teaching. The Pope recommended renewal and updating where necessary, but he rebuked some theologians who were teaching doctrines that were similar to Modernism or were erroneous in other ways. Pius XII died in 1958.

The next Pope, John XXIII, called an ecumenical council to discuss the questions that had been occupying theologians. It convened in 1962 at the Vatican. The bishops and theologians present were divided into groups, usually according to the languages they spoke. They discussed the proposed decrees in their groups and made recommendations. After being rewritten, the decrees were discussed again and voted on by the whole assembly. The format provided an opportunity for the whole hierarchy to agree on constructive recommendations, but it allowed manipulation by national blocs of bishops who wanted their concerns and agendas forced on the whole Church. However, it soon became evident that the final documents did not echo local concerns or limited agendas. Instead they provided a blueprint for constructive improvements in the external structure and organization of the Church, and they also gave guidelines for dealing with new situations and renewing Catholic life. Pope John XXIII died in 1963, but his successor, Pope Paul VI, continued the council and ratified its decrees.

In nations and dioceses where the reforms of the Second Vatican Council were accepted and put into practice correctly, the Church flourished. Poland provides an example of a successful implementation of the council. The primate of Poland, Cardinal Wyszynski, knew that many lay people might be confused and unhappy about changes such as having parts of the liturgy in Polish instead of Latin. Since he was in a hostile political environment under the Communist government, he had to be certain that Polish Catholics would not be upset by the changes. First he discussed everything with his bishops and priests, to make sure that they learned the decrees of the council. Then he insisted that they educate lay people by sermons, discussions, and written explanations. Since Cardinal Wyszynski understood and accepted the council decrees himself, he was able to explain their meaning correctly and to make sure that no erroneous interpretations were adopted. When liturgical or disciplinary changes were instituted, people understood them and saw their benefits. Cardinal Wyszynski's wisdom kept the Church in

Poland firmly united, and Catholics were able to keep their faith. Church leaders in other nations were not always as careful or successful in explaining and implementing the changes recommended by the council.

Discussion Questions

Identify: Pope John XXIII

1. What new currents of theology or needs for change became evident after World War II?
2. How did Pius XII and John XXIII respond to new circumstances in society and the Church?
3. Describe the Second Vatican Council. How were the bishops organized? What were the advantages and disadvantages of this type of organization?
4. What did Cardinal Wyszynski do to prevent Polish Catholics from being confused by the changes after Vatican II?

4. The Church After the Second Vatican Council

The Church has always needed reform. In the past, Church councils have guided Catholics so that they could understand the will of God for the Church and for their lives. The dogmatic definitions of Ecumenical councils, when their decrees have been ratified by the Pope, share the Pope's infallibility in faith and morals. However, people can misunderstand or misrepresent the documents or the meaning of a Church council in the same way that they can misunderstand or misrepresent the Pope's teachings or the words of Christ.

Some Catholics refused to listen to the teachings of the council. Historically, this was not unusual. The Council of

Nicea, which resolved the Arian dispute, did not prevent dissent by those Christians who refused to give up their erroneous views and to accept the teaching of Christ as it had been explained by his Church. After the Council of Chalcedon, many Monophysites refused to give up their erroneous beliefs and misrepresented the teachings of the council. They claimed that it supported their views, when in fact it condemned them. The Council of Trent enlightened Catholics who were honestly confused, but most Protestants who had rejected the Church remained Protestants. Other Catholics, such as the kings and bishops of France, delayed many years in adopting the council's reforms and then put them into practice in a halfhearted way.

After the Second Vatican Council, the bishops in many countries did not realize that they needed to act with caution. Lay people knew about the council from secular and religious news media, but most of them were unprepared for the radical changes in the external aspect of Mass, the other sacraments, and other aspects of Church life that many bishops and priests adopted. To add to the confusion, some of the changes that were put into practice were contrary to the teaching of the council.

Catholics before Vatican II were accustomed to a quiet, prayerful Mass, most of which was in Latin. Music was dignified and often beautiful. Suddenly Catholics were asked to make responses in their own languages to a new order of worship, which was somewhat different from the translations of the old Mass. In many churches the reverent, prayerful atmosphere vanished. New songs, which were often similar to informal popular music and which were frequently disliked by more traditional-minded people, were introduced. In some churches rock music and liturgical innovations abounded. Some priests, in an attempt to make their homilies more appealing, stopped preaching about sin or Catholic doctrines and limited their homilies to psychological self-help with religious overtones. These radical changes had never been imagined by most earlier priests and had not been mandated by the council. Since many changes and liturgical experiments were contrary to the council decrees, a few Catholics suspected that many priests and liturgists had never read the decrees or were deliberately ignoring them.

Many people grew discouraged and even stopped attending Sunday Mass. Even in the most devout countries today, only 30 to 40 percent of the Catholic population attends Mass every week, and in some countries Mass attendance is as low as 10 to 15 percent, even though most of the population is nominally Catholic. Before the liturgical changes, more than 50 percent of the Catholic population in some countries fulfilled their obligation to attend Mass on Sundays and Holy Days of Obligation.

Numerous priests asked for dispensations from their vows. Those priests who were granted such a dispensation were allowed to stop acting as priests, take up other careers, and marry. Vocations to the priesthood dropped dramatically, partly due to misguided experiments in seminary training, contradictory expectations for priests, and discouragement with unpopular changes in the liturgy or with the resistance to beneficial changes by lay Catholics.

After World War II Pope Pius XII and others had recommended that religious orders update their rules, so that they would be able to work effectively in the new social conditions of the twentieth century. Most orders made few changes before Vatican II. The old rules needed adaptation, but the changes adopted by religious orders after the council were often enforced with harshness and a lack of wisdom. Some orders made such drastic changes that they became little more than associations of men and women living consecrated lives in the world. Since there were already secular institutes with vows for lay people, this change compromised the witness of religious life without adding much to the Church. Many monks and nuns asked for dispensations from their vows and left their communities. Young people considering religious vocations saw that many orders were very unstable, which discouraged them from taking permanent vows. Today many religious orders are on the verge of extinction. Scarcely any new vocations replaced the ones who left, and the remaining monks and nuns grew old or died. The confusion in some religious orders indicates that there was a real need for reform, but many of the changes were counterproductive in helping religious men and women live out their love for Christ.

Of course, the changes introduced by Vatican II and resistance to these changes were not the only causes of the decline in Mass attendance and vocations to the priesthood or religious life. Some of these problems were caused by the general hostility toward religion in secular culture, the effects of sin, indifference toward religion, and poor morality among Catholic leaders, neighbors, and families. The security and unity that had been features of Catholic life after the Council of Trent were severely damaged in many countries. Benefits of the changes introduced by the council were not always immediately evident, and Catholic life seemed at times to be suffering from culture shock.

These facts show that the Church has experienced a severe trial, but the beneficial aspects of the legitimate changes are becoming more apparent, and there are many reasons to be optimistic about the future. Most Catholics today find that the new order of Mass—properly celebrated—assists them in prayer, knowledge, appreciating their community, and loving God. Many lay people today are aware of their responsibility, restated and stressed by Vatican II, to live holy lives and to do Christ's work. Dioceses where the bishops and priests proclaim Catholic doctrine fearlessly often have many vocations to the priesthood and religious life and also have strong lay support for the Church. Religious orders such as the Missionaries of Charity, founded by Mother Teresa of Calcutta, have many vocations. The Catholic Church still attracts conversions from other religions and philosophies, and Catholics who turn to God in prayer still find his truth and experience his power and love in their lives.

Modern Catholics have enjoyed a series of wise, holy, and heroic Popes. Pope Paul VI fearlessly proclaimed unpopular doctrines, such as the authority of the Church and the evils inherent in artificial contraception. He traveled extensively and spoke to the United Nations and many other groups. He was often criticized for being too lenient. For example, some Catholics thought that he should not have allowed mistaken liturgical practices and doctrinal errors to take root. Pope Paul was criticized by non-Catholics and many Catholics for not allowing more changes in the Church. These people did not understand that the Church was founded and guided by Christ, who is the unchanging Truth, so they were often annoyed because the Church did not abandon her message and conform to anti-Christian cultural values. Pope Paul VI held the Church together after the Second Vatican Council and continued proclaiming the message of Christ even when doing so brought him great opposition and personal unhappiness.

Pope Paul VI died in 1978. His successor, Pope John Paul I, died unexpectedly about a month after his installation. The next Pope, Cardinal Karol Wojtyla, took the name Pope John Paul II. He was the first non-Italian Pope for hundreds of years, and he came from Poland, which was dominated by the Communist Soviet Union when he was elected. Pope John Paul II was probably one of the most intelligent men in the twentieth century. He spoke at least six languages and wrote so many encyclicals that it will take years for the Church to absorb his teaching. John Paul II traveled to many nations in the world and met most major religious and political leaders. Non-Catholics were very impressed by him, even when they did not accept his message, and he was responsible for many conversions. Many of the people who attended his papal Masses or his gatherings such as World Youth Day were aware of the tremendous spiritual power of these events. Participants usually gained an increased faith and love for God and his Church. Pope John Paul II had a hidden influence on some major political events, such as the dissolution of the Soviet Union into a number of independent nations. He was famous for his personal holiness and his love for every human being. God gave the modern Church one of the most remarkable Popes in history.

Many new religious orders are being founded, and many older orders that remained faithful to their mission are flourishing. Some young people still want to give their lives to God completely, and they often hope to join religious orders and take the traditional vows of chastity, poverty, and obedience. This is particularly true in many poor countries, where social traditions are strong.

When Pope John Paul II died, he was succeeded by Joseph Cardinal Ratzinger, who took the name Benedict XVI, in honor of St. Benedict, the Father of Monasticism in the West, and in memory of Pope Benedict XV, who worked for peace during World War I. Cardinal Ratzinger had worked with Pope John Paul II during most of the latter's pontificate.

There has been an increase in the number of lay associations and devoted lay people. The loss of many monks and nuns to the Church is an incalculable one, but this loss had the good effect of making lay people realize their own call to holiness and possibilities for service of the Church as single or married people. Parents became more involved in their children's religious education. Some founded innovative Catholic schools governed by lay people or home schooled their children.

The ecumenical movement, which began about 1900, encouraged dialogues between different churches and religions to increase understanding and prevent persecution. This movement has not resulted in many major reunifications between churches yet, but it has reduced hated and misunderstanding. Protestants, Catholics, and Jews understand and respect each other much more than they have in the past. The ecumenical movement has been responsible for many charitable projects shared by Catholics, Protestants, and others. For example, the prolife movement is primarily composed of a large number of lay groups organized independently to help stop abortion and to assist women in difficult situations. These groups often include people from many religions working together in true unity and love. Today most religious wars involve a few small sects that are extremely hostile, such as some extreme Muslim sects and a few local Christians. Other wars are given a religious rationale, though they were started for economic or political reasons. Terrorism for religious or political purposes has been condemned by nearly all major religious leaders. Lies and distortions about different beliefs are still being promoted, but they are less common today because most people recognize and condemn them.

Though toleration has increased between most Christian churches, it has decreased on the part of some politicians. Governments founded on ideals of atheism always tried to discourage religious belief, but some countries that were founded with ideals of religious toleration became more hostile toward religions, especially toward groups that will not deny Christ's teaching and accommodate current political and social theories.

The Church today faces many difficulties, but Catholics can be confident that God will care for them, as he has in the past. The Church of the future will be the same Church that Christ established, with the same hierarchy, sacraments, morals, and love of God and others. She will have the same goals of teaching people how to live good lives and leading them to salvation, holiness, love of each other, and union with God. No human being can foresee what God will do to resolve modern problems, but after two thousand years of unexpected solutions to difficult problems, Christians can trust that God will not abandon them.

Discussion Questions

Identify: Pope Paul VI, Knights of the Immaculata

1. Why were changes in the liturgy beneficial in some places but harmful to Catholic life in others?
2. Why did the extensive changes adopted by some religious orders cause a severe decline in numbers and public witness to Christ?
3. What good effects have resulted from the Second Vatican Council?
4. Describe the achievements of John Paul II.

Featured Saint: Maximilian Kolbe

Maximilian was born in Poland in 1894. His parents were devout Catholics. When he was a young boy he was energetic, independent, and reluctant to follow his parents' advice. However, this changed when he was nine. He began praying for hours and turned into a model of family love and obedience. His mother persuaded him to tell her the reason for the change. Kolbe had been worried about her unhappiness regarding his bad behavior. One day he was praying in church about this and asked the Virgin Mary what would become of him. Suddenly she appeared to him and offered him two crowns, one white to represent purity and one red for martyrdom. She asked if he wanted them, and he said that he did. She vanished, but the vision affected Kolbe's entire life and his spirituality.

Maximilian became a priest in the Franciscan order. The community ran a number of colleges, and his scientific and mathematical talents impressed his instructors. He was sent to Rome for doctrinal studies. His teachers there noticed his excellent comprehension and good grades, but they were more impressed by his holy life. He was kind, friendly, and amusing, but his only recreation was visiting Roman churches. Kolbe developed the idea of founding a group called the Knights of the Immaculata, to honor Mary Immaculate. This group showed priests and lay people how to consecrate themselves to Jesus through Mary, to gain her help and protection. These dedicated Catholics focused on prayer, living holy lives, works of charity, and evangelization. They followed Kolbe's spirituality, which was based on his love and trust of Mary. He taught the Knights to accept anything that happened to them as coming from God's hand. Kolbe offered up everything, from unreasonable superiors to the atrocities later inflicted on him by the Nazis, out of his love for God and Mary.

Maximilian suffered from frequent fevers, coughing spells, and headaches. His lungs were so weak that he was unable to preach or teach effectively. He returned to Poland, where he was assigned to a teaching position, then a preaching job.

Since he was unsuccessful at both, his Franciscan superiors gave him permission to concentrate on the Knights of the Immaculata. Kolbe had no money, but he and his companions began printing a small newspaper using donated printing presses and paper. The newspaper published meditations about Mary and stories about the activities of Kolbe's groups. As the paper became more popular, Maximilian acquired more printing presses and associates to run them. The last issue before World War II had a circulation of a million copies in many languages, which was phenomenal for a religious newspaper. It required a small city with seven hundred Franciscans to print it. The lay groups became very numerous and helped strengthen Catholic life and faith before the horrors of World War II.

Catholic Poland was a logical place to begin a successful Marian newspaper, but Kolbe soon expanded his apostolate. In 1930 he received permission from his superiors to found the Knights of the Immaculata in Japan. Bishop Hayasaka gave him permission to begin his venture in Nagasaki, which was the home of fifty thousand Japanese Christians. The paper flourished, and Kolbe attracted many vocations to the Franciscan order and his lay association. The priest hoped to found his Knights in several other countries, including India, but the threat of World War II forced him to return to Poland. In 1945 most of Nagasaki was destroyed by an atomic bomb, a few days after the destruction of Hiroshima. Kolbe's church was one of the few structures that survived the blast, and his associates helped the sick and refugees after the war.

Maximilian Kolbe returned to Poland in 1938. After Germany conquered Poland, he was arrested and sent to Auschwitz, an extermination camp. Many prisoners there were killed immediately, but Kolbe was assigned to one of the work detachments. Prisoners in these detachments received frequent beatings, were given practically no food, and had to work until they died of malnutrition. Most of them despaired, but Kolbe never lost his calm detachment. He comforted the other prisoners and sometimes gave away part of his tiny ration of food.

After many months, a man in Kolbe's barracks escaped. In retaliation, the Germans executed ten men by starving them to death. When the German commander was selecting the men, one of them began weeping and begging to be spared because he had a family. Kolbe asked the German commander if he could take the man's place. "Who are you?" the commander asked. Kolbe replied, "I am a Catholic priest", and amazingly the commander agreed. The man was returned to the line, and Kolbe was sent with the other nine to the small room in which they were imprisoned as they starved to death. Captives in these bunkers frequently screamed or babbled in delirium, but the sound of prayers and hymns were heard from Kolbe's group. The priest was able to motivate his companions to die like Christians and human beings rather than animals. After two weeks, Kolbe and several others who were still alive were executed by injections.

The man that Maximilian Kolbe saved was always grateful. He survived the war, was reunited with his family, and testified at Kolbe's canonization. The Knights of the Immaculata continued to help Christians live good lives and spread devotion to Mary Immaculate. Kolbe was considered a saint because of his holy life and activities before the war, as well as his heroic martyrdom. The twentieth century was so violent and hostile to religion that it gave the Church more martyrs than all the rest of Christian history. Catholics should rejoice that the Holy Spirit can give us faithfulness under persecution, while repeating the prayer of Jesus: "Lead us not into temptation, but deliver us from evil."

14

The Catholic Church in the United States

1. Exploration and Colonization
2. Early American English-speaking Catholics and the American Revolution
3. The Church in the Nineteenth Century
4. Special American Strengths and Problems

Featured Saint: Elizabeth Ann Seton

CHAPTER 14

The Catholic Church in the United States

1. Exploration and Colonization

The Catholic Church in the United States is part of the universal Church, which includes all the Catholics in the world. In addition to being united under the Pope, who is the Vicar or representative of Christ, Catholics are united by being part of the Communion of Saints and the Mystical Body of Christ. As St. Paul said, all Christians are members of Christ. The real Head of the Church is Christ, who governs his Church through the Holy Spirit according to God the Father's eternal plan. No Christian is independent from other Christians, and no national church should be independent from the rest of the Church. Any attempt to separate a local church from the universal Church, united under the Pope, is a serious sin. Such a separation would break the unity for which Christ prayed before he was arrested and crucified.

Every nation with any Catholics has its own religious traditions, which are part of the heritage of the whole Church. Christians usually appreciate the history, customs, saints, and unique characteristics of their own nation in a special way. They should also appreciate the beneficial customs of their neighbors all over the world. Each nation has something unique to contribute, but members of national churches need to avoid the self-centered belief that their own concerns are more important than the welfare of the whole Church.

The Church in the United States has a mixed heritage. The predominant culture of the nation had its roots in England. A few English Catholics survived persecution by English Protestants and settled in the American colonies, and the first U.S. bishop was chosen from their descendants. The U.S. Catholic Church was a genuine branch of the English Catholic Church, though many Catholics in the United States at the time of the American Revolution were from Irish, French, or German backgrounds. They were influenced by early American culture, traditions, and liberties. The Louisiana Purchase added thousands of French Catholics to the United States, and millions of Catholic immigrants from various European countries during the next century brought traditions from many more nations. When the United States acquired Texas, the Spanish Southwest, and California, the American Church gained many Spanish-speaking Catholics, who have had a continuing influence on American practices. In recent years American Catholics have been affected by the influx of Latin American, South American, African, and Asian Catholics and by political events and theological movements in Europe and the rest of the Church.

The first explorers in the United States were Spanish Catholics, who traveled north from Mexico into Arizona, New Mexico, Texas, Louisiana, and Florida in the early 1500s. These explorers were accompanied by Franciscan priests, who hoped to evangelize the Native Americans. One early explorer, Coronado, visited many Native American pueblos in New Mexico, then traveled east as far as Kansas, looking for legendary cities of gold. When he and his expedition turned back, his chaplain, a Franciscan named Juan Padilla, remained with several companions to found a mission. He had some success with the Quivira Indians, but he was martyred when he attempted to travel to other tribes to preach the gospel. His companions survived and reported his death to the authorities in Mexico.

Santa Fe, New Mexico, was colonized by a rich Spanish Mexican, Juan de Onate, in 1598. It soon became a prosperous town, and missionaries converted many of the surrounding Pueblo Indians. In 1680 the Indians united to drive out the Mexican settlers. They killed many Franciscan priests living among them, but the Indians put up no opposition in 1692 when the Spanish settlers returned, accompanied by more Franciscans. During the next 150 years, they expanded into Colorado and Utah and built towns wherever there was fertile land to farm. The Pueblo Indians often lived peacefully nearby. Both nationalities were raided occasionally by hostile Indians, such as the Apaches. New Mexico and the other southwestern states came under the control of the United States in 1846, but they have always maintained their strong tradition of Spanish Catholicism. Today many New Mexican Native Americans are Catholics, but some of them follow their former religious beliefs or attend Protestant churches.

The Spanish monarchs were so committed to evangelization that they paid for the support of many Franciscan missionaries. Florida was a Spanish possession for some time after its discovery by Europeans, and it soon had a network of successful missions to the Native Americans. Spanish expeditions as far north as Virginia came into conflict with early English explorers. Sir Francis Drake, an English adventurer, burned St. Augustine, a Spanish settlement in Florida. It was rebuilt, but eventually English pressure forced out the Spanish missionaries and most of the Florida Indians. Practically no trace of Florida's early Catholic heritage remains.

Early Spanish settlements and missions were founded in Arizona. A Jesuit, Father Kino, explored deserts in Mexico and Arizona and founded a number of missions. After the Jesuits were suppressed in 1773, a Franciscan named Father Junipero Serra founded a chain of missions that extended along the coastal region of California. He imitated the common Jesuit practice of forming settlements with a few Spanish soldiers and lay people to help the missionaries. Native Americans who lived in the settlements usually became Catholics and learned how to support themselves by growing crops or raising cattle. When Mexico secularized the mission lands and later, when California became part of the United States, missions lost their land and much of their influence. In spite of this unhappy outcome, mission churches are popular today as tourist attractions and places of pilgrimage. Junipero Serra was beatified by Pope John Paul II on December 11, 1987.

Most of the early French missionaries in Canada and the northern United States were Jesuits. At first they accompanied French trappers and fur traders, but they soon found that they had more success in converting the Indians if they avoided trading settlements, since the traders were often poor examples of Christian morality. The Jesuits obtained permission from Indian leaders to preach to the people, but it often took years to make any converts. In the meantime, the Jesuits shared the lives of their hosts. They usually had to endure extreme cold, poor food, and the danger of attacks from enemy tribes. A few of them were martyred by being tortured to death, since many tribes routinely executed their enemies that way. The torture was intended to give captives a chance to prove their courage by bearing the suffering without showing any weakness or cowardice. Jesuits who volunteered to serve in the American missions welcomed these hardships as an opportunity to give their lives for Christ. For example, Father Isaac Jogues escaped from the Indians after being tortured and returned to Europe, but after a year he volunteered to go back. He was killed a few years later in 1647. Jogues and seven other Jesuits who were martyred in northern New York and Canada were canonized in 1930. Though the French missions were unsuccessful at first, many tribes eventually became Catholic.

After Canada and northern New York had more French settlements, several groups of French nuns established convents in Quebec and Montreal. They founded Catholic schools or did other charitable work. The Church was organized with parishes, priests, bishops, and a seminary. Fur traders traveled throughout the Northwest, trading European goods for furs, which were shipped to Europe, and a few missionaries continued to travel to newly discovered Native American tribes.

Though France claimed Canada and parts of the northwestern United States, there were not enough French inhabitants to defend the French provinces against the English, who were expanding north from their original settlements in Virginia and Massachusetts. In 1763 the French territories were taken over by England. However, this did not end the activity of French missionaries. The province of Quebec has always remained predominantly Catholic and culturally French.

Louisiana and the southern Mississippi were first explored by Spanish settlers and then were acquired by France, but this made relatively little difference for the Church, since both countries were Catholic. In 1803 the United States bought the territory. Its mixed Creole culture, religious orders, and ancient churches and traditions provide another ingredient in the Catholic heritage of the United States.

Though Catholic missionaries and settlers established a good foundation of churches and often had positive relations with the Native Americans in the United States and Canada, much of their work was swept away by the expansion of English-speaking settlements. It took many years for Catholicism, French and Spanish traditions, and Indian contributions to be accepted as part of American culture. This was a tragedy, but modern Catholics can appreciate the heritage of many nations that contributed to their faith.

Discussion Questions

Identify: Juan Padilla, Junipero Serra, St. Isaac Jogues

1. How are the Catholic Churches in each nation united with the whole Catholic Church, and how is each national Church different from the rest?
2. Describe the Spanish settlements and missionary work in New Mexico and Arizona.
3. Describe the Franciscan missions in California.
4. Describe French missionary activities in Canada and the northwestern United States.

2. Early American English-speaking Catholics and the American Revolution

The English colonies in the land that became the Eastern United States were governed according to charters, similar to the charters given to cities in medieval times or to the charters of business corporations. Individuals who wanted to establish a colony asked the English king to give them a charter, which gave them a grant of land and set up some of the laws the settlers were expected to follow. Since England was three thousand miles away and some of the charters gave the settlers a good deal of independence, English laws were often modified or not enforced in America.

Religious dissenters immediately saw the advantages of this situation. Sects that were outlawed in England might find greater freedom of worship in an English colony. Some of the first settlers in the English colonies were Puritans, who practiced a form of Calvinism that was severely restricted in England. These Pilgrims have become famous because they left England to find freedom of religion. However, they tried to prevent people from different Christian denominations from acquiring any political power in their colony in Massachusetts. Pennsylvania, with religious toleration for all, was founded by Quakers, a small sect with pacifist beliefs that was persecuted in England. Maryland was founded by Catholics. The charter did not guarantee freedom of worship specifically for Catholics. Catholicism was so disliked in England that such a guarantee would have made it politically impossible for the king to grant them a charter. Instead, they established their charter with freedom of worship for all Christians. Though the religious freedom was limited because it was restricted to Christians, the charter was an important precedent. Most of the other colonies were founded for business purposes and followed the same religious laws as England.

Maryland was soon settled by many Protestants, who gained political power and revoked its guarantee of religious freedom. After this, Catholics who lived there were subject to the same legal penalties and fines they had to endure in England, though the laws were less strictly enforced in Maryland. The only place Catholics were really tolerated was in Pennsylvania. Many Irish or German Catholics came to the colonies, but these immigrant groups usually lost their faith after a few generations. No priests were allowed in most colonies, and the Protestants were usually very prejudiced against Catholics. Even if the Catholic settlers refused to compromise, their children or grandchildren often became Protestants, since there was no opportunity for formal Catholic religious education in most colonies. At the time of the American Revolution, there were probably fewer than twenty-five thousand Catholics in the colonies. Most of them were in Maryland or Pennsylvania. There were twenty-five priests, and no bishops. All of the priests in the colonies were Jesuits from England, Ireland, or Europe who had become secular priests after the order was suppressed.

Though there were few Catholics, some of them were able to participate in the political events leading to the formation of the United States. Charles Carroll, a descendant of the original Catholic settlers in Maryland, was one of the delegates who signed the Declaration of Independence. His cousin John Carroll became a Jesuit in Europe and returned to work in Maryland. Many years later he became the first bishop in the United States. Catholics fought in the War of Independence in disproportionately large numbers, considering how few Catholics were left in the thirteen colonies. Several explanations are given for the intense Catholic support of the Revolution.

Even though Catholicism was illegal in most of the colonies, Catholics realized that independence from the British Empire would give them a better chance for religious freedom. The English government was more tyrannical and therefore more hostile to religious toleration than most colonial governments. Catholic France was allied with the American revolutionary government, and French representatives insisted that revolutionary leaders agree to stop persecuting Catholics. Respect for their Catholic allies helped Americans learn to respect the Catholic religion, and many Catholics took advantage of the new situation to join in the fight for freedom.

The principles in the Declaration of Independence and the American Constitution were in accord with Catholic religious principles. The American Constitution provided a practical way to govern people by a lawful authority that would recognize their natural rights. Catholics have always believed that all human beings were created free and equal in the sight of God. Because of this, people have natural rights that may not be violated, such as the right to life, liberty, and the pursuit of happiness. Catholic kings traditionally guaranteed their subjects' rights, though recent absolute monarchs often ignored them. A few Catholic nations were always ruled by elected leaders. Theologians such as St. Thomas Aquinas had outlined principles of government similar to many beliefs of American revolutionary leaders.

Most Americans were unaware of the Catholic foundation to their political beliefs, but Catholics understood that freedom from domination by England should lead to freedom of religion. Their belief was justified. After the Revolutionary War, laws establishing religion were forbidden by the U.S. Constitution, and most state laws that discriminated against Catholics were soon abolished.

Religious freedom in the United States has a special meaning. Ideas of religious toleration changed greatly after the colonies were founded. At first, the ideal of religious toleration usually meant freedom for one's own denomination. After the Revolution people began to realize that religious freedom was a basic human right for everyone. None of the patriots who wrote the Declaration of Independence and the Constitution thought that religion was unnecessary, or that all religions were true, or that it did not matter what people believed. They all believed that Christianity was necessary and beneficial for society. In the Constitution, religious freedom means that the government has no right to make any laws restricting religion. Since the power to tax includes the power to suppress, the government cannot tax religious groups. However, since the government has the obligation to make laws that restrict criminal behavior, some activities that have been considered religious in some societies are outlawed. For example, religions that required human sacrifices would conflict with American laws against murder.

The details of religious toleration are still being debated. For about 150 years after the Constitution was adopted, the government promoted religion in many ways, such as sponsoring Bible reading and prayer in school and making laws against doing business on Sunday. Today public prayer is forbidden in most public schools on the grounds that no one should be forced to listen to someone else's prayer. Many people argue that by this rule the government is preventing the free exercise of religion, which is protected by the Constitution. However, most people who favor having prayers in public schools would not be in favor of giving all groups that consider themselves to be "churches", including groups of witches or extreme cults, a turn at saying public prayers. Saying nondenominational prayers would impose on atheists and be considered worthless by many Christians. This is only a minor example of the complications involved in perfect religious toleration.

Even though the Catholic Church in the United States was soon dominated by large numbers of Irish, German, and French immigrants, the new arrivals quickly adopted American political and cultural traditions. The problems of the Church in the new nation were characteristically American. Priests and bishops were often faced with the double task of persuading local Catholics that they were part of the Universal Church and needed to accept her traditions and teaching, and persuading European missionaries that early Americans had to be handled differently than Catholics in Europe. Legal complications regarding Church property and hostility from Protestants made the situation even more difficult. When John Carroll was consecrated as the first bishop in the United States, he knew that he would spend the rest of his life working to establish basic Catholic institutions and practices.

Discussion Questions

Identify: Pilgrims, Maryland, Charles Carroll, John Carroll

1. Why did the American colonies attract many religious dissenters from England?
2. Briefly describe the history of religious toleration in the American colonies before the Revolutionary War.
3. What principles in the Declaration of Independence and the American Constitution were based on Catholic ideals?
4. Why did many American Catholics fight in the Revolutionary War against England?

3. The Church in the Nineteenth Century

Most Catholics in the United States at the time of the American Revolution had little religious education. Scarcely any of them were confirmed, since there were no bishops in the country. Although there were twenty-five thousand Catholics and twenty-five priests, the influence of the priests was restricted. Priests had to keep a low profile, work during the week to support themselves, and minister primarily to their own parishioners. Transportation was so difficult in the United States that many Catholic immigrants never saw a priest. Under these conditions, it is not surprising that some Catholics had a few strange ideas about the Church.

Before the Revolution, when the Church was illegal, Church property was owned and managed by groups of lay trustees. This was the only possible arrangement during the intermittent persecution in colonial times. However, after the Revolution, some lay trustees believed that they should continue managing Church property and choose the priests, and even the bishops, who would be assigned to them. American Catholics had lived among Protestants for so long that they had forgotten Catholic ideas of religious authority. The trustees were often dissatisfied with their priests because many priests who came to America from Europe after the Revolution were unbalanced, addicted to alcohol, or argumentative. In some cases the priests who were assigned to parishes were driven out by trustees who did not like their sermons or their nationality. Some priests who were alcoholics or were living immoral lives persuaded their trustees to protect them when their bishop tried to remove them.

Bishop Carroll spent much of his life arguing with trustees, but he was never able to resolve the root of the problem, which was their ownership of Church property and their mistaken ideas about authority. Later bishops established legal control over Church property. This helped American Catholics accept the fact that the Catholic Church is based on the authority Christ gave to the Apostles and their successors, not on the opinions of lay people. Disputes between priests and parishioners became unusual after more good priests were ordained, and Catholics became more peaceful and united. Instead of scandalizing their Protestant neighbors with their quarrels, they impressed them with their unity.

The idea that lay trustees should have the ultimate control over Church property and the choice of pastors is called *trusteeism*. This idea was erroneous (though lay control of Church property could be beneficial during times of persecution), but that does not mean that lay Catholics had no role in managing Church property and other affairs. Prudent bishops often employed qualified lay people to assist in decisions about finances and property and tried to find pastors who were suited to the needs of each parish. Most priests were aware that they needed to listen to suggestions from lay people and follow them if they were helpful. Since Vatican II, many parishes have parish councils to advise priests, and bishops usually consult experts on investments and related subjects. This enables lay people to use their management talents for the good of the Church. Priests and bishops are freed from time-consuming business, and their spiritual and temporal authority is safeguarded.

Prejudice against Catholics varied in strength, depending on political events, numbers of recent Catholic immigrants, movements among Protestant denominations, and unpredictable events such as the publication of anti-Catholic books. These factors inflamed the fears left by earlier anti-Catholic propaganda. A few Protestants seem to have believed that Catholics wanted to take control of the United States and establish the Inquisition again. Many people who were too well balanced to believe these malicious attacks were nonetheless afraid that the growing numbers of Catholic immigrants would threaten Protestant domination of the country. Others were prejudiced against Catholics because they thought that the Catholic Church was less Christian than the Protestants or because they disliked Catholic immigrants, who were often poor and had unfamiliar customs, accents, or languages. In some cases American workers feared Catholicism because competition for jobs from Catholic immigrants kept wages low. Later in the century, new Catholic arrivals from Italy, Germany, and Eastern Europe were disliked because Americans thought they might be revolutionaries or anarchists. By this time the Irish were so well established in many places that some of them regarded the numerous Italians as a threat to their jobs and security.

The Irish who came to the United States were not all Catholics, since many Protestants from Scotland had been encouraged to settle in Northern Ireland and then had emigrated to America. Other early Irish immigrants had become Protestants. After the Revolution, Irish immigrants settled in many eastern cities. At first they suffered from discrimination, but compared with the repression in Ireland from the English, America was a haven of freedom. After many years, Irish citizens in some cities began to outnumber Americans from other racial backgrounds. In Massachusetts and New York they became numerous, prosperous, and well organized. They controlled the political government in some eastern cities after 1880, but Catholics and Irish were excluded from many clubs and civic organizations for another sixty years. As late as the 1980s, some Irish Catholic politicians supported antidiscrimination laws and affirmative action partly because they remembered the discrimination they or their parents had suffered in the past.

The assimilation and success of Irish immigrants were accompanied by an increase in Irish vocations to the priesthood. Irish prelates were influential public figures and were often widely respected by Protestants as well as Catholics. Some archbishops from the nineteenth century, such as Cardinal Gibbons, were almost legendary. Along with Cardinal Manning and John Henry Newman, converts from the Anglican Church in England, they helped build a solid foundation for Catholicism in English-speaking nations. However, priests of other nationalities were also influential in the United States. French bishops were responsible for a number of early American dioceses and were assigned to assist the church in New Mexico after the transition from Spanish to American control. A missionary from Bohemia, John Neumann, became bishop of Philadelphia in the 1850s. He was the first canonized American saint, although he was a naturalized citizen. The diverse nationalities of their priests and bishops probably helped Americans understand the universal aspect of the Church as much as any other factor. When the Church became better established and immigrants adapted to American culture, more priests came from families that had been American for many generations. This reduced cultural conflict, but modern Catholics sometimes need to be reminded that their own concerns should be kept in perspective and that the Church is universal.

Discussion Questions

Identify: trusteeism, John Neumann

1. What role do lay people have in managing Church property and parishes?
2. What factors influenced anti-Catholic bigotry?

4. Special American Strengths and Problems

Between 1800 and 1900, many religious orders were founded in the United States or were imported from Europe. They were responsible for establishing Catholic hospitals, orphanages, schools, and colleges. In the first half of the twentieth century, a large percentage of Catholics attended these schools, which were staffed primarily by nuns or priests. Students at these schools usually received an education that was as good as or better than the ones their Protestant contemporaries received in public schools. Catholics frequently attended religion classes and Mass five or six days a week for all twelve grades and college. Catholic schools and churches were the centers of social life for students, their families, and their communities. With all of these advantages, most American Catholics learned a great deal about their faith. Since they often lived in neighborhoods populated by Catholics from the same national backgrounds and had priests who had been well trained in local seminaries, Catholic parishes were usually fairly unified. Lukewarm Catholics were encouraged to practice their religion by their relatives, by priests or nuns who knew them and their families, and by their friends. It is not surprising that Mass attendance was very good and there were many conversions to the Catholic faith from other religions.

Early twentieth-century Catholicism was very dependent on religious orders. Most cities had at least one Catholic hospital, and many schools or other institutions were founded and staffed primarily by priests or sisters. Vocations to contemplative, cloistered religious orders were common. Monks and nuns in these strict groups did farm work, made vestments, baked altar breads, or found other types of manual work to support themselves. They spent most of their time praying. Though their lives were hard, people with true vocations knew that their prayers and sacrifices were bringing God's grace to their families, friends, and country. Contemplative writers showed that Americans could find the same joy from union with God in prayer as contemplative saints in other countries. Non-Catholic Americans were often amazed by the love and dedication of Catholics in religious orders.

In material terms, the sacrifices of these priests and nuns made it possible for Catholics to become successful Americans while retaining their Catholic faith.

Lay groups were also important. The Knights of Columbus was founded in the 1880s as a social and religious organization for Catholic men. The Knights are very numerous today, with many chapters in most cities. They have been responsible for uncounted charitable works, and the group has assisted with the spiritual growth of its members and their families. Another popular group founded in Ireland in the early twentieth century, the Legion of Mary, became influential in America. Legion members met each week for prayer and did evangelization or charitable works in parishes. Third Orders, lay groups connected to various religious orders, promoted prayer, good works, community support, and holy lives. Most churches had an altar and rosary society, which cared for the church, and a St. Vincent de Paul society to help the poor. Lay people were employed by Catholic schools, hospitals, and other institutions, which also needed constant donations of supplies, repairs, and volunteer work from lay people. Students and young adults had many clubs and social activities in Catholic schools and colleges.

Modern Catholics sometimes forget the tremendous contributions of lay Catholics to the Church in the early part of this century because of the great contributions made by people in religious orders. Early Catholics, both lay and religious, were often highly motivated to sacrifice themselves for others and for the Catholic faith. Modern Americans are often less self-sacrificing than their ancestors, and this cultural trend has weakened the dedication of some modern Catholics. However, many groups of dedicated lay people were founded or became more important after the Second Vatican Council.

Though the early Catholic Church in the United States had many good qualities, it had several weaknesses that are still causing problems today. Many Catholics lived in the South before the Civil War, and there were many black Catholics. After the Civil War, the Church was not able to minister to all of them, and they often joined Protestant churches. A few religious orders were formed to educate black people and train black nuns and priests, but there were not nearly enough vocations to fill the need. Several Popes and some bishops and priests spoke out against racial prejudice, but many American Catholics were as prejudiced as other Americans against black people. The black Catholics who persevered in their faith in spite of these obstacles set a good example of heroism for the rest of the Church. In the 1950s many Catholics, particularly priests and nuns, joined in the civil rights movement, and open racial prejudice in the Church has practically disappeared today.

Catholics from Hispanic or Native American backgrounds have had similar problems with prejudice in the United States. In some towns, early Catholics founded separate churches for the Hispanic and northern European Catholics. Different traditional devotions, customs, and languages sometimes made it difficult to combine both groups in one parish. Of course, Hispanic Catholics were not the only nationality that found integration difficult. Irish immigrants, Poles, Germans, Italians, Southeast Asians, and many others have demanded, and often received, churches with pastors who speak their own languages and understand their traditions. The Church today would be more sympathetic to such demands except for the shortage of vocations, which encourages the formation of large parishes that include many nationalities. However, groups of Catholics are free to form lay associations, which could help minorities strengthen their faith and live good Christian lives.

Modern non-Catholic Americans are usually more tolerant of Catholics than earlier Americans. In 1928 the Catholic governor of New York, Al Smith, ran for president. He was decisively defeated, in part because of a vicious campaign of anti-Catholic bigotry. Many Americans seem to have believed that a vote for Al was a vote for a foreign ruler, the Pope, and an evil religion, Catholicism. In 1960 another Catholic, John F. Kennedy, was elected president. Voters accepted his assurances that the Pope would have no say in American politics, and the election was largely free of anti-Catholicism. Since then many Catholics have been elected to office by voters who are predominantly Protestant. Some voters are so anxious for honesty and integrity among politicians that any strong religious background is an advantage.

The Church in America was subject to the same stresses as the rest of the Church after the Second Vatican Council. Liturgies, vestments, Church music, and architecture have changed drastically in the last thirty years. New lay groups have been founded, and new types of worship services and Bible studies are as popular as traditional novenas to saints, Benediction of the Blessed Sacrament, Rosaries, and processions. Changes in religious life and religious education diminished the number and public witness of Catholic schools, though the trend toward closing schools slowed or stopped at the end of the twentieth century, and in some dioceses new Catholic schools were built. A decline in the numbers of priests as well as an increase in the Catholic population have led to the formation of larger parishes, often with as many as eight Sunday Masses. Associations of lay people have become more necessary because the large parishes can be somewhat impersonal. Many old parish groups and social networks were displaced by changes in modern life and have not yet been adequately replaced.

Before Vatican II the church in the United States was well regarded in the past for loyalty to the Pope. Aside from the error of trusteeism, caused primarily by poor religious education and the necessity of surviving under persecution, U.S. Catholics as a group were always faithful to Catholic teaching. Americans, like the rest of the Church, appreciated devotion to Mary and all the saints and the spiritual benefits of Mass and the sacraments. Since the Church was free from conflict for so many years, many devout Catholics uncritically accepted everything that happened after Vatican II, because they believed that the priests, bishops, and nuns would care for the Church.

Few dedicated Catholics today show such uncritical confidence. Most of them know that unless they hold on to their own faith and do whatever they can for the Church, they may lose both. God promised to protect the Church, but it is a historical fact that some countries that were once Catholic are now inhabited by Protestants, Muslims, or people with no religious faith. God did not guarantee to keep his Church safe in any particular country if the Catholics there refuse to defend her. Lay people are as responsible as priests and bishops for the Church, though they have different vocations and spheres of action, and young people are as responsible as their parents. The Church is the Body of Christ, and she needs the wholehearted support of every individual member.

Discussion Questions

Identify: Knights of Columbus, Legion of Mary, John F. Kennedy

1.   Describe the contributions of religious orders to Catholic life in the United States.

2. Describe the contributions of lay people to Catholic life in the United States.
3. What problems exist in the Church today because of past prejudice? What can Catholics do about them?
4. Why were early Catholics more dependent on religious orders than Catholics today?

Featured Saint: Elizabeth Ann Seton

Elizabeth Seton was the first canonized saint born in the English colonies that became the United States. She was raised in New York City as an Episcopalian and married a merchant named William Seton when she was twenty, in 1794. They had five children. The couple traveled to Europe hoping that the change would improve his poor health, but he died there in 1803. Elizabeth became interested in the Catholic Church during their visit to Italy, partly because of the hospitality and faith shown by an Italian family who befriended her. After she returned to America, she became a Catholic in 1805, with the help of the future bishop of Boston. Her family was so angry about her conversion that they refused to give her and the children any financial assistance. In order to make a living, she opened a school in New York. She soon moved to Baltimore, then to Emmitsburg, Maryland, where there were more Catholics. She arranged for the education of her two boys, and she enrolled her daughters in her own school.

Elizabeth Seton was attracted to religious life. In 1809 she took religious vows and founded a religious order, the Sisters of Charity. They established many Catholic schools and hospitals. Mother Seton, as she was soon called, was a remarkable woman. She was intelligent, well educated, courageous, and holy in a practical way. She impressed everyone who met her. When she became a Catholic she found that the Church was her spiritual home. Catholics found that their new convert was a treasure of good judgment and spiritual balance. She said once that she would have liked to live a contemplative life, but she had to make a living. God used all of her talents for the good of his Church in America and saved the rewards of contemplation for the happiness of heaven.

The Sisters of Charity, later also known as the Daughters of Charity, became very influential. Mother Seton's schools became the prototype of Catholic parochial schools, which educated generations of Catholics. Hospitals in her order treated the sick of every religion. During the Civil War the Daughters of Charity and other sisters were so heroic in nursing the wounded, and in giving spiritual and material comfort, that they helped diminish Protestant hostility against Catholics. The order is still influential today.

Mother Seton died in 1821 and was canonized in 1975. The prayer for her feast day reads, "Lord God, you blessed Elizabeth Seton with gifts of grace as wife and mother, educator and foundress, so that she might spend her life in service to your people." This unusual woman exemplifies the contributions to the Church in the United States made by converts from English Protestant denominations. In many cases the converts appreciated the heritage and spiritual life of the Church more than native-born Catholics. Elizabeth Seton was a Catholic for only sixteen years before her death, but she made an essential contribution to the Church.

BIBLIOGRAPHY

The Catholic Church: The First 2,000 Years is written for readers with a limited knowledge of history. The book avoids specialized topics and includes very little information not readily available in numerous historical reference books, biographies, or theological works. Most of the books mentioned in the text can be located in major university or seminary libraries, and many are currently in print. Readers without access to major libraries can obtain papal encyclicals and other types of Catholic literature online. Books can be ordered through online Web sites or borrowed through local libraries by interlibrary loan.

The books listed in this bibliography are predominantly reference works giving additional information on general history, philosophy, biography, or the interpretation of history. The *Catechism of the Catholic Church* is the most readily available, authoritative, and concise overall reference work for Catholic theology, the interpretation of salvation history, and the theological controversies mentioned in the text. A college-level text, *The Western Heritage*, and several other books are included for readers who want to learn more about secular history, but numerous good books on the subject are available. Many books have been written about the relationship of Christianity to culture, philosophy, and political systems; the books included here are given as examples. The other books were chosen because they are well known, easy to use, or found in many libraries.

Aumann, Jordan. *Christian Spirituality in the Catholic Tradition*. San Francisco: Ignatius Press, 1985.

Bunson, Matthew. *Our Sunday Visitor's Encyclopedia of Catholic History*. Huntington, Ind.: Our Sunday Visitor, 1995.

Butler, Alban. *Butler's Lives of the Saints*, new full ed. Collegeville, Minn.: Liturgical Press, 1995–2000.

Catechism of the Catholic Church, 2nd ed. Washington, D.C.: U.S. Catholic Conference, Inc., Libreria Editrice Vaticana, 1997, 2000.

Copleston, Frederic, S.J. *A History of Philosophy*. 9 vols. Mahwah, N.J.: Paulist Press, 1994.

Dawson, Christopher. *Christianity and European Culture: Selections from the Work of Christopher Dawson*. Ed. Gerald J. Russello. Washington, D.C.: Catholic University Press, 1998.

Flannery, Austin, O.P., Ed. *Vatican Council II*. 2 vols. Northport, N.Y.: Costello Publishing, 1998.

Hennesey, James J. *American Catholics: A History of the Roman Catholic Community in the United States*. New York: Oxford University Press, 1981.

Hughes, Philip. *A History of the Church*. 3 vols. New York: Sheed and Ward, 1949.

Hughes, Philip. *A History of the General Councils*. Garden City, NY: Hanover House, 1961.

Kagen, Donald, and Steven Ozment. *The Western Heritage*. 2 vols., 6th ed. Paramus, N.J.: Prentice Hall, 1997.

Kinder, Herman, and Werner Hilgemann. *Anchor Atlas of World History.* 2 vols. Trans. Ernest A. Menze. New York: Doubleday, 1974, 1978.

Knowles, David. *The Evolution of Medieval Thought.* New York: Vintage Books, 1964.

Jungman, Josef A. *The Early Liturgy: To the Time of Gregory the Great.* Trans. Francis A. Brunner. Notre Dame, Ind.: University of Notre Dame Press, 1959.

Quasten, Johannes. *Patrology.* 4 vols. Westminster, Md.: Christian Classics, 1983.

INDEX

NOTES

NOTES

NOTES

NOTES

NOTES

NOTES